Greek Theatre Practice

Contributions in Drama and Theatre Studies
Series Editor: Joseph Donohue

American Popular Entertainment: Papers and Proceedings of the Conference
on the History of American Popular Entertainment
Myron Matlaw, editor

George Frederick Cooke: Machiavel of the Stage
Don B. Wilmeth

Greek
Theatre
Practice.

J. Michael Walton, 1939-

Contributions in Drama and Theatre Studies, Number 3

GREENWOOD PRESS
WESTPORT, CONNECTICUT . LONDON, ENGLAND

Library of Congress Cataloging in Publication Data

Walton, J Michael, 1939–
    Greek theatre practice.

    (Contributions in drama and theatre studies ; no. 3
ISSN 0163-3821)
    Bibliography: p.
    Includes index.
    1. Theater—Greece. 2. Greek drama (Tragedy)—
History and criticism. 3. Electra in literature.
I. Title. II. Series.
PA3201.W35   792'.0938   79-8580
ISBN 0-313-22043-3 lib. bdg.

Library of Congress Catalog Card Number: 79-8580
ISBN: 0-313-22043-3
ISSN: 0163-3821

First published in 1980

Greenwood Press
A division of Congressional Information Service, Inc.
88 Post Road West, Westport, Connecticut 06881

Printed in the United States of America

10 9 8 7 6 5 4 3 2 1

Contents

Illustrations

viii   Illustrations

Preface

The translations used in this book are the author's with the exception of some quotations from Pollux' *Onomasticon*, which are from the translation of 1775. The passage from *On the Art of the Theatre* by Edward Gordon Craig is printed by permission of William Heinemann Ltd.

Thanks are due to numerous colleagues, both students and staff, in the universities of St. Andrews, Denver, and Hull with whom I presented productions of classical plays. In particular I am grateful to Vivien Bridson and John Harris with whom I worked on productions of both Aeschylus' *Libation-Bearers* and Euripides' *Electra* in the Drama Department of the University of Hull.

I must also record gratitude to those who advised me about various aspects of the manuscript, most notably my former colleague Harry Thompson, without whose substantial guidance this book would probably never have seen the light of day.

Greek Theatre Practice

Introduction

Stage-Director: Do you know who was the father of the dramatist?

Playgoer: No, I do not know, but I suppose he was the dramatic poet.

Stage-Director: You are wrong. The father of the dramatist was the dancer. And now tell me from what material the dramatist made his first piece?

Playgoer: I suppose he used words in the same way as the lyric poet.

Stage-Director: Again you are wrong, and that is what everyone else supposes who has not learnt the nature of dramatic art. No; the dramatist made his first piece by using action, words, line, colour, and rhythm, and making his appeal to our eyes and ears by a dextrous use of these five factors. . . .

The first dramatists were children of the theatre.

Edward Gordon Craig, *On the Art of the Theatre: First Dialogue* (London: Heinemann, 1911).

Gordon Craig was never a man to compromise. Retired actor at twenty-six, virtually retired director at forty, he spent his last fifty years writing, theorizing, and devising means of putting off anyone who tried to coax him back into the theatre. Yet Craig was a theatrical seer, and there can be no disputing that many of his visions of the theatre are coming to life sixty, seventy, and even eighty years after he first dreamed them up.

His promotion of a theatre that eschewed realism and considered the individual primarily in his relationship to stage space led him naturally to approve most of those historical periods when the theatre dealt in mighty themes and the essences of existence. The dramatic output of fifth-century B.C. Athens attracted him because it exemplified communal acts of affirmation: affirmation of faith, affirmation of art, affirmation of life itself.

Craig was aware too that Greek tragedy had been ill-served by its accessibility over so many hundreds of years only to scholars. Generations of schoolboys struggling to read twenty lines of Sophocles in an hour were given little encouragement to believe that the meaning they extracted so painfully via variant manuscripts and dubious transcriptions had any relation to a living art.

That the dramatic texts from the fifth century B.C. are merely blueprints for a living performance; that they hide beneath their lines a complex physical action; that they were created to be seen on one occasion only by a large proportion of the entire citizen population of Athens—all of these aspects of tragedy were too often regarded as secondary or ignored entirely both when Craig was writing and indeed since that time.

Even modern critics, aware of the requirements of the stage, have tended to emphasize the poetic form, dramatic as it may be, and concentrate commentary on plot development, characterization, and language. This bias may seem inevitable since there is no way in which the performance of a classical tragedy or comedy can be recreated nor any means found of discovering how the chorus danced, what the actors looked like, and how the action was framed. Yet it is still possible to examine the surviving texts and fragments, scanty though they are, and put flesh on their bones by working out how each of the three great tragedians—Aeschylus, Sophocles, and Euripides—combined the circumstances of production with an acute visual sense to promote theatrical effects.

"The word 'effective'," wrote Humphrey Kitto in *Greek Tragedy*, "belongs not to the classical but to a late stage of the art." The more I read Greek tragic plays, the less I find that I can accept this remark in that otherwise splendid book. I hope to show in the following pages that effectiveness in the theatre was not something of which the Greeks needed to be afraid or ashamed. Indeed, I suspect it was this very quality that ensured the survival of the plays we do have against the work of the large number of tragedians known today only by name. This "effectiveness" was what guaranteed the reputations of the Athenian masters against the florid and bombastic "late stage of the art."

The *Oresteia* was written for a single open-air performance in the spring of 458 B.C. Aeschylus combined the functions, as Craig no doubt approved, of author, director, designer, perhaps composer, choreographer, and chief actor. His greatest reward would have been the knowledge that he had served the dual purpose of contributing to a religious festival and inspiring many thousands of his fellow citizens toward their new form of democratic government. A modern production could emulate few of the conditions of that performance. But for all the differing circumstances between the Great Dionysia of 458 B.C. and any modern production, I firmly believe that Aeschylus employed primarily theatrical weapons that have lost little of their force over the years, if they are properly understood and explored. A single example of his exceptional stagecraft can show the magnitude of this challenge.

When Aeschylus, after devoting two plays of his trilogy to man's earthly relationship with the gods, raises the whole level of the work to the divine in the third play, he takes a reasonable chance. That he appoints as his representative of supernatural power the gods Athene and Apollo is predictable for an Athenian. That he should oppose them with the Furies is an extraordinary gamble. The Furies exist as embodiments of nightmare, dredged up from the recesses of man's deepest fears, and Aeschylus places them on stage for all to see.

Aeschylus takes that gamble. After the trial scene in which Orestes is acquitted and absolved of the crime of matricide, Aeschylus achieves his most daring effect, an effect that could succeed only in performance. Before the audience's eyes he causes the hellish Furies to be transfigured into creatures of radiant beauty. He exorcises them and transforms them into benign deities to watch over an Athens that is not of some almost mythical past but of that very day in 458 B.C.

Is that an incomprehensible concept for a modern audience? Or is it a wonderful challenge to a director to probe into the recesses of man's deepest imagination and suggest in this transformation a universal optimism?

Not all of the surviving plays of Aeschylus, Sophocles, and Euripides reach such heights. Euripides is often mundane by comparison. But each of the tragedians and the comedian Aristophanes created their plays as living works of theatre, depending for their effect on live performance. Yet the conditions of original performance are today so poorly understood that the plays are revived either out of some curious sense of duty or as convenient pegs on which a new writer or director can hang his own ideas.

This book is an attempt to suggest the factors that contributed to the staging of plays in fifth-century Athens. By studying the treatment of the *Electra* theme, common to all three tragedians, I hope to reveal each of these playwrights as an individual, who shared some common conventions but whose work was wholly original. At a time when the stage has once more opened up its boundaries and escaped from the shackles of realism, the quality of the Athenian playwrights can again be appreciated, not only by scholars and students but by directors, actors, and, above all, audiences. Nothing would be less desirable or possible than that I should seem to advocate archaeological reconstructions. Bridges must be built in any modern production of an ancient Greek play—bridges of thought, convention, and expectation for actor and audience alike. What the plays need is a means to performance. The theatre provides such means from its own vocabulary of movement and image.

At the conclusion of the final part of the *Ramayana* staged over the four nights of the midsummer full moon on an open-air stage near Jogjakarta, there is a profound hush. As the last of the masked dancers among the hundred-strong cast disappear from view and the musical gongs of the *gamelan* orchestra finally subside, one is left with the kind of exaltation Athenians must have felt after the Furies, now in reality *Eumenides*, "Kindly Ones," finally processed from the *orchestra*. There, in Java under the shadow of the Siva temple of Prambanan, I became aware of one kind of bridge that could be created to link a modern audience of many nationalities with an epic of great antiquity.

Any such bridges can and must be built in terms of modern theatrical usage. But they can never be satisfactorily built unless they have at least their foundations in the original concepts of the Athenian playwrights. The director of Aeschylus would be well advised to exercise his own imagination and to employ any means of theatrical communication, but primarily to trust Aeschylus—or Sophocles, or Euripides, or Aristophanes.

Seventy years ago Gordon Craig saw the way forward for the

theatre as a return to the concept of theatre that the Athenian play-wrights created. For too long they have stood only as the cornerstone of classical thought. It may well be that through a proper understanding of the "effectiveness" of the Athenian dramatists we may find fresh ways not only to promote classical texts but also to open the door to a new classical theatricality.

Chapter 1   The Playwrights and Athens

In 480 B.C. Persian forces captured Athens and razed much of the city to the ground. The Athenian population had fled to the island of Salamis, just off the coast of Attica, and the small force under seige on the Acropolis had finally been overwhelmed.

Thirty years had elapsed since Athens had expelled Hippias, the last of the tyrants, and Hippias had appealed for help to Darius, king of Persia. It was only ten years since Darius, responding forcefully if tardily, had suffered the minor but humiliating defeat at Marathon, where nine thousand Athenians and one thousand Plataeans had prevented his army from disembarking to march on Athens.

The death of Darius and the succession of his son Xerxes delayed the inevitable return, but the Persian expedition of 480 B.C. was both larger and better equipped. Taking the overland route through Asia Minor, Thessaly, and Macedon, Xerxes marched into northern Greece. Leonidas, with his three hundred Spartans, heroically defended the pass of Thermopylae until he and his men were betrayed and cut to pieces, at which juncture only the Athenian fleet stood between Xerxes and a triumphal march through to the Peloponnese with the consequent subjugation of the entire country.

After Marathon, the city-states of Greece, so often divided, had anticipated the Persian return and formed an alliance against the common enemy. Guided by Themistocles, Athens had built up an impressive navy, and despite the loss of the city, Themistocles succeeded in tricking Xerxes into engaging this Athenian fleet with too little seaway to maneuver their larger ships.

There is no contemporary account of the momentous Battle of Salamis, although Herodotus of Halicarnassus, who was at most ten at the time, gives a full account in Book VIII of his *Histories*. But Salamis day was a red-letter day in Athenian history and came to be used as a handy reference point to link the three major tragedians of Athens. Euripides was born on Salamis day itself, says one account; Sophocles, aged about sixteen, sung in the victory ode afterwards; and Aeschylus fought at Salamis as he had, ten years earlier, at Marathon. Certainly Aeschylus' account in his play *Persians* has the ring of truth to it. Eight years later in the Theatre of Dionysus, a messenger at the Persian palace in Sousa describes his country's defeat:

At that very moment we heard a mighty cry: "On, sons of Hellas. Free your country, free your children, your wives, the shrines of your gods and the tombs of your fathers. The struggle is on and everything at stake." And then from our side rose the sound of Persian voices. The time had come. At once ship battered on brazen ship. A Greek vessel began it lopping off the stern of one of the Phoenicians. Then charge followed charge. The Persians held their own at first but when the crush of ships jammed in the narrows, none could help his fellow. They gnawed at each other with brazen mouths and every oar was shattered. Then the Greek ships, not missing a chance, surrounded and hounded them on every side. Our ships capsized, the sea was hidden from sight, covered by wrecks and corpses, and soon the rocky shore too. We cut and ran but the Greeks hammered and hacked us down with spars, clubbing us as though we were fish. Till night mercifully shut out the scene the sea was all screams and groans. In ten whole days I could not narrate the agony we endured. But this I know. Never before died so many men on a single day.[1]

The effect of such a speech and of *Persians* as a whole, before an audience that must have included many of the combatants—men who had lost friends and kinsfolk—can have few parallels in dramatic history. In overt patriotism, *Persians* provides a fitting opening to Greek drama of the fifth century B.C., even if in content it is atypical.

Aeschylus' *Persians* is probably the earliest Greek tragedy to survive. The composition of six of Aeschylus' extant tragedies can be assigned with some accuracy to the years 472 to 458 B.C., and the remaining play most probably falls within the same period. By 472 B.C. dramatic performances had probably been staged for sixty years, and Aeschylus' own career as a playwright was two-thirds over.

From the years before 472 B.C. a few titles survive, together with some passing references to certain details of special appeal to later historians, but nothing substantial remains. Where tragedy came from, how it developed at specific religious festivals as part of civic ceremonials involving virtually a whole community, what it must actually have looked like in performance—these are questions that can be approached only indirectly. Any attempt to reconstruct the conditions of the first performance of *Persians* cannot profit from critical reviews. Aeschylus left no *Henslowe's Diary* to provide lists of scenic devices, so useful for the assessment of dramatic conventions. Hardly more than half a dozen stones buried under the debris of later theatres indicate the possible size and shape of the playing place for which Aeschylus wrote.

What survives is the play *Persians*, one-quarter of an offering of four by the same playwright written for performance at the Great Dionysia. Of the 1077 lines, a majority suffer from textual difficulties. Of the lost plays in the same group, only 5 lines have come down to us from *Phineus*, perhaps 9 from *Glaucus of Potniae*, and some 20 from the satyr play *Prometheus the Firebringer*.

Persians is a history play, the central action occurring only eight years before its first performance. In this, it might seem to be unique. All other surviving tragedies are situated in or about the period of the Trojan Wars or in the remote past of Argos and Thebes, part myth, part legend, involving gods and heroes celebrated in the epic cycles.

But the central issues of Greek tragedy are immediate, dealing with the process of living in fifth-century Athens. Although the heroic figures seem prehistoric, the treatment, through them, of contemporary issues is of immediate concern. *Persians* serves not merely to glorify the recent past but to strengthen a patriotic resolve aimed toward the future creation of an Athenian Empire.

The history of Athens during the lifetime of Aeschylus, Sophocles, and Euripides has been well charted. Almost all surviving tragedies suggest a lively concern with events of their day, and some references are specific. Sophocles' *Oedipus Tyrannus*,[2] for example, probably performed in 429 B.C., seems to relate directly to Pericles

and the events surrounding the Peloponnesian War. Euripides'
Trojan Women of 415 B.C. would surely have brought to mind in its
audience the recent annihilation of the island of Melos for insub-
ordination. Tragedy was every bit as immediate as Old Comedy,
which made no secret of its political nature and within whose free-
wheeling form Aristophanes made his concerns explicit to later
generations.

In Aristophanes' *Frogs*, Dionysus, as god of the theatre, goes
down to Hades to bring back to earth a playwright to help save
Athens. *Frogs* was first performed at the Lenaia of 405 B.C. less than
a year after the deaths of Euripides and Sophocles. The competition
that ensues in *Frogs* is between Euripides and Aeschylus—not
Sophocles—and Aeschylus had then been dead for over fifty years.
The contrast in attitudes between the dead poets is extreme, and
they find common ground only in the didactic purpose of the playwright:

Aeschylus: Tell me, what should we admire a playwright for?
Euripides: For dexterity, for giving advice and because we make men
    better in the city-states.[3]

In all great ages of the stage, drama has tended to be influenced
by and to reflect the current social and political climate. In no era
was the relationship between the theatre and public life so marked
as it was in fifth-century Athens. The differences of the playwright's
approach to his craft between the first and last periods of the century
are typified by Aeschylus and Euripides. Sophocles and Aristophanes
also mirror artistic and moral attitudes, public and private, offering
between them as clear a view of the Athenian temper as any social
or political historian could have reflected.

This single unifying factor needs to be kept constantly in mind
during the rest of this book. The comparisons between the three
versions of the *Electra* story are carried out in terms of stage performance rather than critical background. But each shift of emphasis
revealed by the playwrights in itself reflects a shift in the awareness
of a whole community as it passes from the triumphs of the cam-
paign against Persia to the humiliation of the defeat by Sparta at
the end of the century.

Such a portrait is painted within the framework of tragic plots that are set, *Persians* excepted, deep in the past or of comic fantasies where fictional Athenians share a stage world with gods, heroes, and celebrities. Old Comedy was more overtly topical, but in the tragedies too the playwrights felt themselves at liberty to comment, however obliquely, on events that were matters of life and death to their watching audience. This was their prerogative as poets; this was their purpose, and Euripides could claim with justification that he and his fellows "make men better in the city-states."

AESCHYLUS

Very little is known of any of the fifth-century dramatists as personalities. Biography was a late art and the series of biographical essays known as the *Lives* are often contradictory and frequently unreliable. Aeschylus, it is thought, was born into an aristocratic family, probably in 525 B.C. His father's name was Euphorion and the family lived outside Athens at Eleusis, where the Mysteries were performed in honor of Demeter. His first play may have been written as early as 499 B.C. but his name is not recorded as a victor's until 484 B.C.

Aeschylus' early years were spent under the tyranny of Hippias and Hipparchus, the sons of Pisistratus, who ruled jointly until the assassination of Hipparchus in 514 B.C. It was during the latter part of the sixth century that the earliest form of tragedy emerged from the "invention" of the first actor by Thespis in about 534 B.C. Tragedy was eventually accepted as a formal part of the festival of the Great Dionysia about the year 500 B.C., and shortly afterwards Aeschylus introduced a second actor.

At the beginning of the fifth century a significant change took place in the visual arts. The earliest style of vase painting was principally decorative and when human figures first appeared they tended to be rigidly posed. Statues dating from the sixth century are relaxed and smiling. The fifth century witnessed a new interest in the plastic arts with the human body viewed as an instrument for action. A dynamic sense of life and liveliness increased in vase painting with black figure giving way to red. The rules of perspective were discovered, and in statuary and sculptured relief, a high seriousness developed. With purpose displayed in every line, the human figure became idealized as man assumed his role as the measure of all things.

At the same time, established religious thought was undergoing change. The influence of sixth-century Ionian philosophers infiltrated the Athens of Aeschylus, Thales, and Anaximenes of Miletus on the nature of matter; Anaximander, who suggested that mankind evolved from fish; Xenophanes of Colophon, whose single god transcended human shape or form—all of these natural philosophers were doubtless known to Aeschylus, as they would have been to all the serious-minded in Athens.

When Aeschylus considered the relationship of gods and men in his plays, he applied an open mind to Hesiod's systematic categorization of the deities. Individually the gods owed their origins, functions, and responsibilities to powers outside man's control or comprehension: earthquake, thunderbolt, sun, moon, lust, war. For Aeschylus this presented problems only as it affected mankind and his moral growth. Thus the gods themselves are perceived in his plays as developing beings. At the heart of the *Oresteia* is the yielding of the old law of blind retribution to the new law of mercy, a moral shift that suggests not agnosticism on the part of Aeschylus but a contemporary search for truth behind the concept of divine justice.

After the victory at Salamis the political changes that marked the transition from tyranny to democracy in Athens were placed in relief by the return to a ruined city. Although the Spartans were allies of Athens and in command at the conclusive Battle of Plataea against the Persians in 479 B.C., they were capable of taking advantage of Athens's weakness once the real enemy had retreated. Athens quickly rebuilt her walls and, with her sea power undisputed, set about establishing Athenian influence as widely as possible. With the declared aim of liberation from Persian oppression, Athens proceeded to make a virtue of extortion. Lists of allies were drawn up of who would pay to the Delian confederacy an annual tribute of money, ships, or soldiers—or all three. Those who failed to cooperate were suppressed, and what started as an alliance for the general good was shortly to be transformed into the Athenian Empire.

Tyrannical as the regime seemed to those outside Athens, within the Athenian state the movement towards democracy accelerated. The Assembly, where any Athenian citizen had the right to speak, was dominated by Ephialtes and Pericles. Under their influence, and in the teeth of opposition from Cimon, the Council of the Areopagus, the last bastion of nondemocratic government, lost nearly all of its powers in 461 B.C., three years before Aeschylus' *Oresteia*. Between the revolutionary legislation and the performance of the *Oresteia* in 458 B.C., Ephialtes was assassinated and Cimon ostracized. The third play of the trilogy uses as its pivot the institution of that same Council of the Areopagus as a court for the trial of murder.

Agamemnon, the first play of the *Oresteia*, deals with the return of Agamemnon with his concubine, Cassandra, from the war against Troy. Clytemnestra, who has already plotted her husband's death, receives him with elaborate courtesy before hacking him to death in his bath. The play ends with Clytemnestra justifying her action supported by her own lover, Aegisthus.

All three versions of the *Electra* story use these events as a background and each opens with the return of Agamemnon's son Orestes to Argos, there to be reunited with his sister Electra. Brother and sister together plan and execute vengeance on Aegisthus and Clytemnestra with the connivance of the Chorus and the aid of either Pylades, Orestes' companion, or of a former tutor.

Aeschylus completed his trilogy with *Eumenides*, which, through the trial and acquittal of Orestes for matricide, and the subsequent conversion of the Furies who have been hounding him, reveals a purpose far beyond the exposition of primitive myth. Sophocles' *Electra*, probably written about forty years later, is complete in itself; so, too, is Euripides' *Electra* (from about 414 B.C.), although his *Orestes*, first performed six years later, takes as its starting point the situation in Argos a few days after the murder of Clytemnestra, with Electra and Orestes still present in the city.

AESCHYLUS' *LIBATION-BEARERS*

Libation-Bearers can stand alone in performance, but the effect of producing it in isolation is to diminish Aeschylus' overall design and intention. His other surviving plays must however be judged separately, the remaining sections of the trilogies and tetralogies being lost. The reader or director should bear in mind that any part of the *Oresteia* is only slightly more self-contained than if it were a single act of a three-act play.

At first reading, *Libation-Bearers* appears to be a particularly static play; not as static as *Suppliants* or *Persians*, but the action can be easily summarized, conflicts between characters are simple, and the outcome is predictable. One could suggest that the play might originally have been performed by virtually immobile actors and chorus. But the text is written so it can be, and might well have been, amplified by elaborate physical presentation of its linked images. Strong emotions predominate in Aeschylus and characters describe their feelings in detail, so any attempt at realistic presentation would be out of place. Demonstration of passion, however, can be as moving as direct imitation of it, and an acting style is required today that enables an audience to be affected by the implications of what is being said or sung, even when the actors do not attempt to identify personally with the characters they are playing.

In *Libation-Bearers* confrontations are confined to the following:

1. A recognition scene between Electra and Orestes
2. A long ritualized *kommos* invoking the help of the dead Agamemnon, which lasts almost a third of the play
3. A short discussion of plans between Electra and Orestes
4. Orestes' greeting of Clytemnestra with news of his own "death"
5. The Nurse and the Chorus
6. Aegisthus and the Chorus
7. The final meeting of Clytemnestra with Orestes and Pylades
8. The escape of Orestes pursued by the Furies, which at this stage only he can see

The Chorus is allocated 452 of the 1076 lines, and only on the one occasion of Pylades' brief intervention does a third character speak in any scene.

Few stage directions are written into the manuscripts of the surviving plays. Occasional marginal notes made by scholiasts indicate some move or piece of stage business, but since these notes were written or transcribed at least as late as the copies themselves, there is no means of assessing their reliability. Some are helpful, some puzzling. Many stage directions are implicit within the lines themselves, but elsewhere they can be inferred from the nature of the situation.

In subsequent chapters I hope to show that these gaps in our knowledge can be filled to a great extent by examining the performing tradition that already existed before Aeschylus and linking it to the internal requirements of the plays in performance. I believe that the function of the chorus in the time of Aeschylus included an element of visual representation of the action indicated in speech by the principal characters. True or not, it is only reasonable to suppose that the choral passages were illustrated or highlighted by movement. Why else should the work of the chorus teacher (*choro-didaskalos*) have been so specialized? The chorus serves as a unifying feature in all fifth-century plays by virtue of its geographical position in the *orchestra* as intermediary between audience and actors. Often the division of choral odes into *strophe* and *antistrophe* suggests no more than the provision of an alternation of voice and dance for aesthetic reasons. Elsewhere *strophe* and *antistrophe* can represent contrary attitudes prevailing in a central conflict or, again, twelve voices advising different courses of action—as when Agamemnon's death cries are heard in *Agamemnon*. They constantly remind the audience that as a chorus they are individually human but, corporately, more than human.

It may seem a risky ploy to apply modern theatrical standards to plays of such antiquity, but a playwright in Athens was always judged by his ability to move his audience. The depiction by vase painters of scenes based on plays, and the way in which the texts themselves are constituted, make it clear that the Greek theatrical experience did not rely upon the spoken word alone. In their graphic and plastic arts, Greek craftsmen made use of color, pattern, and, above all, the spatial relationships among their human subjects. Although no final reconstruction of first performances can ever be attempted, it seems beyond doubt that any stage picture would have been enhanced by grouping, by the interaction of the performers, and by the patterned movement of a chorus that remained in view virtually throughout the whole of a play.

Libation-Bearers certainly has its share of *coups-de-théâtre* as striking although perhaps less obvious than the red carpet of *Agamemnon* or the magnificent transformation of the Furies that provides the climax of *Eumenides*. The unexpected pathos of the old Nurse and her talk of babies, when the Chorus dares not reveal the truth to her; the careful way in which the Chorus avoids alerting Aegisthus without incriminating itself; Orestes hesitating to perform the act of murder when finally faced with his mother until the hitherto silent Pylades speaks with the force of Apollo himself—all of these moments are of supreme theatrical as well as dramatic expertise. They strike a chord in terms of universal human response, even on the page—how much more so on a stage geared to the presentation of mighty subjects. The formality of Aeschylus is classical in the widest sense of the word; his stage world is one of strenuous passions, vividly expressed.

SOPHOCLES

Sophocles was born in 496 B.C. at Colonus, the setting of his last play. The son of an armorer, he both witnessed and contributed to the profound social and political changes of his youth and middle years. Although already sixty-five when the Peloponnesian War broke out, he lived through all but the final defeat by Sparta, apparently writing to the last.

He competed as a playwright at the Great Dionysia of 468 B.C., when he defeated Aeschylus at his first attempt to carry off the prize, the first of many prizes won in a career that spanned the greatest achievements of Athens as well as its decline. He was thought of as a kindly man during his lifetime and after his death. Involved in public life, to the extent of twice being elected general, once reputedly on the strength of writing *Antigone*, Sophocles reflects his political concern in his choice of theme. He is the playwright of the powerful dramatic situation and his sense of purpose, allied to his admiration for mankind, typifies the Athens of Pericles.

After the ostracism of Cimon, Pericles was to remain the supreme political figure in Athens until his death in the early years of the Peloponnesian War. Although personally subject to the whole democratic process of the state, Pericles' authority was undisputed. His influence stemmed principally from his power as an orator. It was Pericles who was chiefly responsible for the building program of the middle years of the century, a program paid for by tribute from subject states.

No style of architecture is more familiar than the columns and pediments of Periclean Athens, whether from the ruins of the classical temple or the neoclassical facades of innumerable town halls and railway stations. The Parthenon, two hundred and thirty feet long and one hundred feet wide, gives an impression—but only an impression—of perfect symmetry. The floor is not level. The columns are not equidistant—those in the corner are not even of the same thickness—and all lean slightly inwards. The illusion however is one of harmony and splendor. The famous buildings on the Acropolis all date from the second half of the fifth century, and to the southwest the Precinct of Dionysus, which includes the theatre, was probably completed during the Peloponnesian War.

From the prosperity of the interwar years came Pheidias' massive statue of Athene on the Acropolis, the bronzes of Polycleitus, and the Poseidon dredged only this century from the sea off Euboea. Decoration, two- or three-dimensional, concentrates on the human figure. Indeed, the sense of perspective in painting emphasizes the individual in a manner that is almost sculptural. Compositions on vases and cups now create a sense of depth, and the static mythological scenes of the previous century tend to give way to depictions of everyday life.

The plays of Sophocles are distinguished by a similar sense of balance and symmetry and lack the extravagances that made both Aeschylus and Euripides legitimate targets for satire. Specific political references are much harder to find in Sophocles, and his attitude to the gods suggests little heart searching, even after the outbreak of the Peloponnesian War.

Fifty years separate the defeat of Persia by Athens and Sparta, and the onslaught upon Athens by Sparta, but they were never entirely trouble-free years. As the Delian League grew into the Athenian Empire, war with the Peloponnese seemed inevitable. An official peace with Persia in the middle of the century accentuated discontent among the subject allies. The signing of a thirty-year treaty of peace with Sparta was unrealistically optimistic and served little purpose beyond affording Pericles the opportunity to prepare Athens for the war that finally came in 431 B.C.

Military activity was principally a seasonal occupation. The Spartans and their allies arrived once a year to ravage the crops in Attica, and the Athenian fleet retaliated with a punitive expedition around the coastal towns of the Peloponnese. Armies spent the winter months recouping their losses, and initially the dramatic festivals were affected hardly at all.

Battle casualties were not heavy but the enforced overcrowding of the city of Athens itself resulted in a severe epidemic of plague. At least a quarter of the city's population died in the four plague years 430–426 B.C., among them Pericles, probably only months after the production of *Oedipus Tyrannus*, a play that opens with the plague-struck citizens of Thebes begging help from their leader.

No one man succeeded Pericles as a figure of dominance, unofficial as his autocracy had been, but the last years of his life witnessed the rise of the demogagues, unscrupulous politicians who openly took advantage of the weakness to which the "democratic" rule of the orator is prone. Cleon, the former tanner, bombastic and ruthless, was the most destructive of these men. Cleon is perhaps the only character in Aristophanes for whom that genial, though trenchant, playwright seems to feel a personal animosity. Even after his death (422 B.C.), which led to the peace of Nicias—intended to last for fifty years and abandoned after less than three—Cleon's political philosophies continued to dominate the Assembly.

If the first ten years of the war were indecisive, the fatal Sicilian expedition of 415 B.C. heralded the final collapse. The army that had set out with such high hopes disintegrated within two tragic years, and very few of its soldiers ever returned to Athens. After Sicily the remaining Athenian allies, no longer to be held down by oppression and the sword, finally cut themselves loose. An oligarchic revolution broke out in Athens itself (411 B.C.), short-lived but indicative of internal dissension. Democracy was restored by the fleet on whose strength alone the future of Athens now depended. When Sophocles died in the autumn of 406 B.C., just after Euripides, the final defeat was only eighteen months away.

At the outbreak of the Peloponnesian War, Sophocles was already an old man. Most of his surviving plays probably derive from this late period, but even then they show little of the disillusion and despair that characterize Euripides' war plays. The dreadful picture of the city under plague, however, at the opening of *Oedipus Tyrannus* is matched by the bleakest lines of all Greek drama from *Oedipus at Colonus*, performed posthumously in 401 B.C.:

Never to have been born at all surpasses everything. But second best, if one has seen the light, to return as quickly as possible whence one came.[4]

SOPHOCLES' *ELECTRA*

Complete in itself, Sophocles' *Electra* has a set of dramatic priorities very different from those of *Libation-Bearers*. The issues of matricide and the resolution of Thyestes' curse on the house of Atreus are virtually ignored. The order of the murders is reversed, shifting the emphasis so Aegisthus, rather than Clytemnestra, features as the murderer of Agamemnon. Electra is on stage at the time of her mother's off-stage death, and any question of remorse or of punishment for Orestes is confined to a passing reference:

Electra: How have you fared, Orestes?
Orestes: All is well that has been done within the house, if Apollo prophesied well.[5]

The Chorus concludes the play with the declaration:

O son of Atreus, after suffering much, you have emerged in freedom with the success of your enterprise.[6]

The conclusion is simple enough but should not be taken to suggest that Sophocles is seeking to dodge the implications of the murder. He has already set his terms of reference, and the morality of matricide is not one of his concerns. The play cannot be regarded as flawed by comparison with the Aeschylean or Euripidean versions, for its omissions are intentional. If anything they return the plot to its Homeric origins although they are designed to centralize the character of the non-Homeric Electra.

The Chorus of Sophocles' *Electra* is given only 225 lines out of a total of 1510. As local women of Mycenae, this Chorus is generally sympathetic towards Electra, but it lacks the dimension of hatred for Clytemnestra, which characterizes the slave women of Aeschylus'

Libation-Bearers. Speaking at the outset in the singular, it, or at least the Chorus leader, treats Electra almost as a daughter:

I came as quickly as possible on my own account as well as on yours, my child. If I do not speak advisedly, have it your way. We are here to support you.[7]

In later exchanges the speeches of Electra are balanced against those of the Chorus. With the appearance of Electra's sister Chrysothemis, the Chorus reverts to the role of peacemaker, although on the whole it is disposed to favor Chrysothemis' attitude of conciliation.

On occasion the Chorus comments on the action as if it is composed of outsiders, sometimes as if personally involved, and sometimes as if completely neutral with no function other than to provide relaxation between long speeches. Such changes are difficult to reconcile. But it is just as true of Sophocles as of Aeschylus that his choruses may change their attitude from line to line. The Chorus does not have a single function within Sophocles' *Electra* and may utter, at one moment, statements that would endanger the members' lives in their real persona and immediately afterwards may cringe before the mildest criticism. It certainly has little direct effect on the play's outcome.

Such a shift of function on the part of the Chorus is hard to accept if we assume that, apart from what it says, it has no significant contribution to make. If it does nothing during most of the action in Sophocles' *Electra* and merely listens like passersby, the identity the Tutor has given it, the members are in no position to comment either on the effect on the royal house of Orestes' supposed death or on the sad position of Electra bereft of her brother. How much the Chorus might have reacted to the conflicts, confrontations, and emotional responses of Electra is considered later, but however such reactions may have been handled originally, the move toward realism in terms of character and motivation does not imply the eclipse of the chorus as a dramatic weapon. It is essential for a director to realize that in Sophocles the chorus was not a tedious old-fashioned device, but a motive force in a play's development.

Any analysis of the plays of Sophocles and Euripides suggests that a less rigid style of performance is required than for the plays of Aeschylus. The emphasis is more firmly placed on individual character, with an added subtlety of response and a greater range of emotion. New use of language, although still poetic, avoids the high-flown and sometimes tortuous imagery of Aeschylus. The lines, in consequence, are easier to speak and may be more rapidly delivered. Aeschylus' *Libation-Bearers* is 1076 lines long; Sophocles' *Electra*, 1510; Euripides' *Electra*, 1359; but they might well all be staged within the same playing time. Euripides' *Electra*, because of the greater lyricism of its Chorus and the subtler shades of emphasis lent by a dialogue that has become almost conversational, could perhaps take longer to present than either of the others.

Sophocles' greater reliance on individual characterization opens the door to a number of devices inappropriate in the plays of Aeschylus. Among these devices is the addition by Sophocles of two characters not used by Aeschylus or Euripides. The introduction of the character of the Tutor makes possible a far more elaborate plot against Aegisthus and Clytemnestra, while Electra's sister Chrysothemis gives an indication of how Electra is treated domestically. Both serve primarily to lend stronger emphasis to the relationship existing between Electra and Orestes. Chrysothemis never actually meets her brother but leaves the stage for good two-thirds of the way through the play. The Tutor clears the way for the recognition scene and keeps guard indoors, but he too is conspicuously absent at the time of the murders themselves.

Aeschylus in *Libation-Bearers* has little interest in Electra, whose final exit occurs before the play is more than half over. He concentrates instead on Orestes, but more on the effect of his deeds than the reasons for them. The individual for Sophocles has intrinsic value and his Electra is a heroic portrait. Sophocles centers on her almost to the exclusion of his other characters, perhaps reflecting an Athens that was in need of heroes. At first encounter this may seem to unbalance the play, but as with the Parthenon, so in *Electra*, individual details of construction may seem flawed, until you stand back and survey from a distance the entire work of art.

EURIPIDES

If Sophocles' work is based on an exaltation of man in his battle against the cruel ironies of existence, Euripides' plays are the work of an iconoclast, living in an age of disenchantment. Although born only twelve (or perhaps sixteen) years after Sophocles in 484 B.C. (or 480 B.C.), living through the decline of Athenian imperialism, he wrote entire plays apparently critical of Athenian political attitudes. Details of Euripides' life are hazy, too, if only because he later suffered from a decidedly hostile press. The comic poets considered him a constant subject for mockery and on numerous occasions paraded in public the reported details of his private life. A joke in Aristophanes over Euripides' mother's vegetable stall, or the unfaithfulness of his wife or wives, was sufficient to supply a *Life* with "authentic" biographical detail. That he was said to have lived as a recluse in a cave on Salamis may imply no more than that he liked to write in peace at his country cottage.

Whatever the truth about his private life, Euripides' writings placed him at the center of controversy throughout his life. While Sophocles was serving the state as general, ambassador, and even treasurer to the Confederacy, Euripides was conversing with Anaxagoras who believed that the sun was not a god but a mass of hot stone, larger and farther away than the moon on whose surface the sun was reflected. Protagoras, grammarian and philosopher, gave readings at Euripides' house from a book, a single quotation from which has survived:

About the gods I have no means of knowing either that they are or are not. For the hindrances to knowledge are many, the darkness of the subject and the shortness of man's life.

The book was banned, Euripides was arraigned for impiety, and Protagoras was deported.

If Athens at the turn of the sixth century was aware of but shrugged off the intellectual probings from Ionia, by the 430s it was playing host to the mood of universal questioning. The Sophists, among whom Socrates was so unreasonably placed by Aristophanes, had begun their teaching. To some they were popular instructors and to others, quibbling pests, but their encouragement to analyze man in all his aspects was seen alternatively as the opening of new doors to the future or as a mark of the decline of empire. If the attitudes sound familiar, it is only because the pattern is recurrent. Only seven short years separated Euripides' death (406 B.C.) in self-imposed exile in Macedon and the condemning of Socrates for "corrupting the youth and making the worse cause appear the better."

Euripides had been writing tragedies for a number of years before any were accepted for performance. Seventeen years more were to elapse before his first extant play, *Alcestis*, was produced in 438 B.C. Earlier in the same group of plays, *Telephus*, which has not survived, provoked an uproar by exhibiting a beggar-king dressed as a beggar rather than as a king. The new mood of realism had arrived, and an experimental day's drama reached its climax when, instead of the traditional satyr play, *Alcestis* was performed. Here was a new type of tragicomedy that dared to challenge established assumptions about heroism and about a wife's responsibilities in the home.

Nineteen of Euripides' plays survive, compared to the mere fourteen of Aeschylus and Sophocles together. This may be in part an accident of history, but it is a fair reflection of the position of respect Euripides held in the following century if not in his own. The small number of first prizes, only four during his lifetime, is an indication of the extent to which he refused to compromise his own advanced views. Sophocles, the former general, who had witnessed the "glories" of war and the defeat of Persia, could hardly have been ignorant of the miseries of war as well. *Philoctetes*, the only play of Sophocles that can definitely be dated within the period of the war against Sparta, while certainly not romanticizing the conflict against Troy, nevertheless does view war as an inevitable part of man's destiny.

Euripides held no such brief. The "war" plays show only the misery of the victims and the degrading effect of war on the victors. *Hecuba, Andromache*, and, above all, *Trojan Women* paint a picture of man that is uncompromisingly stark. Yet *Trojan Women* most probably appeared just before the Sicilian expedition set sail, and it was Euripides who was commissioned to compose the dirge for the fallen two years later. Euripides may not have been the sort of popular playwright who won regular prizes, but there is no indication that his views on war were considered unpatriotic. A small number of the Athenians imprisoned in the Syracusan stone quarries were fortunate enough to become household slaves. Ironically enough, their ability to recite from memory the lyrics of Euripides had made them a desirable addition to Syracusan soirées.

Not all of Euripides' output was as bitter in tone as the three anti-war plays. Euripides' greatest contribution to Greek drama was his ability to confound expectation. He even wrote domestic comedy in the guise of high tragedy. Refusing to accept any reputation at face value, he brought each accepted story to its logical conclusion, in human terms, and only then added the incongruous conclusion that the myth demanded. His characters speak prosily, almost chattily. If they lack nobility, they are certainly believable and psychologically consistent. People not heroes count in Euripides, who is the authentic playwright of Athenian decline, not as its victim, but as one of the few Athenians with courage and ability enough to see the situation as it was. He left Athens for the court of King Archelaus of Macedon a year or two before his death. In later times he was said to have been torn to pieces by the king's hounds after writing the *Bacchae*, but if Aristophanes knew how he died he fails to mention it in *Frogs*.

EURIPIDES' *ELECTRA*

The figure of Electra provides the focal point of Euripides' play of that name as it did for Sophocles. Otherwise, the two Electras have little in common. Euripides refused to see the legend in heroic terms and reversed every preconception about the characters. A far from noble Electra has been married off to a peasant farmer living near the border of the country away from the palace; Orestes is a weak man who has to be goaded into action; Clytemnestra appears as a rather comfortable matron, ashamed of the way she disposed of her first husband, but trying to live it down. The murder of Aegisthus is so unheroic as to break the unwritten moral code at every turn. After inviting Orestes and Pylades to a sacred feast of the Nymphs,[8] Aegisthus is struck down from behind while acting as host to the two strangers. Even the Messenger's glowing account can hardly gloss over the improprieties.

Electra herself is as startling a creation as Euripides ever conceived. Aeschylus had seen her as a wronged and noble woman, Sophocles as embittered and single-minded but justified by the righteousness of her cause. Euripides' Electra is degraded and deranged. She wallows in self-pity and exults in her misery and is either a crafty liar or has ceased to know the difference between truth and falsehood. The Chorus tries to befriend her but she complains of being friendless. She insists that she is forced to get water from the well but refuses her husband's offer of help. Her ravings about Aegisthus' drunken dance on Agamemnon's grave are, she admits, merely hearsay,[9] but they are foreign to the picture of Aegisthus offered elsewhere in the play and suggest improvisation to emphasize her wretchedness. Nor does her description of her mother in any way prepare the audience for the Clytemnestra who arrives to help her daughter after childbirth.

It is tempting to wonder if, after this, any dramatist could have again depicted a "noble" Electra, which may well argue for a production date after Sophocles' version. The long-awaited romantic avenger Orestes, a reality in Sophocles, is a travesty in Euripides. The unquestioning and morally unambiguous conclusion of Sophocles' play is matched by the sourness of that of Euripides, patched up by the appearance of Clytemnestra's two god-brothers and the restoration of the original myth.

As in the Aeschylus and Sophocles versions, it is the Chorus that indicates moral priorities to the audience. With 230 out of the 1359 lines, the proportional contribution of the Chorus in Euripides' *Electra* is slightly larger than that of the Chorus of Sophocles' play. Its role, however, is much more significant. Friendly and sympathetic at the outset in its characterization of local unmarried girls, the Chorus finds itself more and more out of its depth, looking on but taking no part when Electra and the Old Man, with the reluctant help of Orestes, are plotting the murder of Clytemnestra and Aegisthus.

In this *Electra* the Chorus seems to be only vaguely aware of what its "betters" are up to. It seems initially to be witnessing an act of justifiable vengeance, a position that must be maintained to account for its presence at all. It stands for the prevailing attitude to the old story, so Euripides can demonstrate in its bloody fulfillment what a highly dubious moral tale it really is.

From the horrific speech of Electra over Aegisthus' dead body through the entrance of Clytemnestra and up to her murder, the Chorus has little to say, but by the end of the play, it has undergone a change of heart: "You have committed terrible deeds, dear one, against your unwilling brother,"[10] it tells Electra, a condemnation hardly relieved by the brief term of endearment. "Wretched woman," it continues, "how did you dare to look with your eyes at the death of your mother as she breathed her last?"[11] It is rare for any chorus to be as outspoken as this in the delivery of moral judgement. When such a judgement contradicts the previous attitude of a chorus, it gives a clear insight into the playwright's intentions.

Euripides' *Electra*, a complex and frequently underrated play, has many moments that require amplification or explanation through consistent interpretation. An assessment of what the playwright originally required of the actors is harder to make. On stage, a scene may be interpreted not only by the way in which lines are spoken but also by the way in which they are received by other characters. If Orestes were to betray his dismay when recognized by the Old Man, or if Electra were to show disappointment at Orestes' turning out to be her brother, any projection of the scene as a conventional joyful recognition is untenable. The emphasis of any lines suggestive of a subtext is important, even if such lines were originally intended to be taken at face value. Electra on several occasions contradicts herself, and the audience is surely meant to realize this fact. The Farmer's retort to Electra after she says that Orestes and Pylades have come to see her misery, "They will have seen some of it, and you will have told them the rest, I expect,"[12] betrays an almost Chekhovian weariness. He tells Electra she should have invited the newcomers in, and after Orestes and Pylades have accepted the Farmer's invitation, it is her turn to complain to her husband: "You fool, you know how poor your house is. Why did you offer hospitality to strangers who are better men than you are?" He is then packed off to fetch the Old Man, retorting crossly: "A woman can always find something to add to a meal if she tries, and at least fill their bellies for one day."

Realism of this order is a characteristic rarely assigned to Greek tragedy. But it is through the contrast between realistic language and formal performance that Euripides demonstrates his individuality as a dramatist. These lines were delivered by masked actors no less than was the tomb scene in *Libation-Bearers*. These masked actors spoke in verse to an audience numbering upwards of fifteen thousand. Little wonder that Euripides' antiheroic writing provoked the anger of his audience and the mockery of the comic

poets. Euripides' aim was not simply to deal realistically with mythological themes, but to examine the moral principles involved in
terms of contemporary religion and current philosophy. This he
achieved not restricted by established conventions of presentation,
but rather by using these conventions to create surprise effects and
contrast between what the audience expected of its heroic figures
and the sentiments Euripides put into their mouths.

ARISTOPHANES

Although it is the *Electra* plays that I later intend to look at in
detail, this opening chapter would be incomplete without some
consideration of how the work of Athens' premier comic playwright
reflected the age in which he lived. For forty years before Aristophanes' birth in 448 B.C., Old Comedy had been a recognized
festival entry at the Great Dionysia. Nothing, however, remains
except a few titles and fragments for comparison with Aristophanes'
own eleven plays. At a time when the doors of citizenship were
shut fast against all whose parents were not true Athenians, Aristophanes' own claims to citizenship were in some doubt. Nevertheless his comic vision was to project a lively and detailed picture of
Athenian life. His first plays were produced during the Peloponnesian
War, but his work encompasses the final defeat by Sparta and
the partial Athenian recovery of the fourth century, and he con-
tributes the only two examples of Middle Comedy to survive:
Women in Assembly (392 B.C.) and *Wealth* (388 B.C.).

When Sophocles and Euripides died in 406 B.C., the Peloponnesian
War was not yet over. An Athenian victory was still to come in the
sea battle at Arginusae. Afterwards, the Athenian Assembly, fickle
as ever, enfranchised all the slaves who rowed in the battle and
executed six of the eight successful generals for reputedly making
inadequate attempts to pick up survivors. Socrates spoke against
this decision, and Aristophanes mentions the incident in *Frogs*,
where the dramatic competition between Aeschylus and Euripides
is decided not on literary grounds but according to the value of the
advice each playwright gives on Athens' future course of political
action.

One final sea battle, at Aegospotomi, was enough to defeat Athens. The city surrendered in 404 B.C. The walls were pulled down, and a repressive government known as the Thirty Tyrants was installed.

Democracy was restored to Athens in the following year, and in a comparatively short time the city was taking an active interest in the current squabbles between Sparta and Thebes. But the end of the Peloponnesian War saw the end of the classical age of Athens. The constant drain on resources had led to the melting down of statues, and building continued in a haphazard fashion without overall design. The fourth century was to be the age of the philosopher and the orator, of the actor rather than the playwright. Yet within the twenty-seven years of gradual decline from 431 B.C., the theatre produced the main body of the classical repertoire.

Euripides was critical of the conduct of the war in some of his plays. Aristophanes never left the subject alone for long. The war, the generals, and the politicians were a never-ending source of inspiration to him. From the first extant play, *Acharnians*, where the central character makes a private peace for his own benefit, the prosecution of the war obsesses the playwright. *Peace*, in which Peace is rescued from a well down which Ares has thrown her; *Birds*, where two citizens create an aerial city to escape from Athenian imperialism; *Lysistrata*, where the women "down tools" until peace is declared—all have the same preoccupation. Even when the theme focuses some different aspect of contemporary Athenian life, the war is never completely forgotten. The humor can be bitter: the Megarian in *Acharnians* who is trying to sell his daughters because he can no longer afford to feed them offers a savage indictment of Athens' desertion of her allies.

Aristophanes' own political standpoint is not easy to assess. He was after all a writer of comedy, and the temptation to hit at obvious targets may sometimes have outweighed his seriousness of purpose. Consistency alone suggests a deep antagonism toward the pro-war faction, and attacks on individuals may have amused the audiences but seldom the victims.

Most of his abuse is directed against contemporary figures, either in passing reference or by introducing them as stage characters, as happened to Euripides more than once and to Socrates. The community of Athens was dense, and Aristophanes could be confident that his "real" characters would be known by reputation if not by sight. That they were featured in scenes in which they met and conversed freely with gods and heroes, as well as fictional characters, apparently did little to reduce the sting of criticism. After the production of *Babylonians* in 426 B.C., Cleon impeached Aristophanes. Aristophanes reacted by producing in *Knights* (424 B.C.) an even more violently anti-Cleon play. *Knights* won first prize. Cleon was reelected general.

After Cleon's death in 422 B.C. Aristophanes continued to make fun of political decisions and politicians until the end of the war. At certain crucial times he appears to have tempered criticism with expediency. *Birds* produced at the time of the Sicilian expedition and *Lysistrata* produced three years later in 411 B.C. both pose comic situations that have become "classics," but both reduce the potential of the *parabasis* as an opportunity to give vent to the playwright's views on specific issues. Social institutions, philosophical propositions, educational theories, and intellectual posing of all kinds receive no such relief. The unique picture of contemporary Athens tantalizes by a breadth of reference that has defied analysis by future generations. This accounts for his comparatively weak showing in the world's repertoire. Yet his situations, blending as they do wild fantasy and hard politics, have no parallels except perhaps in the plays of Mayakovsky in our own century. *Frogs* with its competition to discover a playwright—Euripides and Sophocles having just died—who will return from Hades to save Athens amply illustrates the hard edge to Aristophanes' nonsense.

Frogs was performed only months before Cleophon, a worthy successor to Cleon, was to urge the Athenians on to their final defeat. The closing lines of the play sound Aristophanes' note of desperation. Selected by Dionysus, not as a better dramatist but as representative of higher ideals, Aeschylus moves off on his return to earth to the accompaniment of the Chorus:

Now as the poet passes triumphant into the light, grant, you powers beneath the earth, good counsel to this city of great and good men. Let us be freed from our anguish at last, and from the onset of war. And let Cleophon fight, and anyone else here who wants to, in their own fatherlands.[13]

It is an ironically suitable conclusion to the Athenian dream of empire that Aristophanes, the poet of peace, should plead for help to the long dead Aeschylus whose paean to Athenian glory in *Persians* opens, for us, the story of Greek drama.

NOTES

1. Aeschylus *Persians*: lines 401–32.

2. Although elsewhere I have anglicized all play titles, I have made an exception with *Oedipus Tyrannus*, there being no English translation that can convey the irony of the Greek *turannos*.

3. Aristophanes *Frogs*: lines 1008–10.

4. Sophocles *Oedipus at Colonus*: lines 1224–27.

5. Sophocles *Electra*: lines 1424–25.

6. Ibid., lines 1508–10.

7. Ibid., lines 251–53.

8. Michael Cacoyannis, in his highly misleading film version of Euripides' *Electra*, presented this feast in honor of the Nymphs as a Dionysiac orgy.

9. Cacoyannis included such a scene.

10. Euripides *Electra*: lines 1204–05.

11. Ibid., lines 1218–20.

12. Ibid., line 355.

13. Aristophanes *Frogs*: lines 1528–33.

Chapter 2 Drama Before Aeschylus

In the previous chapter I referred to Aeschylus' *Persians* and used its early date to look forward to the seventy years of classical drama it heralded. Those seventy years saw far-reaching social and political changes in Athens, the broad outlines of which were reflected in artistic trends throughout the same period. I suggested that the preoccupations of the major playwrights and their differing approaches to their craft by and large reflected the climate of their prime years.

Greek drama did not, however, begin with Aeschylus and if we are to gain any insight into the factors that dictated its early form, and ultimately its whole development as a performing art, we must also look back from *Persians*. We must look not only to the sixty years between the first tragedy and the first extant tragedy, but far beyond that to the religious ceremonials and secular entertainments that all contributed to fostering the dramatic instinct that so suddenly blossomed and flourished in fifth-century Athens. This journey to the darker ages of Greece can be somewhat dispiriting. Few ends tie up, and such patterns as do emerge often seem contrived. Concrete evidence is at a premium.

Some light can be shed by looking back to Homer and the beginnings of Greek literature. In the *Iliad* and the *Odyssey* we feel comparatively at home in the world of the Trojan War, Agamemnon, Clytemnestra, Orestes, and Electra. It is in Homer too that we find the notion of dramatic performance, at least in embryo, as a regular element of social recreation.

Persians was performed in 472 B.C. and has a cast of only four with the Chorus given nearly half of the written lines. No more than two characters ever appear at the same time and only two

scenes involve a duologue. Yet the dramatic form is far from primitive. Speeches like the Messenger's description of the Battle of Salamis
are particularly graphic, but this tendency can be found in all of the
choral odes.

Exactly how, or indeed when, the chorus danced will never be
known. It is generally agreed that all choral passages and perhaps
even the dialogue of classical tragedy had musical accompaniment.
This music may well have been intended not to harmonize with the
voice of the actor, but to provide a fixed rhythmic and tonal element
for him to play the lines against. Equally likely is the possibility
that the lines of the chorus, whether in dialogue or choral ode (the
meter is quite different for each), might have been delivered so as to
enable a chorus to underscore in movement what was being said in
song.

The dance has always been a serious as well as a recreational
activity in the Greek world. In archaic and classical times it was
part of everyday life, still to be seen in the frescoes of Minoan Crete
and Thera and elaborately described in the *Iliad* and the *Odyssey*.
The Greeks danced to demonstrate joy or sorrow; they danced in
procession or display; they danced imitatively, comically, or simply
rhythmically. What is more, they could expect to express themselves
in physical terms by use of feet, hands, and head. In Indian classical
dancing there is a language of gesture and posture that conveys a
wide spread of specific information, and it is not unreasonable to
believe that the fifth-century Greek understood some ancient convention of body language.

In such a tradition the ability to dance a story evolves automatical-
ly, so even Plato, that arch opponent of the theatre, could write in
the fourth century B.C.:

. . . every man is more animated in movement when particularly joyful,
less so when less joyful . . . generally speaking someone who is using his
voice in speech or song cannot keep his body completely still. That is why,
when representation (*mimesis*) of what was being spoken first came into
being, it produced the whole art of dancing.[1]

A "language" of dance, dramatic or nondramatic, clearly was
highly developed. T. B. L. Webster somewhat stolidly itemized

possible variations from representation in vase painting.[2] Unfortunately any attempt to associate these painted gestures with the rhythms of the tragic chorus is doomed to failure. All that the vases can show is that the dance in all periods was notable for the breadth of its style and form, and that the language of gesture (*cheironomia*) was probably well established in dramatic performances from the earliest times. Certainly the choruses of Greek tragedy and comedy had a wide range of emotion and action to convey.

The inescapable conclusion is that whatever most closely links fifth-century drama to its earliest manifestations has as much to do with physical expression as with the spoken word, perhaps more. This needs to be borne constantly in mind when considering forms of ritual and religious ceremonials of all kinds. In all of the miscellaneous pieces of evidence involving the origins of dramatic expression, the one constant feature is dance.

THE ORIGINS OF TRAGEDY

THESPIS

From time immemorial the credit for fathering the "Thespian" profession has gone to a man about whom virtually nothing is known. Evidence of the life and work of Thespis is so slight that there is doubt whether he ever existed. The name certainly seems closely associated with the Homeric term *thespis aoidos* ("divinely inspired bard").

Sir Arthur Pickard-Cambridge[3] collected seventeen early references to Thespis, but the first of these references is in Aristophanes' *Wasps*,[4] written well over a hundred years after Thespis is supposed to have flourished. Of the others, several are clearly derived from one another or from a common source. Four references are worth noting for the classical view of the development of tragedy:

[about 534 B.C.]: From when Thespis the poet first acted who produced a play in the city and the prize was a goat. The *Parian Marble*[5]

Thespis: Of the city Ikarios in Attica the sixteenth tragic poet after the first tragic poet Epigenes of Sikyon, but according to some, second after Epigenes. Others say he was the first tragic poet. In his first tragedies he anointed his face with purslane in his performance, and after that introduced the use of masks, making them in linen alone. He produced in the sixty-first Olympiad [536/5–534/2 B.C.] The *Suda Lexicon*[6]

The *eleos* was a table long ago, on which before Thespis, a single man mounted and answered the choreuts. *Pollux*[7]

They say also that the ancient poets, Thespis, Pratinas, Phrynichus, were called dancers not only because their plays were dependent on the dancing of the chorus but because quite apart from their own poetry they were willing to teach those who wanted to dance. *Athenaeus*[8]

Almost by default, then, Thespis has the best claim to have "invented" the first actor in Athens, but dramatic dance may have emerged elsewhere.

OUTSIDE INFLUENCES

Arion of Methymna, who lived in Corinth about 600 B.C., is credited by the *Suda Lexicon* with having "invented the tragic mode."

Herodotus, in a passage that has exercised the ingenuity of many critics, mentions the town of Sicyon, in the Peloponnese, and the reverence of its inhabitants for Adrastus:

Amongst other tributes to Adrastus, the Sicyonians honoured his sufferings in tragic choruses on Adrastus' behalf rather than Dionysus'. But Cleisthenes returned the choruses to Dionysus, and the rest of the ceremonial to Melanippus.[9]

Pratinas, who came to Athens from the Peloponnese, was later referred to as the inventor of the satyr play (see below). The case for Peloponnesian influence on drama is reinforced by the elements of Dorian dialect used in the tragic choruses of the fifth century.

Despite these possible influences, no dramatic tradition developed in the Peloponnese.

Whatever festivals, celebrations, or dances existed elsewhere in Greece, in the islands, or in Asia Minor, it was Athens that nurtured tragedy. In Athens lived the three great tragedians, flourishing among a host of lesser writers. Most importantly, it was to Athens that the ancient world consistently looked as the center of dramatic activity.

THE DITHYRAMB

The dithyramb was a hymn in honor of the god Dionysus. Sung and danced by choruses of boys and men it was an important feature of the festival of the Great Dionysia together with the performance of plays. Its early history vanishes into a number of obscure references and even Pickard-Cambridge, after fifty-eight pages of carefully sifted evidence, could conclude only that "the history of the dithyramb proves to be a somewhat puzzling and disappointing affair."[10]

No actual dithyramb survives, except possibly among some poems of Bacchylides of the mid-fifth century B.C. There is no reason to doubt the connection of the dithyramb with Dionysus or the attribution of the first literary form to Arion of Methymna rather than to any Athenian poet. Indeed, the performance of the dithyramb in a circular chorus of fifty members, to the accompaniment of a pipe, bears some resemblance to the dramatic chorus as it was later known.

Both before and after Arion, the dithyramb formed part of local festivals in the cities of the Peloponnese, as well as in the islands of the Aegean. The dancers were often presumed to be satyrs, mythical creatures that were part horse, part goat, but mainly human attendants of Dionysus.

THE SATYR PLAY

At the Great Dionysia in the fifth century B.C., a satyr play was presented as a fourth offering after three tragedies from the same playwright. Usually it featured a chorus of satyrs under their leader Silenus, performing a variety of gross and grotesque antics in the name of Dionysus.

Although satyrs were familiar figures of popular mythology from earliest times, later writers attributed the invention of the satyr play to Pratinas, who came to Athens about 500 B.C. at a time when tragedy was already a formal part of the Great Dionysia.

The only satyr play to have survived in its entirety is Euripides' *Cyclops* from the latter part of the century, but there is enough evidence to suggest that traditional features varied little. For the most part the plots revolved round the satyr chorus insinuating themselves into some variation, direct or indirect, of the story already treated seriously in the tragedies of the same group: what, at a much later date, Demetrius of Phalerum was to describe as *hilarotragodia*.

The satyr play to the Danaid tetralogy of Aeschylus, of which the extant *Suppliants* is the first play, was *Amymone*. Although nothing more than the title has survived, the story of Amymone is known from elsewhere. One of the fifty daughters of Danaus, she wounded a satyr with a spear while hunting. Her preservation from rape by the satyr and subsequent submission to her savior, the god Poseidon, no doubt gave a host of opportunities for vulgar horse-play with or without the intervention of Dionysus.

The language in such extracts that survive is surprisingly good, and it is worth emphasizing that in form and theme the satyr play resembled tragedy far more closely than Old Comedy.

TRAGODIA

The word *tragedy* offers a choice of literal meanings based on the Greek *tragodia* itself derived from either *trux* ("new wine") or *tragos* ("a goat").

The second part of the word is associated with *aeidein* ("to sing") and *aoidos* ("a singer", "epic reciter," or "bard"). *Tragodia* is an Attic term not found outside Athens. The association with "new wine" fits in with festivals of the vine and the belief of Horace that early actors smeared their faces with wine lees. *Tragodia*, however, as a derivative of *trux*, is etymologically difficult and usually disregarded.

But what of "goats"? There seem to be as many as a dozen possible explanations why tragedy should be called "goat song." *Tragos* might have been a synonym of *saturos*, a satyr, with participants dressed in goat skins, although a satyr had the ears and tails of a horse not of a goat. Perhaps choruses were sung at a festival in honor of a goat with a goat offered as a sacrifice or prize. Festivals in honor of the goat can still be found in several parts of the world. One such annual event at Killorglin in southwest Ireland involves the crowning of a goat and its elevation on a platform high above the main street. There the goat stays as king of the Puck Fair (see figure 1), while down below the pubs stay open for three days and nights. The atmosphere is hardly tragic, but undoubtedly Dionysiac.

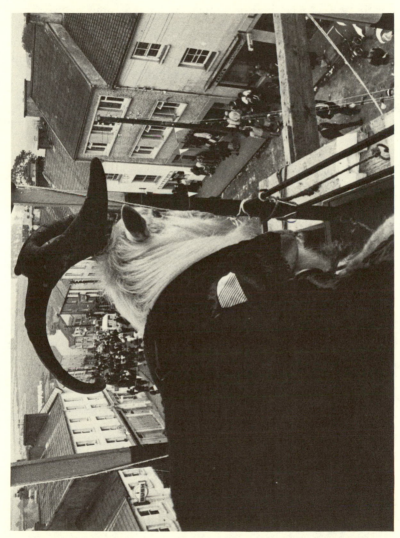

Figure 1. King Puck, The Puck Fair, Killorglin, County Kerry (Bord Fáilte, Dublin)

ARISTOTLE AND THE ORIGIN OF TRAGEDY

By the beginning of the fifth century B.C. the poet Pindar was writing odes (in celebration of victories at the games), dithyrambs perhaps, and individual paeans. Aeschylus was presenting his early plays, none of which have survived, in formal competition at the Great Dionysia. But no one was writing history, political or social. It was left to Aristotle, born nearly a hundred years after the initial performance of *Persians*, to venture the first recorded opinion on the genesis of classical tragedy and comedy.

A philosopher first and foremost, Aristotle wrote works on natural science, ethics, politics, and rhetoric. He also produced a treatise on poetry, the *Poetics*, in which he outlined the difference between epic and dramatic poetry and discussed the background of both.

Aristotle did not see himself as a historian of any sort, least of all as a theatre historian. He was writing simply as a philosopher in answer to his master, Plato, who would have banished all actors and epic reciters from his ideal state on the grounds that it cannot be other than bad for a good man to deviate from his own personality to represent a bad man. Anything dramatic, by being imitation (that is, involving *mimesis*), must by definition be "second best." This world for Plato was, in itself, but a pale imitation of the ideal world of "forms." Drama is thus placed at two removes from reality and in consequence is morally dangerous.

Aristotle in the *Poetics* sets out to counteract the Platonic view, while still accepting Plato's basic philosophic assumptions. The work is in the form of lecture notes and unrevised. Even though Aristotle had access to more plays than have survived into our day, he too lacked historical evidence, and there is no reason to accept any of his views on the history of the theatre as sacrosanct.

After discussing men's instincts toward harmony and imitation, Aristotle continues with résumé of the earliest beginnings of organized drama from which the following points stand out:

1. Cities other than Athens claimed the "invention" of the forms known as "tragedy" and "comedy," although all of the surviving plays are Athenian.[11]
2. These claims were usually linguistic: drama = "something done" but not in the Attic dialect; comedy is derived from *kome* (a "village") rather than *komos* (a "revel").[12]

3. First beginnings were in "improvisation," although improvisation is today such a loaded term that it requires qualification. The Greek *autosche-diastike* could imply anything from "freedom from a written text" to "superficial," "undeveloped," or even "in an experimental stage."[13]
4. Tragedy originated with the dithyramb.[14]
5. Comedy originated in phallic songs.[15]
6. Aeschylus increased the number of actors and was followed in this by Sophocles.[16]
7. The intermediate stage between "dithyramb" and "tragedy" was the "satyr" play.[17] This last idea is challenged by Horace, the Roman poet, in his *On the Art of Poetry*, written just before the birth of Christ. In what is primarily a letter of advice on the art of writing he includes his own understanding of the origins of tragedy:"The playwright who competed in tragic song for a mere goat soon (that is, later) brought naked satyrs onstage and without loss of dignity attempted a comic form."[18]

CHORAL TRAGEDY AND DIONYSUS

The basic objection to Aristotle's belief that tragedy developed from the dithyramb by way of the satyr play is easily stated. All of the evidence from the sixth century on the activities of satyrs suggests revelry and buffoonery, though not unconnected with more solemn aspects of fertility ritual. The satyr play in the fifth century followed this bias.

Tragedy, however, as represented by the plays of Aeschylus, is a highly developed, complex, and totally serious dramatic form, displaying the slightest links only with Dionysus and completely ignoring his reveling companions. In only one extant tragedy does Dionysus figure as a character. This tragedy, Euripides' *Bacchae*, was not produced until after the playwright's death. Far from being a paean of praise to the deity at whose festival it was performed, that play subjects Dionysus to a probing reappraisal in terms of his effect on mere mortals.

If tragedy really grew from the satyr play and both forms existed before Pratinas, it is difficult to account for the gigantic step forward that gave tragedy its serious purpose and form, but that at the same time permitted the dithyramb to retain its traditional nature and purpose at the Great Dionysia.

Traditionally a solution has been supplied by linking tragedy directly through the chorus to the dithyramb. The dithyramb involved fifty singers. *Suppliants* of Aeschylus employed a Chorus representing the fifty daughters of Danaus. Whatever the influence of satyrs, it was long felt that there must be a connection between nondramatic dithyramb and dramatic tragedy. Surely there had been a gradual takeover, when the leader of the dithyramb became detached and turned into the first actor. So *Suppliants*, not *Persians*, always used to be regarded as a primitive tragedy and dated accordingly to about 492 B.C., the perfect transition between fully choral and characterized drama.

R. C. Flickinger wrote first in 1918:

Tragedy and satyric drama were derived from dithyramb and comedy from the comus. Now both the dithyramb and the comus were entirely choral. Consequently early tragedy and comedy were also choral. No other fact in the history of Greek drama is better authenticated both by literary tradition and the extant plays than this. The dithyrambic chorus consisted of fifty dancers and this seems to have been the size of the chorus also in early tragedy. So the chorus in Aeschylus' *Suppliants* (between 500 and 490 B.C.) was made up of the fifty daughters of Danaus.[19]

This conveniently suited the notion of tragedy developing *away* from a use of the chorus. In such circumstances it was only natural to hold that *Suppliants* was the first extant play and the earliest by a number of years. This would leave an appropriate period between the first tragedy (composed, for the sake of argument, by Thespis about 534 B.C.) and early Aeschylus (about 500 B.C.) during which the playwrights explored all the dramatic possibilities afforded by the chorus responding to a single actor playing a number of roles. This would leave a further thirty years between the introduction of the second actor by Aeschylus and the third by Sophocles during which the choral element was gradually downgraded.

In 1952 a piece of papyrus was found at Oxyrhinchus in Egypt where numbers of ancient texts have been preserved in excellent climatic conditions. On it was part of a list of prizewinning plays including the words, "Aeschylus, won a victory with . . . *Danaides*, *Amymone*, second Sophocles." The first two titles have been erased.

That *Suppliants* was the first play in a tetralogy of which *Danaides* and *Amymone* were the third and fourth plays was already known.

That Sophocles first competed in 468 B.C. and won first prize was also known, as was the fact that Aeschylus was victorious in 467 B.C. with the Theban tetralogy including *Seven Against Thebes* as the third play. It transpires that the most likely date for *Suppliants* is 463 B.C., a bare five years before the *Oresteia* and only seven before Aeschylus' death. *Suppliants* is certainly preceded by *Persians* (472 B.C.), *Seven Against Thebes* (467 B.C.), and possibly even *Prometheus Bound*, which cannot be assigned a definite date.

Plainly, then, if *Suppliants* is the most choral of Aeschylus' plays, this is not because Aeschylus had not yet learned any better, but that he wanted *Suppliants* to have the form it has, for good dramatic reasons.

All the preceding argument is far from satisfactory. So complex a jigsaw emerges that most students of drama would be more than happy to leave all the pieces to academics to struggle with, or perhaps reflect that the probable answers lie more in the realm of anthropology than classical scholarship. Many of the scholars who have tried to create a consistent theory of the development of tragedy have themselves adopted a comparative approach. They have sought to draw a throughline from primitive times by reference to other cultures similarly noted for their demonstration of religious ritual in cryptodramatic terms or through the medium of mimetic dance.

Gilbert Murray, one-time collaborator with Granville Barker, looked back to primitive times as well as to the surviving plays.[20] Taking up and expanding Jane Harrison's theory of an "annual spirit" (*eniautos daimon*), whose death and resurrection were related to the seasons of the year and the ritual return of a dead hero, Murray created a formula for a primitive cyclic ritual. This formula, he believed, was carried over directly into tragedy in six stages.

1. *Agon* ("contest"): the Old Year against the New, Light against Darkness, Winter against Summer.
2. *Pathos* ("suffering"): associated with the ritual slaying of the *eniautos daimon*.
3. Messenger: to report the action that has taken place away from the audience's view.
4. *Threnos* ("lamentation"): especially associated with the mixture of emotions implicit in the form "The king is dead. Long live the king."
5. *Anagnorisis* ("discovery" or "recognition"): of the dead *daimon*.
6. Theophany, or resurrection: the dead figure revealed in glory and the conflict implicit in the *threnos* resolved in triumph.

Rituals of this kind are closely associated with sympathetic magic and are found in every part of the world. Early Egyptian drama of this nature may date from as early as 3000 B.C. A type of mimed play from Babylon anticipates the resurrection of Christ in the story of the god Bel who died, went to Purgatory, and rose again on the third day.

Although such nondramatic and even dramatic forms existed elsewhere, there is no evidence for them in Greece, and more particularly none in Athens. L. R. Farnell[21] suggested a tying of tragedy to the combat of "Fair Man and Dark Man" in the cult of Dionysus Eleuthereus in Boeotia, though there is no possible connection with choral drama to be found there. But neither this nor the Mysteries of Eleusis, performed in honor of Demeter and later associated with Dionysus, offer anything that resembles Murray's formula. Even more to the point, none of the extant plays does either.

Far from a joyful epiphany, a majority of tragedies end in lamentation. The coming to terms or resolution of a problem that the arrival of the god suggests in Euripides' *Andromache*, *Hippolytus*, and *Bacchae* (Murray's own examples) bears no resemblance to a resurrection in triumph even if the god is identified with the risen hero. Still less is it true of the *Oresteia*, which chronologically would be a more apposite example.

Once invented it is remarkably easy to fit a formula to almost any play and not only a play.[22] Sir William Ridgeway's answer to the Murray pattern was to beat him at his own game:

But a moment's reflection will convince the reader that the features which Professor Murray takes as characteristic of this ancient ritual drama of the death and rebirth of the Year can be found not only at any moment in human life, but in the whole realm of nature. For example, on a garden lawn is a happy family, two old sparrows feeding their young; enter the lady's favourite cat; she pounces on a baby sparrow (*Peripeteia*); a short struggle (*Agon*), a speedy death (*Pathos*), and the cat retires rending her victim (*Sparagmos*) "tearing to pieces." All under the eyes of little Tommy, who (Messenger) runs in to tell his mother what the naughty cat has done; meantime the parent sparrows are expressing their grief (*Threnos*) in unmistakable terms; the lady comes forth and discovers (*Anagnorisis*) the cat (*Theophany*) returning (possibly with an eye to another of her brood), her former victim lodged comfortably inside the two now in process of forming one body, if not one personality.[23]

Murray later emended his view associating such a ritual with tragedy, while still maintaining its relevance to the development of myth and the worship of Dionysus.

If Murray's theory created more problems than it solved, it had least the virtue of establishing a new dimension in classical thinking. When Ridgeway suggested in his turn that Greek tragedy arose from worship at the tombs of dead heroes because so many people die in tragedy, he was hardly more convincing.[24] George Thomson[25] took the relationship of the totemic society and its ceremonials and saw tragedy emerge from a form of passion play, but it has been left to G. F. Else[26] to suggest, comparatively recently, that such an approach is too theoretical and to reduce the argument once more to the scope of sixth-century Athens and what Thespis may or may not have been responsible for about 534 B.C.

It is here too that I would suggest the all-important link that unites Thespis not to some insubstantial mystery play, but to the very pillar of Athenian culture, the epic poet.

HOMER AND THE BARD

The *Iliad* and the *Odyssey*, wherever located between 1200 B.C. (the Trojan Wars) and 800 B.C., provide, along with various Homeric hymns, the earliest recorded Greek poetry. It is, therefore, in Homer that first associations can be made between an oral and a literary tradition. For fifth-century tragedy these two epic poems—the one concerning itself with a relatively short period in the ten-year war against Troy, the other relating to the return of Odysseus to his native Ithaca—provide an essential background. It is in Homer that one must first seek evidence of the basic skills of the entertainer, skills fundamental to the establishment of any dramatic convention.

Thespis is said to have "invented" the first actor in about 534 B.C. However, a dramatic form can scarcely have emerged overnight. The presence of a dithyrambic chorus from whom the "actor" sprouted appears to provide a convenient link for drama with other kinds of religious dance, but it may well be that other factors were of equal consequence. The actor-chorus relationship has too often been underrated in any consideration of the method of performance of early tragedy.

The epic cycles, particularly the Homeric poems and the nonextant

Theban cycle, provided the essential source material for Greek tragedy. Of all the extant plays, only *Rhesus* (doubtful Euripides) and *Cyclops* (a satyr play) fall unequivocally within the scope of the *Iliad* or the *Odyssey*, but another fourteen plays pass against a background of the Trojan War or the vicissitudes of the House of Agamemnon.

In both the *Iliad* and the *Odyssey*, stories from the present and the past are related by a bard or minstrel. A major, if not the decisive, factor in the development of Greek tragedy may have been the manner in which social entertainment, rather than religious expression, supplied a performance convention. I contend that not only did the actor develop directly from the bard or rhapsode, but that the chorus, which features so prominently in all fifth-century drama, bore initially a physical interpretative function still apparent in the plays of Aeschylus and still influential throughout the remainder of the fifth century in tragedy, satyr play, and comedy.

In the Greek world the term *dance* is used to describe any physical action enhanced by rhythm and action. As Lillian B. Lawler put it, "Further the Greek could, and often did, describe as a dance what we would distinguish as a march or a procession, a child's rhythmic game, a ball game, an exhibition of juggling, tumbling or tightrope walking, or even the gesturing of a tragic chorus."[27] She later went on to suggest that the Greek almost never sang or chanted verse without using an accompanying movement of some part of his body.

Before the funeral games for Patroclus in the *Iliad*, Achilles leads his Myrmidons in lamentation as they drive their horses three times around the dead hero. This is a "dance" whose function is to formalize grief at the level of a solemn game.

The recreational function of dance is described in Book XVIII of the *Iliad*. Hephaestus, the smith of Olympus, has decorated the shield of Achilles. Two joyful dances form a major part of the decoration. The remaining design shows a dance of young men and girls with an interesting refinement:

A large crowd stood round the delightful dance, enjoying it. And a divine bard played the lyre and sung among them while the dancers (or "tumblers") as the song began, whirled around in amongst them in time.[28]

The youths and maidens are dancing to and fro while the bard apparently sets the time for a couple of specialist acrobatic dancers.[29] The word used to describe the actions of the young men and women is *orcheunt'*, from *orcheisthai*, a transitive verb that Athenaeus uses intransitively in a much quoted passage about early drama:

Aristocles, therefore, says that Telestes, the *orchestes*, of Aeschylus was such a craftsman in *orcheisthai* the *Seven Against Thebes* that he made the action apparent simply through *orcheseos*. They do say that the ancient playwrights, Thespis, Pratinas, Cratinus, Phrynichus were called *orchestai* because they not only relied on the dancing to convey the sense of the dramas, but apart from their own work, taught any who wanted to *orcheisthai.*[30]

A few lines earlier Athenaeus suggested that Aeschylus was responsible for his own choreography, and that Telestes was a teacher of dancing (*orchestodidaskalos*), who invented numerous steps, "showing clearly what was spoken with his hands." It is unclear whether all these words with the root *orch* refer to performance or to choreography, but the implication is the same.

Athenaeus is referring to a method of storytelling by means of mime or pantomime and suggesting that it was a familiar mode of expression five hundred years before the emergence of Roman pantomime. The words *orchestes* and *orcheisthai* usually refer to performers, although Plato uses *orchestes* in the sense of "instructor in dance" or "choreographer."[31] Athenaeus also tells us that Aeschylus regularly played the lead in his own plays, so if Telestes fits into the artistic pattern, it may well have been as a choreographer for parts of the tragedy that Aeschylus was unable to oversee because he himself was performing. Actors have frequently directed plays with themselves in central roles, of course, but if the chorus and actor were irrevocably linked, with chorus responding directly to all that the actor spoke, the actor would surely need some kind of outside choreographer to direct the scene.

The exact nature of the bard's performance is clearly of considerable significance here. The bards in the *Iliad* and the *Odyssey* seem to perform much as the bard would have done who himself composed the poems for recitation, and as later rhapsodes who recited passages from the epic poems at the public festivals in Athens. The kind of performance the Homeric bard aims at is not in itself dramatic, but it has dramatic qualities. The effect he has on his audience is also closely akin to that aimed at in tragedy proper.

In Book I of the *Odyssey*, Telemachus, son of the missing Odysseus, is visited by the goddess Athene who gives him encouragement over his future course of action. When she leaves, he returns to the company of suitors for the hand of his mother Penelope:

The famous bard sung to them and they listened in silence. He sang of the sad return home of the Greeks, contrived by Pallas Athene. Upstairs Penelope, wise daughter of Icarius, heard the divine song and came down the steep stairs in company with two attendants. When she reached where the suitors were she stood by a roof-pillar, her bright veil over her face. An attendant stood at either side. Then she burst into tears and addressed the bard: "Phemius, you know many soothing songs which bards have composed, songs of the deeds of gods and men. Sing one of these for your present audience who drink quietly here. But cease from this sad song which tears the heart in my breast, having suffered such grief myself."[32]

In Book VIII Odysseus, who is staying incognito at the court of Alcinous, hears his own story sung. The effect of hearing his former troubles is to reduce him to tears that he can barely hide from his host. As the entertainment proceeds, the king apologizes for how poor his athletes are but says his people excel in the dance:

The nine servants who supervised these matters smoothed the dance-floor and made a circle. The herald approached, bringing Demodocus his tuneful lyre. Demodocus then moved into the centre and around him the young men gathered, all skilled in the dance and beat the dance-floor with their feet, filling Odysseus with amazement at their movements. Soon to his playing the bard added his fine voice, singing of the love of Ares and beautiful-crowned Aphrodite. . . . .[33]

During the telling of the story, Ares, Hephaestus, Apollo, Hermes, and Poseidon all speak in direct speech, all parts being represented by the bard himself. Dancers then take over, and after Odysseus has offered the bard a portion of meat, because "Bards are respected and honoured by all men for the Muse has taught them how to sing and she loves the minstrel fraternity,"[34] he requests the story of the wooden horse. Demodocus is immediately able to oblige.

The status of the bard is of some importance. He is a professional, and his songs are chanted or sung to the lyre. The rhythm he employs is the hexameter in which all the epics are written, and it fits in with music. If dancers are accompanying him, he gives them their time. He also has a privileged position in the household and is treated with almost universal respect. Even Phemius, the minstrel of the suitors, throws himself on Odysseus' mercy with the words, "Respect and pity me. You will regret it later if you kill a bard like me who sings for gods and men,"[35] and after intercession from Telemachus he is spared. The bard has a vast amount of material at his fingertips, much of it topical—"it is the latest song that an audience applauds the most"—and he can sing to order. Clearly, then, he is a privileged performer either wandering from place to place or resident in a great household.

In this sense the Homeric bard was an early version of the German scôp, or "gleeman," who is given the credit for the rediscovery of the narrative tradition that went into abeyance with the fall of the Roman Empire. When the northern scôp joined the mimus of southern Europe in eleventh-century Provence, it was a meeting that already had been anticipated in the Iliad and the Odyssey when the acrobats turned cartwheels to the playing of the bard. The skills of the mime, the tumbler, the jester, are skills that are never entirely lost whatever the prevailing attitude to organized theatre, because they incorporate the basic instinct of the extrovert to play tricks, to entertain, to be the center of attraction among his fellows.

This in turn brings up the whole nature of dramatic performance. At what precise point does a recitation become dramatic? How much is a man who simply tells a story also an actor? How exactly can we define the performance of the bard, if at all, and is he really the precursor of the first actor centuries later?

The bard in the passages quoted relies on two things. First is the imagination of the audience, which he arouses by evoking a specific scene or series of scenes from recent history or from the stories of the Olympian gods. These latter scenes are often discreditable and aim primarily at comic effect, an attitude that may well be reflected in the practice of concluding a group of tragedies with a satyr play.

Demodocus in the Odyssey is sufficiently well informed to recount, in Odysseus' presence, a quarrel between Odysseus and Achilles and the story of the wooden horse, in which Odysseus was very much involved, and provoke no reaction in Odysseus beyond admiration at the bard's skill and grief at the memories the story inspires. He knows his facts and his central purpose is to entertain and perhaps to inform.

The second element of skill in the bard's performance is his ability to convey information and emotion, and in this he most resembles an actor. His delivery is suited to his material and his music underlines what is being said or sung and creates mood. In one specific case, when he sings of the loves of Ares and Aphrodite, the atmosphere is created in essence by the movements of a chorus responding to the lines. This anticipates the central function of the chorus in tragedy. It also suggests that the Messenger speech of a later tragedy might have incorporated a conscious return to a familiar way of telling a story with the help of a chorus—not a lapse into epic, but the epic touch.

In certain key respects the bard's skill is similar to the actor's. The technique consciously acquired by barrister, orator, preacher, or teacher to convince his audience of the point he is making is the same technique as that of the actor. The good lawyer or lecturer knows how to organize physical and vocal resources for maximum effect. Acting, even naturalistic acting, is a physical occupation but it overlaps into many areas of human contact and behavior. The abuse of the term *dramatic* tends to obscure the exceptional features of the actor's performance. The use of the actor's skills is only truly dramatic when the situation is in itself theatrical.

Eric Bentley has described the theatrical situation reduced to its minimum as "A impersonates B while C looks on."[36] To accept this definition would be to forge the final link between bard and actor. The bard in Book VIII of the *Odyssey* who tells the story of Ares and Aphrodite is certainly using *mimesis* and "imitating" another person when he describes the arrival of Ares at Aphrodite's house:

She had just come back from visiting her mighty father Zeus. She was sitting down when Ares entered, took her hand and addressed her: "Come, my dear, let us go to bed together, for Hephaestus is no longer at home. . . ."[37]

Later in the same story the conversation is three- and four-sided among the gods who have come to laugh at the guilty pair pinned to the bed by a net. By employing direct speech, A, the bard, is imitating B, Ares, Hephaestus, Poseidon, and so on, while C, the bard's audience, looks on. Professor Bentley's conditions for the theatrical situation appear to be met.

But something is missing. Although the bard may be representing the characters or "imitating" them, whether he is playing one role or many, he is still recognizable to the audience as the narrator in his own persona. There is no attempt on his part to conceal his own identity or to take upon himself the nature of the person imitated. In this sense *impersonation* is barely adequate as a term to describe the theatrical situation. Aristotle's *mimesis* implies something more.

The "game" that audience and performers play in the theatre may be lighthearted or serious, but it is essential that both sides join in. Except in unorthodox circumstances dictated for the most part by a lack of sophistication, an audience does not accept that an actor *becomes* another person. Disbelief is only suspended by a conscious act on behalf of audience and actor, which is why no performance can exist unless an audience is present. The audience must join in the game. If Eric Bentley's definition of the theatrical situation is emended to read, "A impersonates B while C accepts the pretence," the conscious participation of the audience is seen to be vital, and it ceases to be possible to mistake the performance of the bard for that of an actor. As long as he remains within his own personality as bard, his temporary impersonation does not require full acceptance. His skill can be gauged by the ease with which the audience appreciates not the assumption of character, but the manner in which he tells his story. That ability may be similar to the ability of an actor, but there is still an important step that must be taken before the performance becomes truly "dramatic."

It is now possible to return to the dance. Aristotle paid very little attention to the chorus in the *Poetics*. He does, however, trace the differences between epic and tragic "modes of imitation," and in the final chapter he makes the following statement:

For as though no-one among the audience would understand otherwise, they [the performers] execute a great deal of movement: just as poor flute-players pirouette to imitate a discus-thrower and drag the chorus-leader about when playing Scylla. That is what tragedy is like and that is what former actors thought of their successors. Mynniscus used to call Callipides the Ape for his extravagant action and the same was thought about Pindaros.[38]

Aristotle goes on to condemn tragedy as inferior because epic appeals to an audience who do not need *schemata*. The word *schema* is closely associated with the dance. There is a passage in Plutarch's *Quaestiones Convivales*[39] in which the philosopher Ammonius sets out to define the elements of dance as *phora*, *schema*, and *deixis*. The *phora* seems to be the movement itself; *schema*, the pose; *deixis*, the demonstrative element. Plutarch is a late writer by classical standards, but the significance of these definitions for classical tragedy may be considerable.

Lillian Lawler[40] appreciated that the Greeks were imprecise in their application of the word *schema*, but she could still identify numbers of attested *schemata* in Greek dance with names like "seizing a club," "spin turn," "one after the other," "the high kick," "tumbling." There are many more. Aristotle himself used the word *schematized* in the first chapter of the *Poetics*:

All the arts, i.e. Epic, Tragedy, Comedy, Dithyramb and Music, produce *mimesis* by rhythm, language and harmony, singly or combined. . . .
Dancers imitate character, feeling and action by means of schematized rhythms. . . .[41]

Lillian Lawler commented that "Aristotle obviously does not make the three elements coordinate, but regards *schemata* and *rhuthmoi* (rhythms) as together creating *mimesis*. He could not possibly be speaking of the Graeco-Roman pantomimic dance, of course, which was not developed until the time of Augustus."[42]

I would suggest, however, that the original relationship between bard and chorus *was* similar to that of the later Graeco-Roman pantomime and was carried through directly into early tragedy.

When Aeschylus' *Suppliants* was redated as a late rather than an early play, it was necessary to radically rethink the whole nature of choral tragedy. Of all surviving Greek tragedy, *Suppliants* appears to give to the chorus the biggest share of the action, and this suited the notion that as tragedy developed it moved away from emphasizing the chorus in a steady line down to the last plays of Euripides. The *Bacchae* hardly fits this scheme, of course, having been performed posthumously, but at the top end of the time scale, the years between Thespis (c. 534 B.C.) and the original date for *Suppliants* (c. 490 B.C.) could be seen to be filled by attempts to discover what happened next after the "first actor" had been invented. After thirty years of constant application, Aeschylus had a brainwave and came up with a second actor.

The chorus, however, was never a tedious necessity thrust upon early playwrights unable to think of any other way of writing plays. It was and remained the life and soul of the drama. The decline in emphasis during the fifth century does imply a new set of dramatic priorities as the theatre developed, but Euripides had by no means reached the stage of wanting to dismiss the chorus completely, even when his plays became strongly realistic. For all three tragedians a major function of the chorus remained, I believe, to reflect the rhythm of the play in visual terms, even at times when it had no lines assigned to it.

Bearing in mind the close association between the Homeric bard and his dancers and allowing for the considerable influence of the cyclic dithyramb, it is my contention that, in Aeschylus at any rate, the relationship of actor and chorus was a development from that of the bard and chorus in the *Odyssey* when the chorus danced the story that the bard was singing. In other words, the chorus supplied an extra visual dimension to the story. This also fits with the suggestion of G. F. Else[43] that the second actor was not introduced to supersede the chorus as a source of conflict, but to extend the range of possibilities by the introduction of an outsider.

If Else is correct, the first actor had no direct connection with the chorus except insofar as he initiated choral response. The step that Thespis took in introducing a first actor was simply to develop the action of the bard to incorporate direct impersonation, and to this end he took to wearing the mask. At the point at which "epic" became "dramatic," the scope of the narrative was curtailed. The skill of the dramatist was employed in condensing a story of epic dimension into dramatic form. The second actor emerged so slowly not because it took thirty years for someone to come up with the idea of one character having a conversation with another, but because it took an Aeschylus to identify the several functions of the chorus and create a second actor to feed information to the first.

Early tragedy seems to have involved a single actor who could change character. He shared the spoken word with the chorus, or its leader, and the chorus danced and sang connecting passages while the actor was offstage changing. When the actor had his set speeches, however, the function of the chorus was to dance *during* them to promote their meaning.

Such a theory cannot be proved. It can only be tested against the surviving plays of Aeschylus. Suffice it to say that the descriptive passages of Aeschylus' set speeches and indeed his dialogue between characters are frequently so graphic on the page that they almost serve as directions to a choreographer. Allied to the manner in which Aeschylus displays his theatrical shorthand in visual terms, it seems more than likely that the "effectiveness" of an Aeschylus play in its original production could have been conveyed even to a man who was stone deaf.

If this must remain in the realm of conjecture or implied from the manner in which the plays seem to have been created with per-formance in mind, there is at least some direct evidence for the relationship between actor and chorus with the chorus reacting in movement to the spoken word. It refers not to tragedy, however, but to comedy.

The choruses of Old Comedy were constantly active; of this there can be little doubt. In Aristophanes' *Acharnians*, *Birds*, and *Wasps* there are passages of dialogue that describe what the Chorus is doing. Two scholiasts' notes suggest the nature of choral response; yet few scholars have paid much attention to them. A. M. Dale's dismissive reference in *The Lyric Metres of Greek Drama* is typical: "Here I might mention the curious tradition which appears from time to time in scholia that the *mimesis* of the chorus included expressive dancing to the speech of the actors in a kind of synchro-nized miming."[44] She proceeded to dismiss the idea summarily for no better reason, it would seem, than personal devotion to the spoken word.

The relevant notes appear attached to the texts of *Clouds* and *Frogs* and would have been written by Byzantine scholars at the time of transcription, perhaps based on earlier commentary. At lines 1351–52 of *Clouds*, the Chorus urges Strepsiades to tell it how the dispute arose between the Just and Unjust Causes: "But from where the dispute first arose, you must speak to the chorus." At least this is how we would expect the sense to run were it not for the omission of the definite article so it reads literally "to speak to chorus." The scholiast's note runs: "They used the term 'to speak to chorus' when, while the actor was reciting, the chorus were dancing the speech." This seems to make "to chorus" (*pros choron*) a technical term and implies that for the descriptive passage on which they are inviting Strepsiades to embark, they will provide a danced accompaniment.

The second note is written alongside a passage in the *Frogs* when Aeschylus and Euripides are competing before Dionysus in Hades. Euripides declines to pray to the conventional gods of Olympus and instead asks the help of Aether in defeating his opponent, to which the Chorus retorts: "We are also anxious to hear from you two wise men what harmony (*emmeleia*) of words you embark upon, a warlike path."[45] *Emmeleia* is the word commonly used by Plato, Lucian, and Athenaeus among others for the dance associated with tragedy. Here the scholiast treats *emmeleia* as a synonym for *euruthmia* ("rhythmical order") and adds that the real meaning of *emmeleia* is: "Tragic dancing with the refrain, but some say the accompanying dance to the speeches."

The *Suda Lexicon* gives the same definition as the scholiast without the "some say," and clearly what they have in mind is to differentiate between the refrain, sung by the chorus, and the speeches, spoken or sung by the actors. A different kind of dancing is associated with each, but the important contrast is between the dance that accompanied the choral odes and that which provided a background, or rather a foreground, for the speeches or dialogue of the actors.

That such definitive statements should have been so casually dismissed is strange but may be due to the initial attachment to Old Comedy. It seems at least possible that the scholiasts are referring in passing to theatrical conditions which they took for granted, conditions that can only apply to the chorus-dominated drama of the fifth century B.C.

Certainly *emmeleia* regularly refers to a dance typical of tragedy, as the *kordax* was typical of comedy. *Huporchema* is used to describe pantomimic dance by both Athenaeus and Lucian, but the overlap is only to be expected when dealing with a visual art. Rather it is important to notice how regularly dance was expected to be descriptive or mimetic. The earliest playwrights up to and including Aeschylus were, it seems, considered to be dancers or choreographers no less than they were poets. From earliest times there grew up the codification of gesture known as *cheironomia*. Once established, as in the Indonesian *wayang topeng*, in forms of Indian dance or the theatrical forms of Japan, a single gesture, insignificant in itself, can be "read" by an entire audience.

Such a system of convention was, I believe, the basis of the classical actor's performance. It makes it even more likely that the actor should have developed from the single storyteller than from the composite chorus, whose pattern of movement and behavior was basically corporate.

The relationship between actor and chorus, which I believe evolved from the Homeric bard and his dancers, can be seen as the regular practice with the choral tradition that Aeschylus inherited from Thespis. Substantial traces of it can be seen in the plays of Sophocles and Euripides in the more narrative sections, while the choral reaction elsewhere was intended to convey the mood of and an attitude to the main action rather than a mimed extension of it.

This theory of a close relationship between bard and actor seems to resolve several of the difficulties inherent in the more usual belief that the actor evolved from the chorus. If the first actor did not emerge from the chorus but was always a separate entity, it is possible to accept the dithyrambic influence without wondering why the dithyramb should have maintained its popularity at a time when it had evolved into something else.

Most of all, however, the solution I have suggested is theatrically satisfying. It allows for the manner in which the chorus was later to develop and stresses the advantages in a nonrealistic drama of a closely knit small group in identical masks. It also stresses the extra visual dimension to a performance that is too often considered solely in the light of the spoken word.

NOTES

1. Plato *Laws*: VII 815e–16a.
2. T. B. L. Webster, *The Greek Chorus* (London: Methuen, 1970), pp. 1–32.
3. A. W. Pickard-Cambridge, *Dithyramb, Tragedy and Comedy*, 2nd ed. rev. by T. B. L. Webster (Oxford: Oxford University Press, 1962), pp. 69–72.
4. Aristophanes *Wasps*: line 1479.
5. The *Parian Marble (Marmor Parium)* is a chronological tablet on which are recorded events of importance, including prizewinners in the dramatic competitions in Athens up to the third century B.C. It is incomplete.
6. The *Suda Lexicon* is a late classical encyclopaedia that drew on previous source material which has not survived.
7. Pollux *Onomasticon*: IV 123. Julius Pollux, a grammarian who flourished in the second century A.D., includes in the *Onomasticon* a section on the Greek theatre, much of which is confused and confusing.
8. Athenaeus *Deipnosophists*: I 22a. Athenaeus who flourished about 200 A.D. included in the *Deipnosophists* a history of Pantomime.
9. Herodotus *Histories*: V 68.
10. Pickard-Cambridge, *Dithyramb, Tragedy and Comedy*, p. 58.
11. Aristotle *Poetics*: 1448a.
12. Ibid., 1448a–b.
13. Ibid., 1449a.
14. Ibid.
15. Ibid.
16. Ibid.
17. Ibid.
18. Horace *On the Art of Poetry*: lines 220–22.
19. R. C. Flickinger, *The Greek Theater and Its Drama*, 4th ed. (Chicago: University of Chicago, 1936), p. 33.
20. In J. E. Harrison, *Themis*, 2nd ed. (London: Merlin, 1963), appendix to ch. 8, pp. 341–63.
21. L. R. Farnell, *The Cults of the Greek States* (Oxford: Oxford University Press, Clarendon Press, 1896–1909).
22. In *Chekhov the Dramatist* (New York: Hill & Wang, 1960), David Magarshack attempted to apply the scheme to the plays of Chekhov with implausible conclusions.
23. William Ridgeway, *The Dramas and Dramatic Dances of Non-European Races* (Cambridge: At the University press, 1915), pp. 60–61.
24. Ibid., ch. 1.

25. George Thomson, *Aeschylus and Athens*, 3rd ed. (London: Lawrence and Wishart, 1966).

26. G. F. Else, *The Origin and Early Form of Greek Tragedy* (Cambridge: Harvard University Press, 1967).

27. Lillian B. Lawler, *The Dance in Ancient Greece* (Middletown, Conn.: Wesleyan, 1965), p. 11.

28. Homer *Iliad*: XVIII 603–6.

29. This passage from the *Iliad* is echoed in the *Odyssey* (IV 17–19) during an episode in which Odysseus is relaxing with Menelaus and his neighbors while the bard plays and sings with the dancers.

30. Athenaeus *Deipnosophists*: I 22a.

31. Plato *Euthydemus*: 276d.

32. Homer *Odyssey*: I 325–42.

33. Ibid., VIII 258–67.

34. Ibid., VIII 479–81.

35. Ibid., XXII 344–46.

36. Eric Bentley, *The Life of the Drama* (New York: Methuen, 1965), p. 150.

37. Homer *Odyssey*: VIII 289–94.

38. Aristotle *Poetics*: 1461b.

39. Plutarch *Quaestiones Convivales*: 9. 15. 2. 747b–48e.

40. Lillian B. Lawler, *The Dance of the Ancient Greek Theatre* (Iowa City: University of Iowa Press, 1964), ch. 2.

41. Aristotle *Poetics*: 1447a.

42. Lillian B. Lawler, *Phora, Schema, Deixis in the Greek Dance, Transactions of the American Philological Association*, vol. 85 (1954), p. 158.

43. Else, *Origin*, ch. 4.

44. A. M. Dale, *The Lyric Metres of Greek Drama*, 2nd ed. (Cambridge: At the University Press, 1968), p. 213.

45. Aristophanes *Frogs*: lines 895–97.

Chapter 3 Organization of the Dramatic Festivals

Greece is a hot country, mountainous and waterless over wide areas. Fertile plains and coastal strips were colonized after the Mycenean age by various invaders, but comparative geographical isolation allowed communities to develop idiosyncratically, with marked variation in dialect, custom, and culture. Independent city-states, or *poleis*, grew up all over mainland Greece, the Peloponnese, and the numerous islands of the Aegean. Argos, Corinth, Megara, Thebes, and a half dozen of the major islands including Euboea are all within a hundred miles of Athens.

When the communities began to expand, they were unable to grow larger where they were because their land was simply unable to support increased numbers. They responded by sending out colonists, and daughter cities were founded by Megara, Corinth, and others in areas of Macedonia, Sicily, and southern Italy, forming semipermanent if somewhat strained links with the home *poleis*. Athens was fortunately placed in Attica, an area that was able to accommodate a large farming community outside the city itself. Only in wartime was pressure felt in Athens when the threat of the Spartans forced all the country dwellers into the city with disastrous consequences.

The differences among the Greek cities were exaggerated by trading disputes, and at any one time in the Classical period, almost any combination of *poleis* might be at war with almost any other. Only on the rarest of occasions was any kind of unity fostered in the face of a common enemy. Persia was one such enemy in the early fifth century, but there was no other until the growth of Macedon one hundred and fifty years later.

FESTIVALS

The only times when disputes were temporarily put aside were festival occasions such as the celebration of Panhellenic Games, in particular those held at Olympia. Individual *poleis* all held major internal festivals to celebrate their various patron deities, but since these festivals tended to coincide with major events in the agrarian calendar, they were strictly private affairs. The most magnificent festival in Athens, the Panathenaia, took place in midsummer, with competitions for athletes, horsemen, and musicians. A highlight was the recitation of parts of the Homeric poems by rhapsodes, inheritors of the purely narrative epic tradition of the bards. The Panathenaea concluded with the escorting of the *peplos*, a garment especially woven for Athene by unmarried girls, to the temple of the patron goddess. It is this procession that Aeschylus introduced in the final scene of the *Oresteia*.

At none of these festivals was there a dramatic performance. In Athens, such performances were reserved for festivals in honor of the god Dionysus, a deity excluded from the Olympian hierarchy, but traditionally associated with fertility and wine, and, above all, with the state of ecstasy when normal restraints are looser and the irrational rules. Three of the four Dionysiac festivals in Athens— the Lenaia, the Rural (or Lesser) Dionysia, and the Great (or City) Dionysia—involved dramatic presentation. The Anthesteria probably did not.

The dramatic festivals of Athens belonged to the community and were religious in origin and emphasis. The audiences were not so much spectators as participants, and the physical relationship between auditorium, *orchestra*, and stage area in the Greek theatre emphasized this participation. As with all Athenian festivals, worship was a genuinely communal act, and one that did not preclude laughter or the expression of approval or disapproval at the conduct of affairs. The dramatic contests, no matter how lavish in their preparation, formed only a part of a formal celebration in honor of a god. Thus the contests contributed to civic and religious ceremonial, but did not dominate it.

THE GREAT DIONYSIA

The latest of the dramatic festivals to be instituted, the Great Dionysia, became the most concerned with the theatre. Five days of early spring, sometimes six, were given over to public holiday, usually toward the end of March.[1] At this time Athens welcomed visitors from all over the Greek world and the city felt itself to be on display.

Proceedings began with the statue of Dionysus Eleuthereus being taken from the Old Temple, escorted away from the theatre to a shrine on the road to Eleutherae, and eventually brought back again to the theatre. It was accompanied on its travels by the archons together with priests, officials, and perhaps even the casts of the plays planned for performance. Because the ceremony was Dionysiac, *phallos* poles were also carried. An inscription from the middle of the fifth century requires a new colony to send an annual *phallos* to the Great Dionysia. This would appear to indicate that *phalloi* were sent from all over the empire. Indeed, cities may well have vied with one another to send bigger and better *phalloi*, a gesture certainly in keeping with an occasion that was highly serious but far from solemn. Revelry and dancing were equally a part of the occasion.

Rites and sacrifices were performed along the way, and it was nightfall before Dionysus returned to his theatre, escorted by torches, to be installed in the place of honor facing the *orchestra* for the rest of the festival. Perhaps at this moment a goat might have been sacrificed to give tragedy its name—we do not know. Some time was set aside for proclamations involving those who had earned special distinction for the city or had died in battle. The first day was a long one—noisy, joyful, solemn: the *polis* was on holiday.

The second day was devoted most probably to the dithyrambic contests, each of the ten tribes competing with a group of men or boys. From about 500 B.C. competitions for tragedy probably followed, the plays being performed in groups of four from each of three playwrights. The *komos*, or "revel," that concluded the proceedings acquired formal status when Old Comedy was accepted as an official festival entry in 486 B.C. The exact organization of the festival from day to day is difficult to determine: even now it is not clear exactly how many comic playwrights competed. After the first day, the festival may have been arranged in one of the following ways:

1. *Either:*   day 2: the contest of dithyrambs
     days 3, 4, and 5: the groups of four plays by three tragedians
     day 6: five comedies
2. *Or:*   days 2, 3, and 4: the contribution of the tragedians followed by
        a comedy
     days 5 and 6: one comedy and five dithyrambs

Other variations are possible. If the comedies numbered only three, the festival could be reduced to five days. During the Peloponnesian War, when circumstances may have changed from year to year, Aristophanes' comedies seem to have been performed after the tragedies and the satyr play. The Chorus in *Birds* invites the audience to come and join it:

Nothing's nicer, nothing better than wings. If any of you in the audience had wings, you wouldn't have to sit hungry through those tragic choruses. You could fly off home, have lunch and then fly back for our comedy.[2]

Birds was produced at the Great Dionysia of 414 B.C.

THE RURAL DIONYSIA

The Rural Dionysia[3] was in every way a smaller affair than the Great Dionysia, but to consider it as a single, fixed festival is misleading. Individual *demes*, administrative divisions within the ten tribes, contributed to a number of Rural Dionysias which could include the performance of single plays, notably at the Piraeus, the port of Athens, where Socrates saw Euripides performed.

Regulations seem to have been entirely variable. Tragedy and comedy mingled, with nothing like the organizational rigidity of the Great Dionysia. After the death of Aeschylus and the lapse from favor of the interconnected trilogy, the possibility of putting on single plays may well have become attractive. A new playwright might get his chance to compete away from the glare of publicity attendant upon a major festival. An established playwright might rewrite a rejected play, or a particularly successful single play might be revived despite the practice whereby a production was to be presented only once.

Performances are recorded from the fourth century at Eleusis, Icarion, Aixone, Acharnai, Aigilia, Collytus, Paionia, Rhamnous, and Salamis, by which time numbers of small theatres had been built throughout Attica, and acting had become a full-time profession. It is conceivable that in fifth-century Attica, in addition to the important festivals, there was a host of minor dramatic performances at other times of the year: tryouts, recasts, and revivals, with the choice of play and conditions of presentation dictated by local requirements. Such a system could well have provided employment for actors who were paid for the major festivals from about the middle of the fifth century, but were apparently unemployed in Athens between spring and autumn. More important, the Rural Dionysias might well have functioned as a sort of actors' training ground. One may guess that an actor's training was long and arduous, but unless fledgling actors had access to plays in performance, it is difficult to see how apprenticeships could be served. The Rural Dionysias perhaps provide an answer.

THE LENAIA

No one is sure how the title "Lenaia" is derived. The festival probably had some connection with the Eleusinian Mysteries and again involved processions in addition to dramatic contests. Much of the festival took place outside Athens itself and it has even been suggested that the dramatic performances took place not in the Theatre of Dionysus, but in some other theatre of different shape, age, and location.[4] That there might have been a second major theatre near Athens is an intriguing if unlikely possibility. Comic performance predominated at the Lenaia, but the introduction of prizes occurred later than at the Great Dionysia. At least as many of the surviving plays of Aristophanes were performed at the Great Dionysia.

After Aristophanes was indicted by Cleon for "insulting the state in the presence of foreigners" for his play *Babylonians* (Great Dionysia, 426 B.C.), his immediate stage reply came the following

Lenaia. Dicaiopolis reveals in *Acharnians* the advantages of performing at the lesser of the two festivals:

Don't be annoyed, spectators, if I as a beggar speak about the city in a Comedy. Even Comedy knows what justice is. Nor can Cleon accuse me of speaking ill of the City with strangers present. We are alone here and this is the Lenaia; with no strangers, tribute-bearers or allies: we are alone the winnowed grain, for I consider the resident aliens as the bran.[5]

Only Athenian citizens could attend the Lenaia that took place a couple of months before the Great Dionysia, so the atmosphere of the festival was very different from that of more cosmopolitan occasions. Normally only two tragic poets competed alongside the comedians and the acceptance of the Lenaia as an official occasion, with state supervision, goes back only as far as about 440 B.C. Otherwise its history is obscure, possibly because it was a more parochial occasion.

Listed below are the most acceptable dates of major change:[6]

	Great Dionysia	Lenaia
Introduction of tragedy	c. 534	440–30
Competition for writers of tragedy	c. 502	c. 430
Introduction of comedy	c. 502	443
Competition for writers of comedy	486	442
Competition for tragic actors	449	c. 430
Competition for comic actors	c. 430	442

FINANCE

The fifth century B.C. was the only period of theatre history when plays were created for a single performance. The sense of immediacy that this suggests in terms of the theatrical potential of the plays is frequently overlooked, as is the corresponding freedom from commercial pressures enjoyed by the playwrights. To think of the theatre of Aeschylus, Sophocles, Euripides, and Aristophanes as entirely free from the "taint" of other than sublime artistic and religious motives, however, is to underestimate both the practicality of the Athenians in organizational matters and the constant dependence of the theatre as an institution on its patrons.

It is common knowledge that the financing of dramatic and dithyrambic performance at the festivals of the Lenaia and the Great Dionysia was shared between the state and certain individuals chosen for their wealth. However, a more shadowy individual is involved in theatre organization in Athens, someone usually referred to as the *architekton*, or lessee. The *architekton* may well have functioned in the fifth century B.C., and I have suggested elsewhere[7] that it would have been difficult for the organization of dramatic festivals to have become as formal as it did in the Periclean theatre without him as theatre manager. His existence would fill in numerous gaps not accounted for in the state arrangements of which we have more certain knowledge.

These arrangements can be rehearsed with little controversy, relating as they do to the balance that the state preferred to keep between its own expenditure and the contribution of the wealthier individuals within the state.

The cost of producing a group of plays for performance at the major Athenian dramatic festivals must have been high. This was offset by the concept of the *leitourgia*, or liturgy, by which prominent citizens were required to pay for an item in the national economy for a year. Undertaking, fitting, and equipping a warship was such a liturgy, as was the provision of a public dinner for members of one's *deme*. Undertaking the office of *choregia* was a major liturgy, which could involve a large financial outlay. The *choregia* could bestow a lot of personal prestige, and since the financial burden of liturgies was widely spread, the commitment was not unwelcome.

In any single year a number of *choregoi*, as many as fourteen, would have been needed for the major festivals of the Great Dionysia and the Lenaia. This figure of fourteen is arrived at by assuming that each comedy had its own *choregos*, but even more were needed for the dithyrambic competitions, which, though nondramatic, were just as much a part of the Dionysia as the production of plays.

In the middle of summer the *archon* chose the *choregoi* for the following year's festivals. For someone who thought he was unable to afford the office, there was a way out. A peculiarly Athenian solution involved naming another citizen whose wealth was thought to be greater than that of the *choregos* chosen. If he then agreed to accept the liturgy, well and good. If not, the two exchanged property and the original choice had to continue with his allotted task.

From that moment the *choregos* was responsible for any expenses incurred in the training, equipping, and rehearsing of the chorus. In early times the poet was his own first actor and choreographer, but as the fifth century progressed, the theatre became a profession with its own specialties. After Aeschylus, productions usually employed a professional chorus teacher, or *chorodidaskalos*. The similarity between this term and *choregos* tends to be confusing, but the functions were entirely separate. The *choregos* was a private citizen with no special knowledge of the theatre except as an audience member. His concern was solely with management. The *chorodidaskalos*, who was probably highly paid, and rightly so, had the responsibility of training the choruses for one group of four plays.

The *chorodidaskalos* would have been helped in his task by a good professional musician, another of the expenses incurred by the *choregos*. What with the provision of rehearsal space, the buying or hiring of costumes and masks, and the possible reimbursement to chorus members for time spent at rehearsal, at least in the latter stages of production, the *choregia* initially appears likely to have been a heavy commitment. In addition to the expenses of the chorus itself, the *choregos* was responsible for paying for the attendants, soldiers, and extras variously indicated in the texts.[8]

A further expense falling upon the *choregos* might have been the provision of settings and properties. Altars, tombs, chariots, and carpets decorate the plays and, as "spectacle," might well have been the responsibility of the *choregos*. On the other hand, costume, mask, and possibly hand props were so much the concern of individual actors that each may have provided his own from his fee.

What the *choregos* got for his money was the opportunity, for better or worse, of being associated with a particular production. Patronage of a play with a strong political viewpoint might even have been taken by the audience as an indication of the political stance of the *choregos*, powerless though he was to exercise any direct artistic control. If the play or plays were victorious, he could win a crown for himself and his name would appear in the official records, alongside the names of victorious playwrights and actors. Indeed, so much was the *choregos* associated with a production, that he may have wished, however indirectly, to influence the artistic product, and this does suggest that the allocation of *choregos* to playwright may not have been entirely fortuitous.

As the Peloponnesian War drew to a close, the number of individual citizens able to afford the burden of a *choregia* had diminished, and from about 406 B.C., it was permissible to share the expenses between two or more *choregoi*. This practice was extended through the fourth century until in the last years a state official known as the *agonothetes* superseded the *choregos*.

The name of the *archon* in charge of the festival was also usually inserted in the victory lists—the eponymous *archon* for the Great Dionysia, the *archon basileus* for the Lenaia—but this was for dating purposes. No particular credit redounded to the state official in charge for the success of a dramatic festival, although most of the organization depended upon him and some of the expense was a state matter.

The *choregos* covered the expenses of all performers except the actors, for whom, at least from the middle of the fifth century when they probably first became professionals, the state was responsible. From Thespis and the first actor, to the second and third actors of Aeschylus and Sophocles, the playwright chose his own performers. Sophocles had reputedly such a weak voice that he seldom performed, although custom seems to have allowed the playwright to be his own principal actor, with supporting players picked and perhaps paid for by him until 449 B.C. The year 449 B.C. is the most likely date for the state to have assumed official responsibility for paying actors up to the number of three for each group of plays. At this juncture acting prizes were also introduced, perhaps a consequence of the specialization of the actor's role, and the demand by rival playwrights for individual talents. The state payment for three actors per company may well have been a deciding factor in the casting limitation the tragedians seem[9] to have imposed upon themselves.

The year 449 B.C. was something of a crucial date in the history of the Athenian theatre, if not of its dramatists. Aeschylus was dead by this time, but Sophocles had not yet written any of the plays that have survived him. Euripides had hardly begun his career and Aristophanes was not even born. But this year saw a number of organizational changes, principally involving the new status of actors. About this time, too, Pericles began the rebuilding of the Precinct of Dionysus with the theatre as its centerpiece, not completed until the Peace of Nicias over thirty years later. The new theatre precinct is known usually as the Periclean theatre and Pericles gets the credit, at least from Plutarch, for introducing the "theoric" fund, instituted to ensure that no citizen should ever be excluded from the theatre through lack of funds.

A charge for admission was first instituted either when performances were first given in the Precinct of Dionysus, perhaps in 502 B.C., or in 449 B.C., to coincide with the awarding of prizes to tragic actors. How high the cost of admission was is so variously reported that no certain figure can be suggested. Two obols per day seems the most likely amount, particularly as the second half of the fifth century saw the introduction of the "theoric" fund, whereby the sum of two obols was made available to each citizen to enable him buy a ticket for the theatre. The money was distributed by *deme*, and the system seems to have been the only way of avoiding abuses over the allocation of the tickets.

If the state paid the money to supply the "theoric" fund, who then ultimately received the two obols? Clearly, it cannot have been the state, or there would have been no reason for instituting the fund. Admission charges could simply have been abolished, particularly as it is reliably reported that the rich applied to the fund no less readily than the poor.

It seems clear that as early as the fifth century, probably as early as 449 B.C., the theatre was leased out and, at least at a managerial level, certainly was a commercial enterprise. Although little enough is known of the lessee in later centuries, his function seems indispensable from the time the Theatre of Dionysus was itself run in any more than the most haphazard manner. The lessee never owned the theatre, of course, but I would suggest his responsibilities extended far enough for him to be regarded as a full professional theatre manager.

Having located the limit of his functions, one is forced to admit that information about any lessee is extremely scanty. Three separate Greek words are even used to identify the same job: *theatrones* ("theatre purchaser"), *theatropoles* ("theatre seller"), and *architekton*, which occurs most often. *Architekton* usually means "master builder" or "director of works" or even simply a "leader" or "master." But in a number of later inscriptions, including contracts, *architekton* is the term for the lessee of a theatre, and for this reason it is safe to refer to the lessee from here on as the *architekton*.

In the context of "assigning seats" in the theatre, *architekton* occurs several times in inscriptions from the latter part of the fourth century and from the third century. Only one of these inscriptions mentions the festival itself, and then it is "the Dionysia at the Piraeus" (the Rural Dionysia) where there appear to have been four lessees, not one. One further inscription relating to a contract for the theatre at the Piraeus suggests that failure to keep the theatre in suitable repair would result in the necessary work being contracted for by the state with the bill sent to the lessee.

Despite the lack of direct evidence for the *architekton* in the Periclean theatre, the job that he would have done clearly existed. Perhaps it was in 449 B.C., at the same time the state agreed to pay three actors per company and instituted an admission charge, that it became customary to lease out the Theatre of Dionysus under contract. The *architekton* would then have been responsible for the maintenance of the theatre, involving the employment and payment of stagehands and carpenters if required. He might also have been responsible for control of the audience and front-of-house arrangements.

If he was responsible for the upkeep of the fabric and for staffing the theatre both backstage and front-of-house, he may well have maintained a basic stock of props, scenic units (as required), and even masks, although the hiring of costume later came into the hands of outsiders. Masks were not worn by performers of the dithyramb, but forty-eight new ones for four choruses would have involved far greater expense than the *choregos* apparently incurred.

Even in the earliest years of organized drama, some of the responsibility for the performances may have been delegated by the *archon* in charge.

The cost of running any theatre, ancient or modern, is bound to be high, even when there are no bills to be met for light and heat. High standards were expected in Athens, and the *archon* saw that these standards were rigorously maintained.

The *architekton* appears to have undertaken to attend to the upkeep of the theatre and also to pay a fixed sum of money into the state treasury for the privilege of doing so. In return he must surely have been the man to whom the admission charge was paid. The "theoric" fund offered two obols a day to claimants. Commentators on Demosthenes suggest that only one obol was for admission, the other for refreshment, though such excessive generosity seems hard to credit. Of course the *architekton* may also have held the franchise for providing refreshments in the great hall at the rear of the scenic facade (*skene*), ensuring that he got his hands on both obols, one way or another.

At two obols admission charge per day, the income could have been substantial in a theatre holding at least fifteen thousand spectators, during a festival spread over five or six days. An audience of fifteen thousand paying two obols a day for five days gives one hundred and fifty thousand obols. There were six hundred obols to the mina. One festival might bring in at the box office at least two hundred and fifty minae.

Some indication of the overall costs of production can be found in a speech of the Attic orator Lysias who lived in the second half of the fifth century and the beginning of the fourth century. In making a comparison of the costs of liturgies between the years 410 and 402 B.C., he quotes twenty minae for a men's chorus at the Thargelia and fifty minae for a dithyrambic chorus of men and the erection of a tripod. He also refers to a boys' chorus, fifteen minae; a comic chorus, sixteen minae; fitting up a trireme on six occasions, three hundred and sixty minae; and a tragic chorus, thirty minae.

Accepting the figures of Lysias, the cost to a *choregos* of mounting a tragedy was twenty-five to thirty minae. Depending on the sum payable to the state treasury, the profit margin of the *architekton* could have been reasonable. If he paid all expenses of upkeep and production, apart from chorus and actors, perhaps it would not have been so lucrative. Backstage staff must have included dressers and a stage-management crew of at least four to work the stage machinery and handle mundane jobs such as opening and shutting doors.

The policing of the auditorium was at this time not the problem it later became. From the introduction of seat prices, tickets may have been sold in advance. Tokens have been found, cheaply made and resembling coins, which seem to indicate the block of seating but not individual seats.

This three-way splitting of expenses between *choregos*, state, and *architekton* has no direct parallel today. A modern provincial touring theatre, however, might be expected to assume the responsibilities of an *architekton*, and the backer of a show frequently has no more direct influence over the artistic product than did the *choregos*. Today national and local subsidy can often provide at least the equivalent of the actors' salaries for a new play. The real difference in artistic and monetary terms lies in the fact that the Greek *playwright* was unhampered by the need for or even the possibility of commercial success. A play might receive a second performance in exceptional circumstances, but the author was under no pressure to consider any more than the needs of a single audience on a single day.

The winning *choregos* could expect a crown of ivy. A similar prize was awarded to successful playwrights and actors. Victors might expect a financial reward as well. Every playwright who "gained a chorus" won a prize, but the cash value in the fifth century is not known. In the latter part of the fourth century, a sum of ten minae for victory in the dithyrambic contest at the Piraeus was customary, an improvement at least on a basket of figs, the traditional prize in pre-Aeschylean times.

Any cash reward was secondary to the honor of a victory. The ceremonial crowning of playwright, *choregos*, and (after 449 B.C.) actor was performed by the *archon* before the entire audience as a fitting climax to the festival. The crown and an inscription in official records gave evidence of the favor of the god and bestowed an honor similar to that of a victory in the Olympic games.

The total cost of a dramatic festival has been variously estimated.

As has been shown, there might have been a turnover as high as five or six hundred minae, which is ten talents or the equivalent of about five hundredweight of silver. Such a sum would pay for the upkeep of the rowers on a warship for two years or purchase three hundred slaves. With such sums of money involved, there can be no surprise to find a middleman, the *architekton*, in it for the profit. Nor should it be surprising how successful he was in keeping details of his responsibilities and his profit margins well out of the limelight.

DRAMATIST AND FESTIVAL

Although unhampered by modern commercial pressures, a dramatist did not write solely to please himself, nor, whatever his reputation, could he ever assume that his work would "gain a chorus." When the *archon* had made his decision and the *choregos* had been chosen, the playwright could at least be sure of one of the prizes when his play or plays were finally performed. Sophocles himself was turned down by the *archon* on one occasion, and Aeschylus, Euripides, and Aristophanes may well have suffered the same indignity.

Censorship was rare, nor can there have been any absolute requirement to conform to the submitted text. In the case of Aristophanes, where immediate response supplied much of the fun, the author's initial working text may have been very free indeed. The author, as director, could rewrite and incorporate new material right up to the last moment.[10] The outrageous fashion in which both living and dead characters are treated by Aristophanes did lead to several attempts to curb Old Comedy. But freedom of speech was so deep-rooted an Athenian ideal that suppression was likely to fail even in the short run.

Restraints of some kind may have been occasionally enforced during the Peloponnesian War. It is difficult to imagine what authority could have restrained the ebullience of Aristophanes, particularly during the address to the audience in Old Comedy known as the *parabasis*, where the poet spoke directly through the leader of the chorus. Aristophanes' advice to leading politicians is frank, honest, and sometimes physically impossible. Yet *Lysistrata*, perhaps the fiercest antiwar play of all, has no *parabasis*. By that stage of the war, with the democratic government of Athens in abeyance, no doubt even Aristophanes had to control his tongue. Certainly the comedy of the following century was more subdued and contained a progressively smaller political element. For most of Aristophanes' working life, despite his early brush with Cleon, he prided himself on his artistic freedom.

The *archon*, then, selected the plays perhaps on submission of the whole work, perhaps on the evidence of no more than a synopsis. The association of a particular *choregos* with a particular dramatist may have been personal preference initially, but in the latter part of the century was almost certainly decided by lot. A lottery was the only real safeguard against possible abuses, when so much personal prestige was involved for both playwright and *choregos*. The *choregoi* for dithyrambs first drew lots to ascertain the order of precedence and then selected their musician accordingly. As the chorus in tragedy and comedy was just as heavily dependent on its musician and choreographer, a similar procedure may well have been adopted.

During the period when the playwright was his own actor, selection of other actors was a straightforward matter. Before the institution of prizes for acting in 449 B.C., the association of specific actors with specific playwrights does not appear to have caused dispute. The protagonist could still have selected his acting colleagues so the playwright could write with specific actors in mind, as often happens in the theatre today.

But the Athenian love of chance was not long to be denied, and the lot was introduced for selection of actors too. Perhaps with the growth of professionalism among actors, a desire to rise in the hierarchy overcame discretion. The possibility of bribery may have removed the sense of fair competition. At any rate, the state itself finally chose three protagonists and allocated them by lot, one to each tragic poet. A similar process presumably developed for comedy.

The competing playwright was by the middle of the fifth century, therefore, triply dependent on luck. First, he was associated by lot with a particular *choregos*; second, the *choregos* was awarded his musician by lot (although he chose the members of his chorus); third, the main actor was chosen by lot although he himself remained free to choose his fellow actors. The performers then remained the same throughout the tragedies and possibly in the satyr play also.

By the Lenaia of 418 B.C., and possibly at the Great Dionysia in the latter years of the fifth century, a protagonist could appear for more than one playwright in the same festival. The squabbles that must have arisen over priorities and rehearsal time are mercifully lost in time.

The members of choruses, at least for the Great Dionysia, were amateur, chosen from among the citizen population. As a tragic chorus numbered twelve or fifteen dancers and the comic chorus, twenty-four, it is likely that the same group performed in all four plays submitted by one playwright, although the level of ability required must have been great. In the *Oresteia*, for instance, Aeschylus or Telestes would have been training a group of male amateurs who were required in the course of the same day to represent old men of Argos, captive Trojan slave women, Furies (female?), and satyrs (decidedly male). The likely rehearsal period was at most four months, although the gap of only two months between Lenaia and Great Dionysia may indicate a shorter time.

Artistically the Athenian playwright was faced with a number of imponderables. In rehearsal, however, he was able to exert control as both director and choreographer if he so desired. Young playwrights sometimes preferred to rely upon the experience of an older hand. Posthumous revivals of plays, although uncommon, may have required a director in the modern sense. In comedy, with its extended stage action and scope for "business," the employment of an outside director seems to have been a regular practice. The first three plays of Aristophanes—*Banqueters, Babylonians,* and *Acharnians*—were brought out under the name of Callistratus.

With plays cast and preparations under way, the process of rehearsal no doubt proceeded much as rehearsal for any production at any time—inspiration, aggravation, depression, excitement, last-minute panic—but the ancient Greeks had no opportunity to ease their way into a long run, no chance of living down first-night notices. Everything depended on that single performance.

PUBLIC PERFORMANCE

In the week immediately preceding the festival, the preliminary ceremony of the *proagon* took place. The *proagon* perhaps did no more than serve the purpose of a program with an introduction to cast and actors and a few notes from the author himself. Playwrights, *choregoi*, actors, and choruses gave a kind of preview or "trailer" of the plays to be performed, either in the theatre itself or in the roofed Odeon of Pericles. Summoned in turn by a herald, the playwrights introduced their subjects, theme, and company before a restricted audience. Costume and mask were not worn, and the ceremony served a more functional purpose than the mere whetting of public appetite. It informed the public about the plays they were going to see.

It is still misleadingly asserted that a Greek audience knew exactly what was going to happen in any play simply from the title. This is far from the truth. The virtual limitation of theme to traditional myth might seem to indicate at least some prior knowledge on the part of the audience. An audience who had come to see an *Oedipus* would know Oedipus' family background and the story of his marriage. They would expect a Pentheus or a Hippolytus to end up in shreds, Agamemnon axed in his bath. But that is likely to have been the sum of their knowledge. The audience can have had no sense of watching yet another production of *Oedipus* or *Electra* as a modern audience might feel seeing *Hamlet* or *Macbeth* for the fifth time. Sophocles' *Oedipus Tyrannus* closes with Jocasta hanged and Oedipus blinded and driven into exile, deprived of his children. Euripides' *Phoenician Women* opens in the same city of Thebes, at least ten years later. Oedipus' children are now adult, the first character to appear is Jocasta, and only at the end of the play does Creon send Oedipus into exile. The variations endemic in myth made for diverse emphases within existing stories. Euripides made the unorthodox treatment of a familiar story his trademark. The Helen of his play of that name is not the unfaithful wife who absconded to Troy with Paris, but an innocent who was spirited away to live chastely in Egypt for ten years while a replica, fashioned out of air, wrought havoc among Greeks and Trojans.

Aeschylus, too, seems to have been distinguished for originality: he may even have been the first to embroider the Orestes story with matricide, a refinement adopted by both Sophocles and Euripides in their treatment of the Orestes myth.

After all the preliminaries, sacrifices, processions, and various performances during the festival itself, the prizewinners were chosen.

At the great festivals selection of prizewinners was left, as might have been expected, at least partly in the gift of the gods. Before a festival began, each tribe put forward a number of names of potential judges. From among these names, one representative of each of the ten tribes was then selected and presumably found himself occupying one of the seats reserved for officials and guests. After the performances each representative made his selection, wrote it down, and deposited it in the voting urn. The *archon* then selected, at random, five votes, and prizes were awarded accordingly. Whether each judge attempted to place all plays or chose a single winner we do not know, nor do we know what happened if equal votes were cast for two sets of plays. Although the process may seem haphazard, it did ensure that all the plays had been seen by all the judges and that no single judge could be praised or blamed for the final verdict.

Even when plays were no longer connected in trilogies, it was still a group of plays that was judged, and not a single play. This goes some of the way toward accounting for decisions surprising in retrospect. *Oedipus Tyrannus* was part of a group placed only second, although Sophocles took first prizes regularly, as had Aeschylus. Euripides was awarded only five first prizes, one of them posthumous. As a revolutionary dramatist who frequently angered audiences, his lack of success can hardly be surprising, especially when the judges might have comprised, for instance, a gym teacher, a banker, a lawyer, a saddle maker, and a sea captain. Prizes for actors were probably awarded by the same judges and decisions, no doubt, every bit as hotly disputed in the following months.

THE AUDIENCE

The nature of the festival must have affected the mood of the audience. Athenians attended the theatre, not as a place of general entertainment, but as a place to go on certain special occasions during the year, and their expectations and behavior would have influenced the conventions of attendance that developed. Fourth-century lawsuits indicate that bad behavior and fighting were not infrequent, but that even trifling misdemeanors could bring the offenders into court. State officials were eventually appointed, and their job was to maintain order and to keep rival *choregoi* and chorusmen from one another's throats.

Reaction to the plays was noisy, enthusiastic, and sometimes actively hostile—a state of affairs that appears to have been quite acceptable. Tragedy and comedy were always strongly political in Athens, and it is worth recalling just how recently the works of "subversives" like Euripides and Aristophanes were banned in their native city: indeed, an audience in modern Athens is quite liable to rise as one man, cheering and applauding a sentiment of which they approve.

Stories abound of fifth- and fourth-century Athenian audiences booing, clapping, throwing nuts and fruit, exacting encores, and eating and drinking noisily in mid-performance. In this respect, the comedies of Aristophanes provide a mine of information. When direct address is part of the playwright's and actor's technique, no secret is made either of the reasons for competing or of the methods used to ensure a favorable hearing. Distribution of sweets and fruits among the audience seems to have been common, if only because this is a stratagem to which one of Aristophanes' characters refuses to stoop. Xanthias in *Frogs* suggests exploiting some rude stock jokes, to appeal to the lowlier elements, but Dionysus stops him. Considering the number of rude stock jokes that Aristophanes does use, the humor of his rivals must have been far from subtle.

Because of such widespread sexual and excremental humor, Victorian critics chose to believe that women and children would have been banned from attending comedy, but tragedy, being more uplifting, would be regarded as acceptable. Even if the moral point were consistent, performance of tragedy was always followed by a satyr play in which the *phallos* was worn, and the amount of physical comic business was as blatant as in comedy proper. The parade of simulacra of the *phallos* at all major festivals was a matter of homage to the fertility of nature, and even private houses had the figure of a Herm outside the front door, complete with erect penis.

Aristophanes in *Birds* might seem to imply that women were not present when the Chorus suggests that a further advantage of wings would be the ease with which one could fly off from the theatre to commit adultery; but this hardly suggests that women were not *allowed* to be present at the Great Dionysia. It merely shows that some women were not there.

Apart from citizen women, there were also the *hetairai*, noncitizens who according to Athenian law were not permitted to marry citizens, but whose status was often more than that of mere courtesans. Their influence could be widespread in the city, and the liaisons they formed were sometimes more permanent than a formal marriage, which might be annulled by renunciation before witnesses. Drawn from all over the Greek-speaking world, the *hetairai* were often highly educated and were readily accepted into the community. Their presence among the audience is suggested in later times, but citizens' wives might also have attended: why else should Alcibiades be said to have amazed men *and* women by his clothes when he was *choregos*?[11] Or why should the *Life of Aeschylus* suggest that at the entry of the Furies in the *Oresteia* women had miscarriages and little boys died of fright?[12] Why should Aeschylus in *Frogs*[13] say that all decent women committed suicide on seeing Euripides' *Bellerophon*, if none of them was present to see it? Why should Plato refer on no fewer than three occasions[14] to the detrimental effect of the theatre on women and children? Plato also refers to slaves as part of the fourth-century audiences with which he was familiar; no doubt at Rural Dionysias, at least, even slaves were allowed to watch plays.

No reasonable evidence exists to indicate that women, either freeborn or *hetairai*, were excluded from the theatre. What seems possible is that a special block of seating was set aside for them, and the citizen women who wanted to attend may have been segregated. In the prevailing conditions this would have been a convenient arrangement. The auditorium was divided into blocks and theatre tickets were associated with these blocks. The auditorium was therefore adequately controlled, a control exercised initially by tribe.

The first play most probably started at daybreak. Three tragedies, a satyr play, and a comedy would take at least six and one-half hours to perform continuously. Performances may have been continuous, but it is more likely that intervals occurred, particularly in such a large theatre from which egress was difficult.

The calls of nature that Aristophanes is so fond of mentioning must have affected the most retentive bladder, especially when its owner found himself sitting in March on a stone seat. The Athenians were not overly fussy about where they relieved themselves, but in a theatre with the geography of the Theatre of Dionysus, even with drainage channels, fifteen thousand people necessarily had to be able to leave the auditorium from time to time.

At least half an hour could have elapsed between plays in a connected trilogy or even an hour. Even with two hours between satyr play and comedy, the comedy would have concluded before dark. This would allow time also for the sale and consumption of refreshments. The long hall behind the *skene* is presumed to have provided shelter against a sudden shower. Perhaps a more regular use was to house stalls where food and drink could be bought. One might perhaps expect Aristophanes to have referred to this somewhere within the extant plays, but he is surprisingly circumspect about the drinking habits of an audience who had set out to celebrate Dionysus in all his functions.

The audience consisted of ordinary, everyday Athenians, and the picture painted by Theophrastus in the *Characters* may be a fair reflection of some sections of those audiences who wept, cheered, and voted prizes at the first productions of playwrights who had died at least thirty-five years before Theophrastus himself was born:

The Shameless Man "books places at the play for his guests without paying his share, and then takes his sons along the next day, and even their tutor."[15]

The Disgusting Man is one "who lifts his clothing and exposes himself in front of respectable women. And in the theatre, when others stop applauding, he starts, and hisses those whom everyone else is watching. And when everywhere else in the theatre is quiet, he lifts up his head and belches to make the audience turn round and look at him."[16]

The Dim-Witted Man "going to watch a play, is left alone in the theatre at the end, fast asleep. And when he has to get up in the night after a heavy dinner, misses the right door on the way back, and is bitten by the neighbour's dog."[17]

The audience for a dramatic festival was a cross section of the whole Athenian community. However much the audience appreciated the plays or showed their disapproval, they were judging the plays by immediate impact. Indeed, there must have been few who understood the complex theology of Aeschylus or the contemporary philosophy of Euripides. Whatever the intrinsic merits of the plays, success or failure depended on capturing the imagination of the crowd and exciting its emotions. To this the entire festival occasion made its contribution.

NOTES

1. During the month of *Elaphebolion*, between the middle of March and early April.

2. Aristophanes *Birds*: lines 785–89.

3. One such festival is described, perhaps parodied, in Aristophanes' *Acharnians*.

4. Margarete Bieber, *The History of the Greek and Roman Theater*, 2nd ed. (Princeton, N.J.: Princeton University Press, 1961), p. 52.

5. Aristophanes *Acharnians*: lines 496–508.

6. Dates are based on the register of victors at the Great Dionysia and on other inscriptions, including the *Parian Marble*.

7. J. Michael Walton, "Financial Arrangements for the Athenian Dramatic Festivals," *Theatre Research International* 2, no.2 (February 1977): 79–86.

8. Euripides' *Hippolytus* has a chorus of huntsmen in addition to the main chorus. Aristophanes uses a secondary chorus in *Frogs* for the single sequence that gives the play its name.

9. See chapter 6.

10. This surely accounts for the half-hearted references in *Frogs* to Sophocles who inconveniently died in the Autumn of 406 B.C., two months after the death of Euripides, and when *Frogs* would already have been approved for production the following year.

11. Athenaeus *Deipnosophists*: XII 534c.

12. *Life of Aeschylus:* 9.

13. Aristophanes *Frogs*: lines 1050–1051.

14. Plato *Laws*: II 658a-d, VII 817c; and *Gorgias*: 502b-d: as noted in A. W. Pickard-Cambridge, *The Dramatic Festivals of Athens*, 2nd ed., rev. by John Gould and D. M. Lewis (Oxford: Oxford University Press, Clarendon Press, 1968), p. 265.

15. Theophrastus *Characters*: IX.

16. Ibid., XI.

17. Ibid., XIV.

Chapter *4* The Theatre

Looking down from above the theatre at Epidaurus, it is easy enough to appreciate that the focal point of the theatre is the circular *orchestra*, or dancing place (see figure 2). It was here that the chorus regularly performed, creating patterns on the lightly paved surface in front of and apart from the main acting area.

The physical relationship of the three distinct parts of the Greek theatre—*skene*, or stage building; auditorium; and *orchestra*—dictated the construction and performance of its drama. The *skene*, with the area immediately in front of it, provided a place for the actors to enter from and perform and exit to, both framing and setting their actions. The auditorium followed the line of the *orchestra* around its leading edge, thereby supplying what is virtually an end-stage view of the front of the *skene*. The *orchestra* provided a large open space where the chorus could have either a view of the actors similar to the view that the audience had or a view of the audience similar to the view that the actors had. In this way the circular *orchestra* served to link stage action with the auditorium and the chorus could be either spectators of or participants in the stage action or even both at once.

It is to Epidaurus that one must go to get any kind of impression of what the Theatre of Dionysus might have looked like in the latter part of the fifth century B.C. The theatre at Epidaurus was built, as it happens, in the fourth century when modifications were already taking place in theatre building elsewhere, but Epidaurus was one of the few sites to remain free from later reconstruction. The principal difference from the Theatre of Dionysus is the isolation of Epidaurus from a large community. The theatre in Athens was only part of a complex, constructed between 449 and 416 B.C.,

Figure 2.   The Theatre at Epidaurus (by Courtesy of Costis Livadeas)

that included the Odeon of Pericles, where the *proagon* was held, the old temple that had been a feature of the precinct in earlier times, and a long hall running from east to west, its floor level below the flat *orchestra* but reaching as far north as the terrace wall behind the *skene*. All of this would have been visible to the spectator in the auditorium of the Theatre of Dionysus (see figure 3).

Epidaurus is still a working theatre, used for revivals in modern Greek of Athenian classical drama. Performances of Greek tragedy and comedy no longer take place in the Theatre of Dionysus in Athens. The theatre is still easily accessible to tourists but only as an archaeological site, so little does it resemble the theatre for which Aeschylus, Sophocles, Euripides, and Aristophanes created their plays.

THE PERICLEAN THEATRE
Precinct of Dionysus c.415 B.C.

Provisional Plan

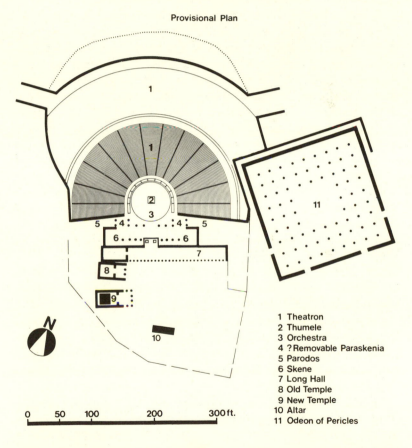

1 Theatron
2 Thumele
3 Orchestra
4 ?Removable Paraskenia
5 Parodos
6 Skene
7 Long Hall
8 Old Temple
9 New Temple
10 Altar
11 Odeon of Pericles

0   50   100   200   300 ft.

Figure 3. The Periclean Theatre. Provisional Plan of the Precinct of Dionysus (Lee Elliott)

Classical revivals in Athens today are often set in the nearby Roman theatre of Herodes Atticus but this is a poor guide to the theatre of the fifth century B.C. Modern summer festivals do manage to accommodate classical revivals among a large number of other activities on the wide stage and within the semicircular *orchestra*, but succeed only in emphasizing the difference between Greek and Roman theatre building.

A Roman theatre was constructed on the principle that an audience in one-half of a purpose-built unit attended for the express purpose of looking at the other half. In consequence the *orchestra* was semicircular and regularly used to house important spectators; *parodoi*, or side entrances, were covered over; and the facade was three stories high with its topmost tier parallel to the level of the back of the auditorium. Romanization eventually overtook the Theatre of Dionysus, which accounts for its present form, but not before it had undergone radical changes from the theatre known as the Periclean theatre, completed sometime during the Peace of Nicias (421 to 416 B.C.).

Many early theatres elsewhere in Greece were also remodeled, but in the last thirty years, due mainly to the efforts of Costis Livadeas and the *Nea Skene* company, much of the "provincial circuit" has been revealed. Theatres at Dodona, Gythion, Argos, Eretria, Thoricon,[1] Cos, Amphiareus, Ithome, Megalopolis, Nicopolis, Patras, Pherae, Piraeus, Philippi, Rhodes, and Thasos all owe to Livadeas the revival of drama in their precincts for the first time in two thousand years.

Only two Greek theatres have been in regular use in this century. Delphi has the most impressive setting, perched high above the valley with a view plunging down to the Gulf of Corinth. But Delphi was only a small theatre with a comparatively late horseshoe-shaped *orchestra*.

All of which makes the survival of Epidaurus the more remarkable. Its geographical position must account at least in part for its freedom from Roman influence. Far from the nearest large town, the theatre of Epidaurus served as a complement to the shrine of Asclepius, god of healing. The remains of the temple form part of a precinct where the physically infirm were brought to be "touched" by the god. It seems reasonable to suggest that the theatre was built to provide a spiritual counterpart to the hall of healing.

For all the undoubted value of this fourth-century site, large questions about its architecture and working practice remain un-answered. The *skene* did not survive the ravages of time and its destruction removes one vital potential source of information on the actual look of the scenic facade, its decoration, and the settings for performance. Principles of staging practice, rather than direct evidence, must dictate how we proceed in discerning any scenery the Greek stage may have employed, especially when we return to Athens.

THE EARLIEST THEATRE

The theatre at Epidaurus resembles in its basic outline what archaeology tells us was the shape of the Theatre of Dionysus in the last part of the fifth century B.C. This Theatre of Dionysus, however, was part of a reconstruction that took place under Per-icles. It is at one remove from the Theatre of Dionysus for which Aeschylus created the *Oresteia*, at two removes from the first theatre in Athens for which Aeschylus probably wrote his earliest plays.

Perhaps there were even earlier theatres, as long as the term *theatre* is not taken to imply a purpose-built, architect-designed playhouse. Such a concept bears no relation to any early Greek theatre and perhaps to no theatre in Athens before the end of the fourth century B.C. or even later. What we must look for is not so much a theatre as a simple playing place. Even so, evidence is at best tentative.

Attempts have been made to associate the circular threshing floor of the Greek village with the earliest *orchestra* or dancing place. Similarly, a case has been made for attaching a theatrical purpose to certain flat areas, bounded by shallow steps on two or three sides in Cnossos and Phaestos on the island of Crete. Perhaps some kind of performance did take place in such areas, but there is nothing to show they were dramatic.

In Athens itself some development can be mooted through the likely homes of early tragedy. Horace, although writing five hundred years after the event, asserts that Thespis performed his first plays on wagons.[2] A wagon does give an elevation for the performer and provide physical boundaries for him, but it also implies a mobile performance. The grammarian Pollux, writing two hundred years later than Horace, suggests that the first actor stood on the *eleos*, which seems to be the same as the *thumele*, or sacred altar, located in the center of the Periclean *orchestra*. Both writers are so vague, however, as to suggest they had little direct evidence themselves.

Originally, the festivals must have required a simple theatral area. With the Greek word *theatron* deriving from the Greek for "to see," the most convenient theatral area would have been a place where as many as possible could congregate to watch what was going on. For any nonprocessional spectacle, whether it be a dog fight or a football match, an audience is likely to group itself around the focus of attention. The bard , or actor, needs control of his audience and prefers to frame himself against a background. This background can itself acquire a specific dramatic function, thus forcing the audience to confront the performer rather than surround him.

From there we can only say that the first theatre in Athens seems to have been a fit-up affair in the *Agora* with scaffolding seats. By the time tragedy had become a regular part of the Great Dionysia, it was staged either in the *Agora* or within the Precinct of Dionysus Eleuthereus, where the Theatre of Dionysus now stands. The move to the precinct may have been the result of a collapse of artificial seating during a performance (to which several later writers bear witness), and certainly the slope of the Acropolis provided natural accommodation for large numbers of spectators. (See figure 4.) Beyond this, the only feature of this second theatre clearly indicated by archaeological remains is the *orchestra*, ninety feet in diameter.

Many critics believe the earliest plays of Aeschylus required no further setting and that the *skene*, serving as a background, was not added until later times. The word *skene* means, literally, a tent and a tent is believed to have served as an entrance and dressing room for the one or two actors. Reconstructions of this first Theatre of Dionysus almost all suggest the barest of acting areas, devoid not only of decoration but even of a "frame" for the actors. That such a concept is quite out of the question for the *Oresteia* is not likely to provoke much dispute, but I hope to show later that there may have been similarity in terms of staging convention between the first productions of the earliest plays of Aeschylus and the latest plays of Sophocles and Euripides.

Figure 4. The Acropolis from the Air (R. Schoder, SJ)

THE PERICLEAN THEATRE

During the spate of building initiated by Pericles from the middle of the fifth century, which included the Parthenon, the Erechtheion, and the Propulaia, the Precinct of Dionysus was radically altered and the Athenian theatre acquired its third form. The completed Periclean theatre probably remained more or less constant until the construction of the Lycurgan theatre, with its stone *skene*, in the latter part of the fourth century.

The renovation of the Precinct of Dionysus appears to have had several immediate effects on the theatre, apart from providing a complex that must have altered the overall view from the auditorium. Fortunately, enough has been excavated to give a reasonable picture of what these new features were. The circular *orchestra* was reduced from a diameter of ninety to seventy-two feet (perhaps as little as sixty-four feet) and pushed back into the hillside. The rake of the auditorium was made steeper, and more space became available at the far side of the orchestra to allow for stage buildings. The auditorium may also have now been fixed and formalized with paved seats and arranged in sectors (*kerkides*), perhaps thirteen, allowing one for each of the ten tribes and three more for either free women or noncitizens. With a minimal allocation of space, this produces a full house of no more than seventeen thousand persons. The Periclean Theatre of Dionysus is that to which Plato referred in speaking of an audience of thirty thousand, so it may have been possible, in the fifth century, for those who wanted to sit or stand on the hillside above and beyond the last row of seats, to get a free, if imperfect, view.

The reshaping of the *orchestra* and the building of the long hall seem principally aimed at providing extra room for the *skene*. Stage building and stage alike, although still removable, were required to be of a new solidity to accommodate the demands of the playwrights. Directly behind the *orchestra* and between the *orchestra* and the wall is an area with a solid foundation twenty-six feet wide by nine feet deep, which archaeologists date to this time. An opening of almost as great a width carried on through the terrace wall, from where it went right up to the hall or even through it. The surface of this solid area contains two large holes of different size. The terrace wall behind it shows the remains of eight out of what were probably ten post holes—and that is all. From such scanty material an attempt must be made to reconstruct the *skene* and *proskenion* (the area in front of the *skene*), for which Sophocles and Euripides wrote most of their extant work and for which Aristophanes wrote all of his.[3]

THE SKENE

Although the spatial relationships of the main areas of the Periclean and pre-Periclean theatres can be pinned down, the details of the scene building and the way in which it was used are largely conjectural. Not until eighty years after the death of Sophocles and Euripides was a permanent stone *skene* built for the Theatre of Dionysus. Until then it was made of wood, as most of the great stages of the world have been made of wood. Being wooden it was removable and temporary. This factor alone must have had considerable influence on the way in which the *skene* was used to represent the variety of backgrounds required by the playwrights.

Two later writers, Vitruvius and Pollux, wrote about what they termed "the Greek theatre" without specifying to what period between the sixth century B.C. and the third or second century they were referring.

Vitruvius was an architect, more or less contemporary with King Juba of Numidia, whose *History of the Theatre* disappointingly has failed to survive. Vitruvius died in about 15 B.C. slightly earlier than Juba. The ten books *On Architecture* cover construction of temples, private houses, various types of machines, and decorative devices. Book five offers a comparison of his Roman theatre with what he simply terms the "Greek theatre."

His strict geometric divisions show that Vitruvius appreciated the relationship of *orchestra* and *proskenion*, and he does compare the semicircular Roman *orchestra* with the circular Greek one, typical of the fifth century B.C. He also makes mention of acoustics and of a colonnade behind the scene building in case of bad weather (presumably the long hall). His most controversial remark, however, concerns the "stage" (*logeion*), which he says was narrow in the Greek theatre and between ten and twelve feet high.[4]

Vitruvius was an architect and he was a professional. His figures are so precise that his complex diagrams were to provide models for Renaissance architects, and his advice, "Whoever uses these rules, will be successful in building theatres,"[5] was taken as gospel. When, therefore, he describes a stage between ten and twelve feet high, it is beyond dispute that there was something he called a "stage" of this size during some period, even if it was not the fifth century B.C.

The *Onomasticon* of Julius Pollux[6] is such a curious hotchpotch of fact and fantasy that it is difficult to find in it any consistency. Book four does include the following definitions:

1. The separate parts of the theatre are a little gate, archway, channel, wedges of seating (*kerkides*), *skene, orchestra*, stage (*logeion*), *proskenion, paraskenia, huposkenia*.[7]
2. The *eleos* was an ancient table on which, before the time of Thespis, one individual stood to answer the chorus.[8]
3. The second story (or "double roof") was either, on one occasion, a top-floor room in a royal palace, such as that from which Antigone surveys the army in *Phoenician Women*, or, on another occasion, a tiled roof (?) from which they (?) threw things. But in comedy, the second story was for brothel keepers to look out or old women or wives to watch the action.[9]

Pollux may have been unduly influenced by familiarity with the elaborate facade of the theatre of his own time, but in these remarks there seems less with which to take issue than most authorities would suggest. Even so, here and elsewhere in their discussions of stage machinery, both Pollux and Vitruvius appear to have in mind as the "Greek theatre" not the Periclean Theatre of Dionysus with its wooden *skene*, but the fourth-century Lycurgan theatre with its permanent stone *skene*. Later modifications made at a time when the chorus had become insignificant in the drama may well have been designed to accommodate spectators in the *orchestra*, a development that would have led to the adoption of a high stage to relieve sightline problems.

The Periclean *skene* cannot be reconstructed by recourse to later stone theatres in places far from Athens. Vase paintings, however, have survived, both Greek and Italian, that show mythological characters in what look like dramatized scenes. Each uses a simple structure of Ionic columns and a pediment as a background to the composition. Although many of the scenes themselves do not occur in extant plays, such a convention might be aimed at demonstrating that a scene is theatrical, and that a background construction of this form is associated with the theatre. The majority of such vases date from the fourth century; only a few are from Attica.

Of two vases that clearly do show theatres in action, one in particular accords with Pollux (see figure 5), suggesting twin side porches (*paraskenia*) with an acting area (*pro-* or *hupo-skenion*) between double doors. By the time of the Hellenistic theatre, *paraskenia* were a regular part of any stage building. They served to centralize the action by limiting the extent of the stage. In Roman times they also covered side entrances. There is good reason to believe that in a less elaborate form, *paraskenia* were features of the Periclean theatre. Although several later theatres managed to do without them, archaeological evidence testifies to their incorporation into the Lycurgan Theatre of Dionysus. If they merely confined the action, *paraskenia* might have provided a throughway for the actor who entered by the *parodos* and proceeded on to the stage instead of into the *orchestra*.[10]

Figure 5.   *Skene* and *Paraskenia*, a Fourth-Century Scene
(Paris, Musée du Louvre, Photograph M. Chuzeville)

Each *paraskenion*, as it appears in figure 5, takes the form of a portico with double doors behind, which brings us to another possible feature of stage decor. *Prothuron* is a term meaning "porch," or "portico," and is believed to have indicated in the theatre the covered area in front of a central stage entrance. The "theatrical" vases often frame scenes against this kind of background. Indeed, the majority of Greek temples are built in such a style (see figure 6), and with three or four steps ascending to them from the level ground, they create the sort of raised area required by actors. The two holes in the central foundation of the Periclean theatre might well have been intended for wooden posts to support a *prothuron*. The *prothuron* need have been no more elaborate than either one of the two *paraskenia* in figure 5, but its scenic function was probably specific.

Even the number of doors in use in the Greek theatre is in dispute. It is difficult to restrict the action to the use of *parodoi* plus a single central entrance, unless this one entrance is presumed to lead on occasions to more than one area of a house or temple. Some Greek houses conformed to this style of building, but the Italian vases suggest at least two doors, with a flat roof between. Some of the plays themselves seem to require three doors.

From Aeschylus onwards, an upper level is a fairly standard requirement of the plays. Some distinction seems to be made between an upper area for humans and an upper area for gods. The conclusion of Euripides' *Orestes* involves Orestes, Pylades, and Hermione on the roof of the palace with Menelaus beating at the doors below. Apollo eventually appears to restore the myth to its recognizable form, but presumably does not enter from the same point as the humans nor does he position himself beside them. Even if Apollo appeared on the *mechane* (see below), it is clear that on some occasions the *skene* required a flat roof.

Visual evidence exists to indicate a raised stage in some performances in classical times.[11] This feature of the Athenian theatre, or the lack of it, has caused much controversy, but the issue can be simply stated.

Vitruvius tells us that "the Greek stage" was between ten and twelve feet high. No detailed examination of the ancient texts is required to show that access between *orchestra* and the scene building is essential, with regular movement between acting area and *orchestra*.

Figure 6. The North Porch of the Erechtheion (by Courtesy of
Prof. R.A. Tomlison)

Even allowing for the possibility of ramps leading from the *parodos*, or of large flights of steps descending from stage level, a stage ten to twelve feet high is out of the question for the fifth century. One might think that Vitruvius is muddled in his prescription of a ten-foot stage, were it not for the fact that a "stage" of such dimensions has been found in Hellenistic theatres elsewhere. By the third century B.C., however, contact between actor and chorus had been curtailed—if indeed a chorus was still used.

Other evidence for the existence of a stage is worth noting. Horace tells us in his *On the Art of Poetry* that Aeschylus "built a stage on beams of moderate size."[12] Horace is not a reliable historian, of course, and several of his remarks about Greek theatre are suspect. Plato talks in the *Symposium*[13] of Agathon going up on to the platform (*okribas*) in the theatre. The passage is usually thought to refer to events at the *proagon*, but some critics identify this *okribas* as the stage of the Theatre of Dionysus. Others refer to several phrases found in theatrical contexts that suggest the use of the terms *go up* and *come down*, *from the skene* and *on the skene*. These allusions need not be interpreted as anything more than theatrical jargon akin to modern *upstage* and *downstage* although mention of the steepness of a path[14] cannot be thus explained.

Having argued away the high stage, Margarete Bieber (among others) found it a relatively simple matter to dismiss any kind of elevation:

The most important thing to bear in mind when reading Greek plays is that in the classical age there was no such thing as a raised stage.[15]

As far as visibility is concerned, no great problem existed. But sightlines created by the relationship of auditorium to acting area are considerably affected by the juxtaposition of actors and chorus. When either group encroaches upon the area reserved for the other, as with the entrance of Agamemnon in his chariot in *Agamemnon*, or of the Chorus issuing from the temple in *Eumenides*, the playwright is invariably seeking a surprise effect. Even without the remarks of Plato and Horace, the elevation of the actor seems essential not merely on grounds of visibility, but to distinguish his basic function from that of the chorus. If Pollux is to be believed, the earliest actor perhaps sought the natural elevation of the *eleos*, but the only reason for the actor's ultimate "retreat" to the rear of the chorus and *orchestra* is that he thereby acquired greater maneuverability and prominence.

Two steps ascending to a low platform would be enough for the actor's purpose; six would be too many. Although classical Greek has no word for "stage,"[16] and although no evidence for the existence of such a structure survives other than the holes in the foundations of the Periclean theatre, the solution offered above is the most theatrically viable one and is also in keeping with a stage area made entirely of wood. Such an area would be sufficiently variable to accommodate the individual requirements of a large number of plays.

SCENES AND MACHINES

Several devices for aiding scenic effect were in use in later times. Pollux talks of the following:

periaktoi: prism-shaped scenic units
ekkuklema: a platform on wheels
mechane, or *geranos*:   a crane for the introduction of celestial figures.

He refers to ornamentation of the *skene* (or *proskenion*[17]) by means of *pinakes* ("painted panels") set between columns and to three doors in the *skene* used according to the rank of the character. He also notes some rather bizarre devices, most of which seem highly improbable for the Classical period:

Charon's steps: for ghosts to ascend from hell into the middle of the *orchestra*
anapiesma: a kind of trapdoor for the lifting up of a river
stropheion: for showing either heroes translated to heaven or those who died in a storm or in war
hemikuklion: for a remote view of cities and men swimming
bronteion: a thunder machine with pebbles poured into urns
keraunoskopeion: a lightning machine that may have worked in a number of unlikely ways, one of which involved catapulting a plank with a flash painted on it very fast into a trough
theologeion: an upper platform for gods
distegia: a second area for scenes on roofs.

Odd though these devices may sound, the first three he mentions have supporting evidence from elsewhere.

The noun *ekkuklema* ("a thing wheeled out") is not found before Pollux, but the verb "to wheel out" from which it is derived occurs twice in the plays of Aristophanes. In *Acharnians*, Dicaiopolis has called on Euripides to borrow some tragic props, but Euripides is working and cannot see him:

Euripides: I've no time.
Dicaiopolis: Have yourself wheeled out.
Euripides: Not possible.
Dicaiopolis: Please do.
Euripides: Well, I'll get wheeled out. But I haven't the time to get down.[18]

In *Women at the Thesmophoria*, Euripides comes with Mnesilochus to ask a favor from Agathon:

Euripides: Agathon's coming out.
Mnesilochus: Where is he?
Euripides: This is him, the one being wheeled out.[19]

The connection of both scenes with Euripides might suggest that the *ekkuklema* was invented by Euripides, but it may well have been used much earlier.

In all probability the *ekkuklema* was a small platform on runners on which a tableau could be set, or upon which a body or piece of furniture could be introduced into the action. It may be that a revolve turned on a central pivot from inside the *skene*, and that more than one could be used, but in practice a simpler arrangement fits all the occasions where an *ekkuklema* is required. A rectangular platform would be set in position behind the central double doors, to be propelled forward either manually or by means of some kind of winch when the doors were opened. The amount of room available in the Theatre of Dionysus would have been restricted to something less than the width of the doors and no more in depth, but such a space would have been ample for any of the tableaux in the plays.

Manuscript notes added by scholiasts suggest the use of the *ekkuklema* in several other plays including Aristophanes' *Clouds*, in the scene where all the philosophers inside the "thinking shop" are displayed. In tragedy there are specific references to the use of the *ekkuklema* for the tableau of slaughtered sheep in Sophocles' *Ajax*, for the dead Eurydice in *Antigone*, for Phaedra in Euripides' *Hippolytus*, and even for the complex choral entrance in Aeschylus' *Eumenides*. Indeed, the three plays of the *Oresteia* all require a "tableau" or "reveal." In each case the *ekkuklema* is suggested to stage an interior scene that would be considerably obscured for most of the audience unless it was wheeled out.

On numerous other occasions in ancient Greek tragedy and comedy staging problems can be conveniently solved by assuming the use of the *ekkuklema*. For instance, Aristophanes' *Clouds* opens with Strepsiades and his son in bed: nothing simpler than to wheel them on "asleep" and then once they have got up, to wheel the beds off again. The *ekkuklema* was undoubtedly part of the basic equipment of the Periclean theatre and in all probability of the pre-Periclean too.

The machine by means of which gods were "flown" in is the device that is hardest for the modern mind to accept, and Aristophanes himself uses the *mechane* in a humorous context in two important scenes. In *Peace*, Trygaeus, swaying dangerously up to heaven on the back of a dung beetle, shouts to the operator (*mechanopoios*) to take care not to drop him—and with good reason if the *mechane* was set, as Pollux states, as far away from the *skene* as the stage-left *parodos*. In *Women at the Thesmophoria*, Euripides, a character in the play, swings to and fro in an attempt to rescue Mnesilochus, while pretending to be Perseus with his winged sandals saving Andromeda from the sea serpent. No doubt the real Euripides' *Andromeda* staged just such a scene, but so elaborate a use of the *mechane* seems to have been rare. Its more customary use was for the introduction of the gods who so often conclude an Euripidean play. The Latin term *deus ex machina* stems from this function of the *mechane*, when an unexpected extra character is introduced into a play to resolve an impasse.

Whether the *mechane* was used before the time of Euripides is doubtful. Some critics believe the entire chorus of Aeschylus' *Prometheus* was flown in by crane but the idea is extremely far-fetched and no other play of Aeschylus or Sophocles requires the machine.

Evidence for the use of *periaktoi* in Roman times is not in dispute. Vitruvius suggests the use of six *periaktoi* in the Roman theatre, three being placed at either side between the side entrances and the end of the stage.[20] Shaped like a prism, a *periaktos* provided three separate scenes, turning on its axis to display alternating sides to the audience. Assuming a surface area of a *periaktos* of roughly four feet across by eight feet high, its value to the classical theatre becomes clear. The possibility of showing a change of scene by rotating a three-sided unit is a sophisticated refinement of the fixed painted panel, or *pinax*. Pollux talks of a further use of a *periaktos* "to introduce sea-gods, and things too heavy for the *mechane*."[21] This sounds much more the function of the *ekkuklema*, although elsewhere he does mention that the panels on the three sides of a *periaktos* were detachable, a plausible development from the use of *pinakes* slotted into gaps between pillars.

The three faces of the *periaktos* might have represented simply tragic, comic, or satyric scenes,[22] although there seems little reason for their being introduced merely to inform the spectator what genre of play he was watching. If, however, the three sides gave a direct representational view of a scene as Pollux hints, or more plausibly an emblematic view, this would imply that an actual change of location could be indicated: Delphi could be seen to change to Athens in *Eumenides*, Ajax's tent to become the seashore in *Ajax*. Few such changes occur in extant Greek plays, but new settings could have been used for each play in a group. Certain gods might have been associated with a particular environment so Athens, for instance, might have been indicated by the depiction of the goddess Athene on one *periaktos* and by a representation of the city itself on the other. Pollux again seems to support such a conjecture when he talks of a distinction between right and left *periaktos* for "things from outside the city" and "things from the city."[23]

The majority of modern critics reject the use of *periaktoi* until at least the fourth century, although the possible use of painted panels in the Periclean theatre in relation to background and scenery needs further consideration. The time lapse between the fifth century B.C. and the careers of Vitruvius and Pollux, and the vagueness of their terms of reference, suggests that neither is overconcerned about the stage conditions of the first performances of the classical tragedies, but that their information relates to possible revivals during the subsequent one, two, or even three centuries. We should, however, be wary of treating their work in too cavalier a fashion. Much of what they have to say is reliably reinforced by observations from elsewhere. If much of the rest is decidedly dubious, this is all the more reason for treating the "grey" areas with respect as well as skepticism.

STAGE SETTINGS

The Periclean *skene* was almost certainly a wooden construction but little direct information survives relative to the staging of plays. Texts do provide some indication of what authors expected their audiences to see or to imagine. How far imagination and vision coincided eventually emerges as the basic issue. At one extreme are the views of the majority of Victorian critics. The Victorians saw Greek theatre in terms of nineteenth-century representational settings. At the other extreme are the opinions of more modern commentators who believe the ancient theatre saw no need to translate into fact any of the features noted in the texts: once mentioned, these are thought to have existed effectively in the audience's imagination. Such a line of reasoning removes the necessity for even a background setting for early Aeschylean drama.

The work of each of the great playwrights demonstrates how difficult a task it is to differentiate the literal from the figurative. Before considering the *Electra* plays, let us examine a few other examples that demonstrate the range of requirement.

The action of Aeschylus' *Prometheus* takes place on a mountain where, during the opening sequence, Prometheus himself is nailed to a rock. Prometheus first hears rather than sees the Chorus, which is identified as the winged daughters of Oceanus:

What sound, what invisible scent flies towards me, sent by god, or mortal, or a mixture of both? Has it come to this mountain at the end of the earth as a watcher over my troubles or what does it want? . . .

Ah, what is this whirring of wings I hear close by? The air whispers with the light beating of wings.[24]

After they have come into view, Prometheus invites them to listen to his troubles "alighting on the ground" and the Chorus replies:

And now with light foot, leaving the swift-moving seat and the pure air, pathway of birds, I set foot on this rough ground.[25]

Oceanus enters almost immediately:

I have come to the end of a long journey in visiting you, Prometheus, directing this winged bird by my will but without a bridle.[26]

Towards the end of the play Hermes threatens Prometheus with thunder, lightning, and earthquake, and when Prometheus defies Hermes, the latter warns the Chorus:

Move from this place quickly lest the deafening of thunder stun your senses.[27]

The last speech of the play is given to Prometheus himself:

And now in actual fact, not merely in word the earth has been shaken. The noise of thunder from the depths roars, the bolts of lightning flash all round and whirlwinds swirl the dust. The blasts of all winds display their opposing strife and leap at each other. The upper air is confused with the sea. Such blasts against me from Zeus for certain cast fear upon me. O holy mother, O air revolving the common light of all, you see how unjustly I suffer.[28]

Did *Prometheus* require a dummy figure for its protagonist, the arrival of the entire Chorus on the *mechane*, and a final earthquake effect complete with thunder and lightning to engulf Prometheus? Peter Arnott, comparing the earthquake with similar scenes in Euripides' *Madness of Heracles* and *Bacchae*, wrote: "To present such effects realistically would require the combined resources of Bayreuth and Drury Lane."[29] But is it enough to state that a "thing can either be described or shown, and there is no need to do both,"[30] and conclude that nothing occurred to reinforce the spoken word? The problem is ultimately insoluble, but if *Prometheus* is not viewed in isolation, some sort of staging pattern emerges.

Prometheus was certainly performed in the pre-Periclean theatre and is among the earliest, if not the earliest, play to survive. Aristophanes' *Wasps*, Euripides' *Ion*, and Sophocles' *Philoctetes* were written in that order between 423 B.C. and 409 B.C. At the opening of *Wasps*, Procleon is attempting to escape from his house to serve on a jury. His son Anticleon gets his slaves to guard Procleon, and a net has been thrown over the house because the father has already tried to climb out along the drainpipe:

Anticleon: One of you, come round the back quickly. My father's got into the kitchen and is scuttling about like a mouse. Mind he doesn't pour himself out of the wastepipe from the boiler. And you, lean against the door.

Xanthias: Right, boss.

Anticleon: Lord Poseidon, what's that noise in the chimney? Who's that?

Procleon: I'm just a little bit of smoke.

Anticleon: Smoke? From what wood?

Procleon: Fig.

Anticleon: By Zeus, that's the most pungent there is. Get back in. Where's the chimney lid? Down you go. I'll put this log on too.[31]

Procleon then tries to push open the door, to pry up the tiles on the roof, and finally to escape under a donkey, a parody of Odysseus' escape from the Cyclops' cave. Finally, when the Chorus arrives, Procleon gnaws through the net:

Chorus leader: Now, tie one end of the rope to the window, and the other end round yourself, and lower yourself down.[32]

So he escapes.

Euripides' *Ion* is set in Delphi, and when the members of the Chorus make their entrance, they reveal that they are newcomers to Delphi. They immediately start to express their admiration of the set:

Chorus: Not only in holy Athens have the courts of the gods such fine pillars, and the worship of Apollo such respect. Here before Loxias himself, son of Latona, stands out the shining double temple-face.

Look here, where the son of Zeus is slaying the Lernian hydra with his golden scimitar. Look over here, my dear.

Yes, I see, and close by some other is lifting a flaming torch. But who's story is being told? Is it one I have told in my embroidery?

I am looking everywhere. Look at the battle of the giants on the marble wall.

Yes, we can see it, friends.

And do you see brandishing the Gorgon shield over Enceladus. . . .

I see her, my own goddess, Pallas Athene.

I ask you, you who stand by the temple, is it lawful for us to pass the threshold of this sanctuary with bare feet?[33]

Sophocles' *Philoctetes* opens with Odysseus and Neoptolemus searching for Philoctetes on the coast of Lemnos:

Odysseus: Your task is to help me find a cave with a double entrance ("with two mouths"), the sort to provide two seats in the sun in winter, or a gentle through-breeze in summer to bring soothing sleep. Further down on the left you should see a little spring if it still flows. Go quietly and let me know whether he is still in the same place, or has roved elsewhere. Then I will let you know what we must both do.

Neoptolemus: Lord Odysseus, it has not taken long; I think I can see the cave you mean.

Odysseus: Above or below. I do not see it.

Neoptolemus: Up there. I can hear no sound of movement inside.

Odysseus: Look and see if he is asleep.

Neoptolemus: It is empty: no one here. . . .

Odysseus: This is clearly his house, and he cannot be far away.[34]

All the foregoing scenes appear to require fairly solid sets and sets that resemble in some detail the given descriptions. Would any dramatist be likely to write such scenes to draw his audience's attention to the fact that none of the things mentioned really exists in physical form, onstage? Does not Euripides' *Ion* set in Delphi (the audience and Chorus being actually in Athens) suggest some sort of theatrical in-joke? If *Ion* is correctly dated about 418 B.C., might not the audience have been sitting for the first time in the fully completed precinct, after some thirty years of attending plays presented in what was virtually a building site?

A. W. Pickard-Cambridge offered the following as a setting for *Philoctetes*:

The background itself, the front of the temporary wooden *skene*, would be painted to represent a cliff, and the cave would be the upper part of the central doorway, the lower part being blocked; a rough path led up from the *orchestra* level to the mouth of the cave. Whether the spring which was between the beach and the cave was represented (e.g. by a niche in the rock) we do not know. All this would require only easily contrived adaptations of the conventional facade, aided by appropriate scene-painting.[35]

Peter Arnott pointed out how unnecessary such elaboration is, but went on to suggest that no scenery at all was used:

There is no setting in tragedy or comedy that could not be represented by the basic arrangement of *skene*, altar, stage and steps, helped out by a little imagination.[36]

Surely it is unsatisfactory to claim that settings were thus stereotyped, when on so many occasions playwrights emphasize physical details and are at pains to stress simultaneously that their plays are passing in a theatre. "There is no evidence that any form of painted scenery, apart from a permanent architectural facade, was used in classical times,"[37] states Arnott, in a purposeful attempt to break down nineteenth-century preoccupation with realistic settings. He is forced to admit, however, that in Aristotle's *Poetics* a statement exists to the effect that Sophocles introduced *skenographia*.[38] Vitruvius associates decoration of the *skene* with Agatharchus' work for Aeschylus, and elsewhere Agatharchus is credited with the discovery of the principles of perspective.

SKENOGRAPHIA

Skenographia is a tantalizingly simple term whose literal meaning is virtually no help in determining what Aristotle took it to be. "Writing on a tent" in a theatrical context can only refer to some kind of scenic decoration: but what kind? There is a world of difference between "painted scenery" and a "painted scene building."

If *skenographia* means "painted *skene*," the implication must be that Sophocles' plays were presented against a flat wooden background, painted to resemble something specific, a temple, seashore, palace, or some such locale. What then did Aeschylus and his predecessors use? I have already suggested that the actor needs a frame of some kind but an undecorated wooden wall would hardly have appealed to the Greek eye. The provision of a literal *skene*, a tent, could have provided a place to come from and go to and still have been sufficiently large to be accepted as a proper background, but the surviving plays suggest no such transition.

The noun *skenographia* and the verb *skenographein* are in the main late usages, often in a comparison of what is real and what is imaginary (that is, "skenographic"). By the late fourth century the *skene* of the Theatre of Dionysus was a permanent stone structure on which it would not have been possible to paint directly. It would have been possible to paint on removable wooden panels and one is forced to admit that if the term *skenographia* is used with any consistency, it refers to representational scenic painting. I would suggest that what Sophocles introduced was a series of painted panels, incorporating emblematic devices, to fit between the wooden columns of the three-dimensional Periclean *skene*. Perhaps Aeschylus too had recourse to a three-dimensional background, but one that was less precisely defined.

Aeschylus creates settings in the most unspecific of language. It is sometimes difficult to work out if he has any one location in mind, but this imprecision is intentional. It is in the nature of Aeschylean drama, and presumably in that of the pre-Periclean theatre, to create scenes in terms of nonrealistic setting, but not without any background.

Detailed description of background appears to coincide with the beginnings of the Periclean theatre, although the *Oresteia* of 458 B.C. is fairly specific in its references and draws the attention of its audience to features of the set and to the complexity of the stage picture. Audiences are happy to accept as legitimate stage devices whatever is introduced as such and is thereafter used with consistency, and the inclination of the theatre is almost invariably toward some kind of visual reminder. The Chinese theatre offers a well-known scene of a river crossing by a young girl and an old ferryman. Despite the fact that the majority of the scene is mimed, the old ferryman still carries an oar. In Chinese Opera an army has always been a collection of banners, and a plain table has been a bed when someone lies on it.

Nearer home, an understanding of the emblematic tradition is essential to a study of medieval art and drama, including an appreciation of color values, backgrounds, and groupings of characters: a small tree indicates that a scene is set on earth; a town is represented by a tower with a door below. Items of costume and even hairstyle identify the characters of medieval art, and a complex system of iconography dictated medieval dramatic presentation.

A tacit acceptance of stage conventions makes the mode of representation recognizable and acceptable. The Jacobean play *Two Noble Ladies* includes the drowning of two soldiers, and stage directions indicate what happened:

First Soldier: What strange noise is this? (*Thunder. Enter* two Tritons with silver trumpets)
Second Soldier: Dispatch, the tide swells high. What fiend is this?

   (*The Tritons seize the soldiers*)

First Soldier: What fury seizes me?
Second Soldier: Alas, I'm hurried headlong to the stream.
First Soldier: And so am I, we both must drown and die.

   (*The Tritons drag them in, sounding their trumpets*)[39]

The acknowledgment of the simple setting is most clearly expressed in Plautus' *The Brothers Menaechus*, based probably on an Athenian New Comedy of the fourth century:

Prologue: This city is Epidamnus, as long as this play lasts anyway. In another play, it will be another town. Just as the families change in the houses—they may be occupied by a pimp one day, young man next, old man the next, poor man, beggarman, king, parasite or clairvoyant.[40]

The above examples stretch the goodwill of an audience without ever really taxing it. But there are limits. In all verbal drama (some dramatic dance is almost self-sufficient) a director tries to avoid certain things. An audience is unlikely to accept an actor announcing "Here I lie" while he is standing firmly on his two feet, or "I look down from the roof" when he is plainly standing at ground level. The actor may not have to be perched on a proper roof, but a token elevation "stands in" for the real thing. A mime artist may succeed in creating the illusion, but his art depends upon making the invisible visible, and an actor in a play relies on tokens.

This sense of convention needs careful consideration in connection with the earliest plays of Aeschylus no less than in the last plays of Euripides. Set pieces, accessories, properties, and costumes of the actors were all likely to have had a specific importance whose meaning was clear enough to the audience, familiar with symbolic as well as literal values. It is quite possible to imagine every surviving Greek play as having been staged in the Theatre of Dionysus with basically the same setting. This could have comprised a *skene* of columns, with one or more entrances between them, and with a solid roof. The addition of a pediment would lend the whole the appearance of a temple facade, in the same fashion as the "theatrical" vases delineate temple porticos. But this facade would in itself be no more than an emblematic stage setting.

In the time of Aeschylus, this *skene* could have been less elaborate, perhaps no more than the outline of columns and pediment painted on a background. Because the audience had no expectation of a theatre of illusion, it would be perfectly comprehensible for Prometheus, tied to a frame on an *ekkuklema*, or even between pillars of the set, to be assumed to be tied to a rock on a mountaintop. When the Chorus is advised to stand back from Prometheus, the members give themselves adequate room to "dance" the earthquake as Prometheus describes it. Significantly, they do not have the last lines of *Prometheus* (as is customary), perhaps because the earthquake dance has already attained its climax with their headlong exit up the *parodoi*. Thus Prometheus is left to conclude the play and then to be withdrawn on the *ekkuklema* into the *skene* through the central entrance. If Aeschylus' theatre of the imagination could stage an earthquake so simply, the description of the entrance of the Chorus, and even that of Oceanus, could indicate a figurative dance, all part and parcel of a theatre tradition, familiar to the entire audience.

If, by the time of *Prometheus*, the columns were already of solid wood, *skenographia* was perhaps employed for decoration of panels (*pinakes*), to fit between the columns on either side of the main entrance. The main entrance would itself be concealed by the *ek-kuklema* until the finale of the play, backed by a "rock" to which Prometheus was tied.

Such suggestions must be tentative, and many alternative settings have been posited for this particular play. If a basic principle can be established for the time of Aeschylus, however, any staging problems of the Periclean theatre can be easily solved. What was a rudimentary arrangement on an ad hoc basis in the pre-Periclean theatre would have inevitably undergone modifications in the Periclean precinct, which permitted more room for a semipermanent *skene* and also provided postholes for a framework of wooden pillars. The *skene* must have been substantial enough to harmonize with the permanent building of the hall and surroundings without looking prefabricated, when actually representing a palace.

To this basic acting area, scenic units could have been added. Both *Wasps* and *Philoctetes* seem to imply the existence of double entrances. These entrances could have been accommodated by the addition of *paraskenia* in the manner indicated by the Italian vase (figure 5). If double entrance is to be interpreted as a double door in a central position, no *paraskenia* need have been used. Instead, a *prothuron* could have been added, perhaps depending on whether the *ekkuklema* was to be used. If an elaborate roof was required to show a two-storied building with a window and chimney hole (as in *Wasps*), this extra element could be added. Even doors could have been removed, perhaps to be replaced by a curtain before the cave of Philoctetes or by open access. In any circumstance it would have been a simple matter for a competent carpenter to add scenic units. The theatre may even have possessed stock sets of *paraskenia*, *prothura*, and stage steps. All that was necessary was for the playwright to explain the location of his play, which characters usually do, and to provide in the space between the columns some visual reminder of what the *skene* was supposed to represent on this particular occasion. Such a ploy is theatrically satisfying and surmounts any problems presented by a change of scene in plays such as *Eumenides* and *Ajax*. It does this simply by the presentation of a new emblem, the work of a moment, especially if instead of single panels between the columns a *periaktos* is pivoted to display any of three panels of equal size.

The test of such a theory of setting lies in its ability to accommodate the majority of plays that require such a setting. With the *Electra* plays as a reference, an examination of staging requirements can now be made.

NOTES

1. Thoricon has an *orchestra* that is rectangular rather than circular or horseshoe shaped.

2. Horace *On the Art of Poetry*: line 276.

3. Some critics believe the dramatic performances of the Lenaia took place not in the Theatre of Dionysus but in the Lenaion itself. In *The History of the Greek and Roman Theater*, Margarete Bieber supplied a provisional reconstruction of the setting for Aristophanes' *Frogs* in an endstage arrangement. This fails to convince. The relationship between actor, chorus, and audience in Old Comedy is based no less than in tragedy on the tripartite nature of the theatre itself. Aristophanes' Lenaia plays show no significant difference in terms of stage presentation from those written for the Great Dionysia.

4. Vitruvius *On Architecture*: V 7. 2.

5. Ibid V 8. 2.

6. See chapter 2, note 7.

7. Pollux *Onomasticon*: IV 123.

8. Ibid.

9. Ibid., IV 129–30.

10. Traces of ramps at Epidaurus indicate that that theatre employed such entrances.

11. A number of vases, depicting in the main comic scenes, clearly show a wooden platform stage, often with steps up to it. As evidence for the Theatre of Dionysus, they can be disregarded but they do give a record of a fit-up farce theatre in the Classical period. See A. D. Trendall and T. B. L. Webster, *Illustrations of Greek Drama* (London: Phaidon, 1971), III 6. 1, IV 1, IV 11, IV 13, IV 14, IV 17, IV 20, IV 21, IV 24, IV 26, IV 27, IV 35.

12. Horace *On the Art*: line 279.

13. Plato *Symposium*: 194b.

14. As in Euripides *Electra*: line 489.

15. Bieber, *History*, p. 73.

16. The word *logeion* is used by Vitruvius and Plutarch.

17. The precise meaning of *proskenion* and *huposkenion* is difficult to pin down. As far as the Periclean theatre is concerned, it seems safest to identify the *skene* as the vertical scenic facade and the *proskenion* as the area in front of the *skene*. *Huposkenion* ("the area beneath" or "adjacent to the *skene*") is most plausibly defined as the area below the high stage of the Hellenistic theatre.

18. Aristophanes *Acharnians*: lines 407–9.

19. Aristophanes *Women at the Thesmophoria*: lines 95–96.

20. Their exact position is located by Vitruvius in a diagram.

21. Pollux *Onomasticon*: IV 126.

22. Such scenes are depicted in the frescoes of the Roman villa of Publius Fannius Sinister at Boscoreale.

23. Pollux *Onomasticon*: IV 126.

24. Aeschylus *Prometheus*: lines 115–26.

25. Ibid., lines 278–81.

26. Ibid., lines 284–87.

27. Ibid., lines 1060–62.

28. Ibid., lines 1080–93.

29. P. D. Arnott, *An Introduction to the Greek Theatre* (London: Macmillan, 1959), p. 44.

30. P. D. Arnott, *Greek Scenic Conventions* (Oxford: Oxford University Press, 1962; reprinted, Westport, Conn.: Greenwood Press, 1979), p. 123.

31. Aristophanes *Wasps*: lines 138–48.

32. Ibid., lines 379–80.

33. Euripides *Ion*: lines 184–221.

34. Sophocles *Philoctetes*: lines 15–31, 40–41.

35. A. W. Pickard-Cambridge, *The Theatre of Dionysus in Athens* (Oxford: OxfordUniversity Press, Clarendon Press, 1946), p. 50.

36. Arnott, *Conventions*, p. 106.

37. Arnott, *Introduction*, p. 38.

38. Aristotle *Poetics*: 1449a.

39. As quoted in Andrew Gurr, *The Shakespearean Stage* (Cambridge: At the University Press, 1970), p. 121.

40. Plautus *The Brothers Menaechmus*: lines 72–76.

Chapter 5 Staging the Electras

AESCHYLUS' *LIBATION BEARERS*

Aeschylus' imprecision in locating the scenes of his plays was due, I have suggested, not to a lack of interest in mundane detail, but rather to a sophisticated awareness of the neutrality of the *skene* in the theatre of his time. It was this assumption that the *skene* was identified and brought to life principally by specific reference that had become old-fashioned by the latter part of the century, and that allowed Euripides to make fun of Aeschylus' stylized approach to the recognition scene in his own *Electra* (see chapter 8).

All three plays of the *Oresteia* require the *skene* to represent a building at some time. *Libation-Bearers* is often thought to incorporate a scene change during the action, but I intend to show from the text itself that this is unnecessary.

In the opening lines of *Libation-Bearers*, Orestes is praying to Hermes of the underworld. The manuscripts are deficient, and these first lines are supplied from a quotation in Aristophanes' *Frogs:*

Hermes of the underworld, guardian of my father's power, be my saviour and helper, I beseech you. I have come back and returned to this land. I beg my father to hear, at this mound of a tomb. . . .[1]

Even if the text were more sure, it would still not be possible to work out exactly how the play opened. The actors could not be discovered and the audience must have seen them enter before any lines were spoken.

Orestes has returned from abroad and calls upon his father's help "at this mound of a tomb." The tomb is clearly important and needs to be visible to the audience for what it represents. Vase paintings indicate it could have stood at least five feet high (figure 7).

Figure 7. Electra at the Tomb, a Fourth-Century Scene (Paris, Musée du Louvre. Photograph M. Chuzeville)

Such a unit would have provided not only a visual focus for the play but a central scenic piece against which to compose key moments such as the offering of libations, the recognition, and the *kommos*.

References to this tomb[2] occur in the first part of the play:

Electra: . . . as I pour this offering on my father's tomb.[3]
Chorus: I will speak reverencing your father's tomb as [though it were] an altar.[4]
Chorus: Pour out tears . . . on this protection against evil.[5]
Electra: I see this lock of hair upon the tomb.[6]
Electra: [The lock of hair] . . . an adornment to this tomb.[7]
Electra: I will reverence this tomb above all else.[8]
Electra: Hear this cry . . . as you see these your children seated at [*or* on] your tomb.[9]
Orestes: I pray to the earth and my father's tomb.[10]

Only one further reference is made to "the edge of the funeral mound,"[11] this by the Chorus after the assumed set change has taken place and the scene moved to before the palace. Peter Arnott noted the predominance of early references to a tomb but commented as follows:

If a particular scenic feature is only casually mentioned, and most of the time taken for granted, we may assume that it is realistic enough to need no explanation. When, on the other hand, it is repeatedly identified, we may assume that it is not recognisable without such identification. . . . We may therefore safely say that some other feature does duty for the tomb, and that this feature is probably the stage altar.[12]

This is one of many attempts by Arnott to prove that a stage altar, set at the edge of a low stage fronting the central doors, was a permanent feature of the theatre.

The references to the tomb, however, are not intended by Aeschylus to remind his audience, periodically, that what they see to be one thing is meant to be something different. The tomb is a theatrical device for maintaining a visual focus during the early part of the action. It serves as a constant reminder of Agamemnon, whose murder governs the development of the entire trilogy. By retaining the action in close proximity to Agamemnon's tomb and by constant reference to it, the author induces his audience to recognize it not as a solid feature of the theatre, substituting as a tomb, but as a visual focus around which the events of *Libation-Bearers* revolve. The tomb need never be removed from sight. Dramatically speaking, sound arguments can be made for its remaining constantly in view during Orestes' planning and execution of vengeance upon Aegisthus and Clytemnestra, and perhaps as a counterpoint to the tableau of their slaughtered bodies.

Indeed, it is difficult to discover where the notion of two separate settings originated. The palace is mentioned in the second speech in the play when the Chorus enters: "I come, sent out from the house,"[13] and Electra invokes the spirits "that watch over my father's house."[14] The anxiety of the Chorus in case Orestes and Electra may be overheard indicates that they are standing just outside.

More references to the palace are made while the plot is being hatched:

Orestes: Like a stranger, having all the equipment, I shall come with Pylades here to the gates at the threshold [*or* of the inner courtyard] . . . and if none of the door-keepers will receive us . . . we will wait in such a way that anyone who passes by the house will wonder and say "Why does Aegisthus turn away the suppliant from the house if he is at home and knows about it?" But if I shall cross the outermost threshold of the gates. . . .[15]

After this Orestes and Pylades withdraw from the stage to disguise themselves before approaching the door.

Orestes: Boy, boy, hear the knocking at the outer door. Who is inside, boy; and again I say "Who is at home?"[16]

When Clytemnestra has heard the message, she instructs a servant:

Clytemnestra: Escort him to the hospitable men's quarters of the house and his attendants and fellow-traveller.[17]

After Aegisthus has been murdered, a servant gives the news:

Servant: Alas, alas for my stricken master. Alas again for the third time.
Aegisthus is no more. But open up as quickly as possible, and release the gates of the women's quarters from their bars.[18]

No further references are made to the palace or tomb and certainly
nothing to suggest any difficulty in a single setting for the whole
play, although the position of the tomb relative to the *skene* still
presents a difficulty.

Arnott's theory that the altar was a permanent feature that could
be used to represent a tomb would be more plausible were it not
for his situating the altar in front of the main entrance, where its
presence would render scenes in several plays virtually unstageable,
notably those requiring the use of the *ekkuklema*. If the altar was
located to one side of the main door, together with a statue of a god,
in the position where shrines were often placed, before private houses,
it could have replaced one of the *pinakes* and itself have served to
help identify the location.

In *Libation-Bearers* the tomb could have been set between pillars
of the *skene* or even painted on a *pinax*, where as a more substantial
unit than an altar it could have been given as much prominence as
the play required. A much more acceptable idea is that the tomb
was a free-standing unit in front of and below the stage area, sufficiently far from this to avoid impairing the function of the central
entrance but close enough for the actors to have had access to the
tomb without needing to intrude too far upon the *orchestra*. This
would have provided not only the visual focus welcomed earlier
but a central scenic piece against which to compose key moments
in the play, the offering of libations, the recognition, and the *kommos*.
Statues of the gods could have been positioned as far away as the rear
boundary of the *orchestra*, but they would much more reasonably
have been placed between the columns, either painted on panels or
sculpted.

ENTRANCES AND EXITS

It is far from clear whether *Libation-Bearers* would have needed
three or five entrances. The *parodoi*, although regularly used by
the chorus, also represent roads. Pollux distinguishes between the
right *parodos* ("audience right") leading from the country, the

harbor, or the city, and the left *parodos* for those arriving from anywhere else. He follows this with the information that of three doors in the *skene*, the center door opened onto whatever was of most importance in the set (palace, cave, and so on), and the door on the right was provided for the second actor, the one on the left having a poor appearance, either leading to a deserted temple with no house at all behind it or, in tragedy, to a prison. Applied to the surviving plays, this principle serves only to create problems, but there may well be the germ of a real convention contained in Pollux. In the Theatre of Dionysus, the city of Athens was stage left; "abroad" was stage right. The stage-left and stage-right *parodoi* may well have reflected this. Certainly entrances that one would expect to be made along a *parodos* are often allowed for by five or more lines between recognition and entry into the action. The playwrights make similar provisions for the long exit, the two *parodoi* being a good fifty feet from the central door. This leaves the doorways in the *skene* solely for entrances from indoors, and incidentally this makes it quite possible for most plays to be set with a single central entrance.

Libation-Bearers might still have used three doors. Orestes and Pylades would have made their first entrance up the stage-right *parodos*. The Chorus in all probability accompanied Electra either literally from the house or coincidentally with her entrance by processing up the stage-left *parodos*. Until Orestes knocks at the door of the palace, no suggestion is given that more than one door is needed. Clytemnestra's entrance was clearly from the central doors, but when Orestes and Pylades are invited inside, references first to "men's quarters" and then, later, to "women's quarters" clearly open up the possibility of two other entrances. From here on each director is on his own. Did Clytemnestra, her attendant, Orestes, his attendants, and Pylades all go out the same way after Clytemnestra had given her instructions? Or did Clytemnestra retire by the way she had come, her attendant taking Orestes and Pylades in at a side door? Alternatively, did Clytemnestra perhaps exit by a different door (to the "women's quarters") to that from which she had entered, while Orestes and Pylades were led into the palace through the central door? Any solution has important effects on the action immediately following the death of Aegisthus.

The Nurse Cilissa enters after the next choral ode. Where did she come from? If she came from a door that indicated her station in life, it could hardly be the one through which Clytemnestra had recently entered the palace. The Nurse, however, has received her orders from Clytemnestra, and it is reasonable that she has come from conversing with the Queen. The only other possibility is that the Nurse came from the third door, but such complications begin to resemble the penny under the glass trick: the characters are constantly appearing from the doorway where you least expect them.[19]

The Chorus announces who the Nurse is:

I see here the nurse of Orestes in tears. Where are you going to, Cilissa, passing the gates of the house? [or "where are you walking to, close to the house?"][20]

At the conclusion of her short scene the Nurse exits to fetch Aegisthus, who is away from the palace. A long exit seems to be intended for the Nurse along the stage-left *parodos*, toward the city as opposed to toward the country, from which Orestes and Pylades first made their appearance.

Aegisthus must have entered from the direction of the Nurse's exit (almost certainly the same actor would have played both parts). A nice dramatic contrast suggests itself between the slow, sad, old woman and the brisk, exultant king, a contrast ironically heightened by the audience's special knowledge of the real situation.

Aegisthus would have entered the palace by the central entrance: this is essential for the later revelation of the body. After his death cries are heard, a servant enters with the news, and this servant should also have come from the central entrance and the scene of the murder. He calls for help:

But open up as quickly as possible and release the gates of the women's quarters from their bars.[21]

Clytemnestra enters almost immediately, presumably from the "women's quarters." To be consistent she should have come from the same door by which she previously made her exit. If this is the central door used by the Servant, why did the Servant appear on stage in the first place? Clytemnestra calls or her axe and the Servant probably exits at the same time. He is not referred to again and could have left by any of the doors. A slight hiatus suggests he used the central door with time to get clear before Orestes and Pylades emerged from killing Aegisthus.

Orestes and Pylades drive Clytemnestra into the palace, there to be murdered in turn. The bodies are now revealed, in tableau. The remainder of the play presents no real difficulty.

Three possible settings can therefore be suggested for the original performance:

1. A scenic facade with a single entrance, by means of which all the different parts of the palace could be reached
2. A two-door facade, the second leading to the women's quarters.
3. A three-door facade with one of the side doors leading to the women's quarters, the other to the men's.

No evidence can be found as to which of the three possibilities Aeschylus favored. Indeed, the production problems raised by any of the solutions confirm the impression that Aeschylus was no more literal minded in his *mise-en-scène* than in any other aspect of his theatre.

My own preference accordingly must be not for the setting that solves the greater number of immediate problems, but the one I opted for in production because it most added to a dramatic tension that has survived without strain the years of changing theatre convention. The first and third plays of the trilogy need only one door. I have suggested in chapter 4 that there was no reason why in the Periclean theatre pieces should not be added or removed from play to play, and I would surmise that Aeschylus used three entrances from the *skene* in *Libation-Bearers*. The compelling reason for this is not that the palace architecture needs to be worked out geographically with women's and men's quarters, but that the buildup of characters and action in the latter part of the play is too great for a single entrance to contain.

SOPHOCLES' *ELECTRA*

If the *Electra*s of Sophocles and Euripides are both to be assigned to a late date,[22] the Periclean theatre would have been by then complete and would have afforded perhaps wider scope for the playwright in terms of scenic possibilities. Sophocles' *Electra* opens with the following speech from the Tutor:

Son of Agamemnon, once commander-in-chief at Troy, now it is possible for you to cast your eyes upon what you were eager to see. For this is the ancient city of Argos that you longed for, the hallowed precinct of the maddened daughter of Inachus. And this, Orestes, is the Lyceian marketplace of the wolf-slaying god; and on the left, the famous temple of Hera. Where we have come to, here believe you see golden Mycenae and this is the deathly house of the sons of Pelops. . . .²³

The speech is certainly a full description and one that seems to imply a detailed set. The Tutor can "see":

1. The ancient city of Argos and the precinct (or "grove") of Io
2. Apollo's marketplace.
3. The temple of Hera
4. Mycenae
5. The palace of the sons of Pelops

Unfortunately such a description tells us nothing: it is too detailed. All or none of the features described might be visible to the audience. Some of them might be represented realistically or emblematically, with others left to the imagination. To discover what Sophocles' *Electra* requires for a setting, the entire text must be considered.

At line 51 Orestes announces that he will offer libations at his father's tomb, and he has to leave the scene to visit the tomb. When Electra enters, she refers to herself as lamenting "before my father's doors."²⁴ Chrysothemis, Electra's sister who has come from indoors, asks Electra why she is standing and talking "at the way out from the hall."²⁵ The word for "hall," *thuron*, is a rare one that usually implies an antechamber or vestibule rather than the whole house.

When Clytemnestra has already been on stage for a hundred lines arguing with Electra, she gives orders to an attendant:

Lift up the offerings of fruits, you who stand beside me, so that I may offer to my lord here prayers that will free me from the fear that I now feel. Phoebus our protector, hear my hidden prayer.²⁶

The presence of an altar and/or statue of Apollo is implied, although how it is situated relative to the scene building is not clear. Apollo is being addressed as god of the household, so his altar or statue would logically be expected to be close to the palace.

The Tutor, on his second entrance, asks the Chorus if this is the house of Aegisthus,[27] and the Chorus confirms that it is. Much later Orestes hears someone about to come out of the house, and the Tutor emerges, criticizing Orestes and Electra harshly for making plans so publicly.[28] If he had not kept guard at the doorposts (stathmoisi), declares the Tutor, the plotters would have been discovered, thus implying that only one door needs to be guarded and so presumably only one door is in use.

Orestes then urges Pylades to accompany him indoors, but first to salute "my father's seats of the gods, such as dwell here in the place in front of the gates."[29] After suitable respect has been paid, they enter the house and Electra prays to Apollo for help. The word "seats" (hede), which Orestes uses, can have no greater significance than "the place where they are situated," but it might also be used for "shrine" or even "seated statues." "The place in front of the gates" (propula) is a secondary form of propulaia, a term used for the gateway of Egyptian temples. Propulaia is also the name of the temple built by Pericles just before the Peloponnesian War on the west side of the Acropolis and at the entrance to it. The term propula would be likely to carry visual associations for an Athenian audience, and it suggests a plausible background for this play with the portico, prothuron, prominently placed to set off the central action. The Propulaia was probably completed about 432 B.C. and might even have served as a model for the skene during the intermediate stage of the construction of the Precinct of Dionysus and before its completion.

Orestes and Pylades are urged to pass through the area opposite the doors (antithuron),[30] the reference being no more than an instruction to them to return indoors at the approach of Aegisthus who himself demands that the gates be opened to display what is inside.[31] The phrase is condensed into two words that give the clearest possible indication of the use of a reveal with the body of Clytemnestra, dead under a sheet, and with Orestes and Pylades standing beside it. No matter what the form of staging, this reveal must be brought forward into the center of the acting space and little doubt exists (as with the tableau of bodies at the end of Libation-Bearers) that the scene is written for the ekkuklema.

Apart from a few passing references to the palace, the set is not elsewhere mentioned.

ENTRANCES AND EXITS

At the opening of Sophocles' *Electra*, the Tutor, Orestes, and Pylades have come from abroad and probably entered up the stage-right *parodos*, as did Orestes and Pylades in Aeschylus' *Libation-Bearers*. The general principle that the stage-right *parodos* is used for entrances from abroad and the stage-left *parodos* for the city is by no means immutable, but the dialogue makes it clear to an audience which *parodos* indicates which direction. When they hear Electra offstage, Orestes, Pylades, and the Tutor exit, Orestes going with Pylades to look for his father's tomb.

It is normally assumed that the Tutor must have gone off in a different direction from that taken by Orestes and Pylades. Orestes and Pylades, however, are not familiar with the place; otherwise the Tutor would not have had to point everything out to them, nor can they be assumed to know where Agamemnon's tomb is. They must also time their arrival back at the palace at an appropriate moment after the Tutor has gained admission. It is more reasonable to assume that the three left the scene together.

When Orestes is making his plans, he refers to a bronze urn he has hidden in the woods, which he says he will bring back with him. In stage terms, he indicates that he must leave by the way he has come. Agamemnon's tomb lies then on the same side, or "abroad," although one might have expected it to be on the "city" side, stage left. This leaves the stage-left *parodos* free for the use of the Chorus.

Electra enters from the palace. The Chorus does not speak until line 121, but functions in such close association with her in this scene as to indicate that its entrance coincides with that of Electra. The members are identified as local women from Mycenae and accordingly would have entered along the stage-left *parodos*. The change of rhythm in Electra's first words from the iambics of the opening scene indicates a lyric lament with musical accompaniment, and the musician enters perhaps leading the Chorus. All later entrances and exits could have been comfortably managed with one central doorway, and no obvious difficulty is presented in assuming it also accommodated the *ekkuklema*.

The minimum setting required for *Electra*, then, is a palace background with a single entrance. It is surely out of the question to visualize an original setting incorporating all the features referred to in the text: the old city of Argos, the marketplace of Apollo, the temple of Hera, the city of Mycenae, and the palace. Even more dubious was Sir Richard Jebb's analysis:

Coming from Phocis, the travellers have reached Mycenae by the road from Corinth, and are now standing on the high ground of the Mycenaean citadel, in front of the palace.

The old man, looking southward, points out the chief features of the landscape. (1) The Argive plain which lies spread out before them to the south and west. (2) The *agora* and temple of Apollo Lyceios in the city of Argos, distant about six miles to the south. This temple was the most conspicuous object in the town (*Pausanias* 2.19.3); and it may be supposed that a person standing at Mycenae could see the building, or part of it. (3) The Heraeum, correctly described as being on the speaker's left hand. Its site was S.E. of Mycenae, at a distance of somewhat less than two miles.[32]

Even assuming the dullest pedantry on Sophocles' part, it is hard to believe that many members of the audience would either have been able to identify the actual spot where the Tutor was standing or had any wish to do so.

A rather more acceptable notion is that individual features of the Precinct of Dionysus were pointed out so Sophocles used the entire precinct as his set, including the old temple, the long hall, and perhaps even the Odeon and the Acropolis itself. Of the five landmarks mentioned, however, only one is important to the play and that is in plain view: the facade of the palace set in the *skene*. If features of Argos were represented on painted panels between the pillars to the sides of the central door, such features would at least account for their being mentioned in the first place. Altars or statues could have been placed to the side of the central doors, but would have been obtrusive if placed in front of them. The requirements of the play can be served quite simply as soon as it is appreciated that Sophocles was not trying to persuade the spectator that he was anywhere other than the Theatre of Dionysus, watching a play.

Aeschylus and Sophocles illustrate with great clarity in their *Electra* plays both how much and how little it was incumbent upon Greek playwrights to give physical representation of the scenes where the plays are set. So does Euripides but, predictably, he presents a somewhat different set of problems.

EURIPIDES' *ELECTRA*

The play must first have surprised the audience when they discovered that they were confronting not the royal palace, but a farmhouse. The farmhouse could only have been revealed in one of two ways. Either the set was representational enough for the audience to comprehend the location of the action before the play even started, or they became aware of the "farmhouse" only as the fact was made known by textual references. If a representational set was originally used, the surprise lay not so much in the setting itself as in the fact that Electra lived in such lowly surroundings. If the alternative suggestion is correct, the set was recognizable only as a theatre setting with little to distinguish it from that provided for Sophocles' play.

The prologue from the Farmer identifies the country as Argos. He addresses the audience directly and tells of the war against Troy and its outcome, the adorning of Argive walls with spoil, and the murder of Agamemnon in his own home. Initially, no indication is given about who the speaker is or how he relates to the story. In time, he announces that Electra has been given to him as a wife, and it becomes clear that this place is where the two of them live. From here to the end of his speech, the Farmer talks of his poverty and his unworthiness to sleep with Electra, who is still a virgin, as she herself keeps pointing out. Nothing, however, is said about the house itself. Until it becomes clear indirectly that this is the home of a peasant, the text gives no indication that the set might not be a palace. By the time Electra enters, no reference has yet been made to the set as anything but a "house." The Farmer replies to her determination to fetch water herself with the words, "The spring is not far from the house."³³ The word for house used here, *melathra*, has the grander meaning of "halls," but significantly it is the same as is used to refer to the cave dwellings in Sophocles' *Philoctetes* and Euripides' *Cyclops*.

When Orestes and Pylades enter, Orestes announces that instead of going inside the city walls he has come to the frontier of the country,³⁴ so he can quickly recross the border if anyone recognizes him. He fails to mention the house. The Chorus arrives and announces that it has come to visit Electra at her "rustic courtyard":³⁵ any literal translation turns the original into "country seat," but as used in Homer, the word for "courtyard" (*aule*) would imply a double door opening into a central courtyard surrounded by buildings.

Electra complains that she lives "as an exile from my father's house in the home of a labourer on these high crags,"[36] but from what is said elsewhere about the set, it is clear that Electra is not living in a hovel. Electra's husband may be poor by royal standards, but he does at least own a farm. Her house is up in the hills and it is deserted, and although Electra has already been at great pains to exaggerate her discomfort, her only complaint so far about her dwelling is that it is not *the* palace.

Electra catches sight of Orestes and Pylades as they step from their place of concealment. The literal translation is odd:

Some strangers, holding family beds, are rising from ambush to the house.[37]

"Holding family beds" seems to mean "having a resting-place beside the family gods." If this is so, the hiding place appears to have been beside either an altar or perhaps a statue of a household god. Electra does not have time to reach the house before the two men intercept her, when her reaction implies a direct appeal to Phoebus Apollo, perhaps another statue at the other side of the door or even the place of concealment to which she retreats as her way indoors is barred.

Orestes asks about her condition:

Electra: I dwell far away [from the city] in this house here.
Orestes: Some ditcher or cowherd deserves this house.[38]

This is the first time the lowliness of the building is referred to, but it is Orestes who speaks of it in such contemptuous terms. In a long speech Electra then tells Orestes, without recognizing him, what news he should take back to her brother:

Tell him in what sort of clothes I am lodged, with what filth I am weighed down, beneath what roof I live [cast out] from my father's house, weaving my own clothes at the loom or else have my body naked and go without, having to carry water from the river myself, without a feast on sacred occasions, cut off from dances. I shrink from married women, being still a virgin. . . .[39]

The remarkable thing is the mild tone in which Electra refers to her home. After all, the majority of her complaints are known by the audience to be unjustified since Electra refuses help from her husband and declines invitations from the Chorus to go to a festival, even when it offers to give her a dress.

The only good reason is that the house is there in full view, onstage, and despite Orestes' reservations does not look like a hovel. At no time has Electra spoken of it as such. Her husband seems to confirm this:

Who are these strangers I see at the gates? For what reason have they approached my rustic gates?[40]

With the arrival of the Old Man, the possibilities afforded by this kind of theatre are extended. "How steep the approach is to this house,"[41] he announces, and several commentators see the need of something to climb to justify the remark. A ramp up to the stage has been suggested or perhaps a steep incline up the *parodos*. But what is important is that the speaker's extreme age is physically demonstrated. Perhaps the lines were said as he reached the step to the main acting area and began to climb. This would be perfectly in accord with stage practice, but it would not be incongruous in this kind of theatre for flat ground to be referred to in this way when the setting has been announced as "in the mountains," and the Old Man has greatly exerted himself to get there with the things he is carrying:

Nevertheless I must drag along my bent back and backward-sinking knee to my friends.[42]

Later when the murder of Aegisthus has been carried out, Orestes catches sight of Clytemnestra approaching. As she does not enter for twenty-five lines, even though she is coming in a carriage, Orestes must "see" her well offstage, beyond the *parodos*. After the scene with her mother, Electra persuades her to go indoors with the words:

Step inside our poor house. Take care you do not soil your clothes on the smoky roof [*that is*, house].[43]

The purpose of Electra's line is primarily to taunt her mother with the difference in their modes of dress.

Such realistic details are typical of Euripides' stage technique, but are still quite in keeping with the use of the *ekkuklema* on which the bodies of Aegisthus and Clytemnestra were presumably presented in tableau. So, too, with the Dioscuri, Castor and Pollux, whom the Chorus announces:

But who are these who appear over the top part of the house, spirits are – they, or from the gods in heaven?[44]

An upper story is not required elsewhere in the play. Either the Dioscuri were deposited on the roof at this juncture or they delivered their lines in midair from the *mechane*.

ENTRANCES AND EXITS

The arrangement of entrances and exits is hardly more complicated than in Sophocles. The Farmer who delivers the prologue presumably enters from his house. Electra enters at line 53: since she is carrying a water jar, she too would have come from indoors, and she speaks ten lines before the Farmer addresses her. It is improbable that the Farmer exited at the end of the prologue, to return only ten lines later. On the other hand, it is curious that the pair should both have come from the same entrance since Electra does not appear to notice the presence of her husband until he addresses her. The prologue may of course have been delivered from the *orchestra* or from the side. Electra may even have come from a different door, although a second entrance from the *skene* is not needed again and is never referred to. Most probably the play proper started with the arrival of Electra, the Farmer creating the transition from the prologue by his change from direct address to the audience to dialogue with his wife. Electra could have left at the end of her speech or waited five lines until the Farmer exited to go ploughing. Electra is going to fetch water and the Farmer's line does have the sound of a parting shot:

Well go on, if you want. The springs are not far from the house.[45]

What is difficult to explain is how Electra and the Farmer could have departed along opposite *parodoi* when Orestes and Pylades immediately arrive from abroad, that is, up the stage-right *parodos*. That they should have passed either Electra or the Farmer is frankly ridiculous; yet if Electra also used the stage-right *parodos*, leaving the left free for the Farmer, even five lines is scarcely enough to cover Electra's departure. Electra's next entrance is back from the spring, with water, and the Farmer later returns from ploughing, having been seen approaching the house by the Chorus. Even the constant references when the play opens to the fact that it is still night cannot really resolve the difficulty without an awkward hiatus.

If Orestes and Pylades, on their entrance, did not pass either Electra or her husband, three possibilities remain. The Farmer reentered the house and left by a back door, much as it is sometimes believed an *angiportum* was used in Roman comedy[46]—this despite his next appearance being along one of the *parodoi*. Alternatively, he used Pollux's "third door," which did not lead indoors. As neither of these accords with the much more literal stagecraft of Euripides, one has to assume that the Farmer did use the same *parodos* as Electra, his exit so timed through five lines that he did not appear to be accompanying her. The problem is very different from that posed by the Servant and Clytemnestra in *Libation-Bearers* (see above) and nicely emphasizes the differing dramatic techniques of the two playwrights.

Orestes and Pylades could then have entered unobstructed along the stage-right *parodos*; the Chorus could freely have entered up the stage-left *parodos*, with the only remaining complication being the arrival of Clytemnestra. Clytemnestra is on her way to visit Aegisthus (who has already been killed offstage) and should come from the *parodos* other than that from which most of the play's entrances are made, so as not to pass the spot where he has been murdered. But by this time the contrast created between stage-left and stage-right *parodoi* is more important than the strict locality suggested by each, and if the Farmer, Old Man, Messenger, and the procession with the dead Aegisthus have all used the stage-right *parodos*, Clytemnestra must logically have used the stage-left *parodos*.

In terms of what needs to be represented, Euripides' *Electra* poses no particular difficulties. The *parodoi* and a single central entrance are all that is required. Electra does not harp on the squalor of her house, because her house is not squalid. In keeping with what has been said elsewhere, the central entrance would be flanked by wooden pillars, the double doors assumed to open onto a courtyard.

An emblematic tradition would have made it possible for a deserted mountainous area to be indicated on painted panels. An altar or statue completes the set, although its use as a hiding place makes it improbable that it would have been positioned in front of the doors. Probably a statue of Apollo was located in front of or between two of the columns not containing a painted panel. Accepting the convention that columns and a door imply no more than the fact that here is a stage, all other references to setting fall into place. No *prothuron* would have been needed because this is a poor man's house, and the mere fact of the removal of the *prothuron* would be sufficient to indicate that it is not a palace.

CONCLUSION

No description exists of a setting for any production in the theatre of classical Greece. In the absence of any direct evidence, one can at best trade conjectures. Competent carpenters and stage crews could well have created a completely new setting for each play. This is, after all, what is done today at Epidaurus and Delphi or at the theatre on the Lycabettos, when classical plays are presented there. It has already been remarked that the fifth century saw a move toward a type of realism, with emphasis shifting away from Aeschylus' drama of the imagination.

Later, however, the Theatre of Dionysus was rebuilt in stone and thereby became permanent, although some variety of setting could still be achieved. No less solid are the surviving fourth-century theatres in other parts of Greece, and a large proportion of these theatres presented plays that were originally written for the Theatre of Dionysus in Athens. The latter can therefore be fairly taken as an archetype suitable for adaptation to meet local conditions elsewhere. This similarity of basic design demonstrates not only that the Theatre of Dionysus was the model, but that its conventions of setting were accepted as a universal standard.

In the fifth century the wooden *skene* was probably erected for each festival and taken down from year to year. The wooden *skene* may have varied and may have had features revised from time to time, but this basic facade may be assumed to have furnished the background for all plays written during the period, with set pieces added or removed for individual plays.

The staging of Aeschylus seems to require the emphasizing of certain specific features within a neutral area. But neither *Persians*, *Seven Against Thebes*, *Suppliants*, or indeed *Prometheus* would suffer from performance in front of a set similar to that required by the *Oresteia*, which may itself not have differed greatly from the semipermanent background created for the Periclean theatre.

Sophocles' plays present some important problems. *Antigone*, *Electra*, *Women of Trachis*, and *Oedipus Tyrannus* all have a palace or house as a background, but *Ajax* opens in front of Ajax's tent and later moves to the seashore. *Oedipus at Colonus* takes place in front of a sacred grove. The surviving portions of the satyr play *Ichneutai* indicate a cave setting similar to that of *Philoctetes*, a passage of which was quoted earlier.

Euripides sets most of his plays before some kind of building: a palace for *Alcestis*, *Medea*, *Madness of Heracles*, *Hippolytus*, *Orestes*, *Bacchae*, *Phoenician Women*, and *Helen*; a temple for *Children of Heracles*, *Iphigeneia in Tauris*, *Suppliants*, *Andromache*, and *Ion*. *Trojan Women*, *Hecuba*, *Iphigeneia in Aulis*, and *Rhesus* are set in front of a tent (the action of *Rhesus* occurs entirely at night) and *Electra*, before a farmhouse. Only *Cyclops* has a cave setting, although *Andromeda* (no longer extant) seems to have taken place on a seashore.

All Aristophanes' plays need a house or houses in the background —their occupants vary from scene to scene. *Wasps*, *Clouds*, *Lysistrata*, *Women in Assembly*, and *Wealth* can all be confined to a single street; *Acharnians* and *Knights* have a scene on the Pnyx; *Women at the Thesmophoria*, a scene at the Thesmophoreion. *Peace* requires a house on earth, a scene in Heaven, and a cave into which Peace has been thrown; *Birds* starts with no more than a doorway in a rock and is gradually transmuted into Cloudcuckooland, the city in the air. In *Frogs* a street in Athens gives way to the River Styx and Pluto's palace in Hades. In every case, the setting was probably implied by certain scenic features that were given specific identification by the characters within the play. These features could themselves be reinforced by sizeable properties such as pyres, tombs, couches, and altars. When carried logically through into the performances of the actors, staging techniques of this sort appear entirely appropriate in a theatre that relied for its dramatic effectiveness as much, I believe, upon the visual elements of its presentation as upon the spoken word.

NOTES

1. Aeschylus *Libation-Bearers*: lines 1-5, as supplied from Aristophanes *Frogs* 1126–28, 1172–73.

2. *Tumbos* and *taphos* are used interchangeably for "tomb."

3. Aeschylus *Libation-Bearers*: line 92.

4. Ibid., line 106.

5. Ibid., lines 152–55.

6. Ibid., line 168.

7. Ibid., line 200.

8. Ibid., line 488.

9. Ibid., line 501.

10. Ibid., line 540.

11. Ibid., lines 722–23.

12. P. D. Arnott, *Greek Scenic Conventions* (Oxford: Oxford University Press, 1962), p. 60.

13. Aeschylus *Libation-Bearers*: line 22.

14. Ibid., line 126.

15. Ibid., lines 560–71.

16. Ibid., lines 652–53.

17. Ibid., lines 712–13.

18. Ibid., lines 875–79.

19. The various possibilities and the arguments of former commentators are discussed by Oliver Taplin in his comprehensive *The Stagecraft of Aeschylus* (Oxford: Oxford University Press, Clarendon Press, 1977), pp. 343–44 and 349–51.

20. Aeschylus *Libation-Bearers*: lines 731–32.

21. Ibid., lines 877–79.

22. Few persons dispute that both plays are late, but more question whether the Sophocles version was produced before or after the Euripides version.

23. Sophocles *Electra*: lines 1–10.

24. Ibid., lines 108–9.

25. Ibid., line 328.

26. Ibid., lines 634–38.

27. Ibid., lines 660–61.

28. Ibid., lines 1322–30.

29. Ibid., lines 1374–75.

30. Ibid., line 1433.

31. Ibid., line 1458.

32. R. C. Jebb, *The Electra of Sophocles*, abridged ed. by G. A. Davies (Cambridge: At the University Press, 1905), p. 53.

33. Euripides *Electra*: line 78.

34. Ibid., line 96.

35. Ibid., line 168.

36. Ibid., lines 207–9.

37. Ibid., lines 216–17.

38. Ibid., lines 251–52.

39. Ibid., lines 303–11.

40. Ibid., lines 341–43.

41. Ibid., line 489.

42. Ibid., lines 1139–40.

43. Ibid., lines 491–92.

44. Ibid., lines 1233–34.

45. Ibid., lines 77–78.

46. See William Beare, *The Roman Stage*, 3rd ed. (New York: Methuen, 1964), app. C.

Chapter 6 Conventions of Performance

Until the middle of the fifth century B.C., when prizes for actors were probably first introduced, acting hardly merited the title of "profession." In Athens the playwright had originally appeared as his own protagonist, but with the introduction of second and third actors the functions of author-director and actor seem to have been separated. As the century progressed, the range of parts available to actors became more extensive. The commonplace and sometimes deeply subtle sentiments of Euripides superseded the grandiloquent dramatic poetry of Aeschylus and the actor's emotional scope was extended:

He's just a savage-creating, stubborn-mouthed fellow uncontrolled, unbridled, unfettered in speech, indefatigably bombastified.[1]

So says Euripides, as a character in Aristophanes' *Frogs*, mocking Aeschylus, his rival for the bardic chair in Hades. "And you say this to me," replies Aeschylus in a fury, "you gossip-monger, you beggar-maker, you rag-stitcher?"[2]

By the fourth century the actor had come into his own as a virtuoso performer whose presentation of a play from the classical repertoire drew audiences into the theatre. Fifth-century actors were dealing chiefly with new material, where the interpretation of the character by the playwright was uppermost in the minds of the audience. Comic fiction though it may be, the dispute between Aeschylus and Euripides in *Frogs* illustrates the difficulties faced by an actor who at successive festivals might have had to perform in a revival of the *Oresteia* and in Euripides' *Electra*. The Orestes of *Libation-Bearers* cannot be played in the same manner as the Orestes of either *Electra* play, even allowing for a masked actor playing in a similar set with the same basic physical relationship to the audience. The craft of the individual playwright is as much revealed in what he requires his actors to put over as his approach to the plot.

Critical commonplaces about the nature of Greek acting are based in the main on the entirely erroneous belief that the mask is inflexible and a positive handicap to an actor wishing to project any but a single dominant emotion. A proper understanding of the process of the physical acting that must accompany the mask is essential for any reasonable assessment of the nature of the original performances. True, voice was regarded as important, and in later centuries comparisons were made between the art of the actor and the art of the orator. Peter Arnott represented the majority view when he wrote:

> The actor's concern was chiefly with his voice, the most important part of his professional equipment. In such a theatre this was inevitable. When playing to an audience of fifteen thousand or more, the actor could hope to convey little by visual subtlety.[3]

I hope later to demonstrate that this is a misconception and to suggest that the visual aspect of an actor's performance would have been at least as important as the quality of his vocal delivery.

Whatever else people may or may not know about Greek tragedy in performance, they have nearly always been given to understand that all physical action took place offstage, that all comedy and tragedy was performed by a maximum of three actors who shared the parts among themselves, and that these actors performed wearing high boots, with padded costumes and in exaggerated masks. In all probability none of this is true for the fifth century B.C. Such apparent conventions are worth investigating in some detail in order to build up a true picture of the common external characteristics of Greek tragedy, as well as how the plays of Aeschylus, Sophocles, and Euripides may have differed from one another in stage presentation.

OFFSTAGE VIOLENCE

That violent action for the sake of it is undramatic is pinpointed by Horace writing in *On the Art of Poetry*:

The mind is less stimulated by what is taken in through the ear than what is brought before the trustworthy eyes—what the spectator can see for himself. But you should not bring onto the stage what should take place off-stage. You should keep out of sight many of the things to be narrated later. Medea should not murder her children in full view of the audience. . . .[4]

Horace's reason is that he personally would be "incredulous and repelled,"[5] and his refinement has been extended to embrace the Athenian audience as a whole in order to explain the apparent lack of action in Greek tragedy.

Roy Flickinger in his *The Greek Theater and Its Drama* was concerned with the performer himself. The latter, Flickinger declared, was in the position of a priest and thus for religious reasons would not have been allowed to appear to kill another actor even in imitation.[6] It has also regularly been suggested that scenes of violence required greater changes of facial expression than the mask could convey.

It cannot be denied, however, that far from all violence being enacted offstage, Greek tragedy does contain scenes of physical assault, suffering, and even death, to be presented in full view of the audience.

The plays of Aeschylus offer mainly threats of violent action. Apart from Prometheus being chained to his rock, later to be engulfed by an earthquake, Aeschylus lays less emphasis on stage action than on the relationship of actors and chorus.

In the plays of Sophocles the name character in *Ajax* commits suicide in full view of the audience, and this occurs in what may be Sophocles' earliest extant work. Heracles writhes in agony through 300 lines of *Women of Trachis*. Philoctetes is in pain almost throughout the play bearing his name, even fainting. At one point he engages in a physical struggle with Neoptolemus. In *Oedipus Tyrannus*, Oedipus has the old herdsman's arms twisted until he reveals the truth; in *Oedipus at Colonus*, Antigone is dragged off by Creon's soldiers and Creon himself tries to remove Oedipus by force.

In the plays of Euripides suffering and death are commonplaces of the onstage action. Alcestis in *Alcestis* is brought out into the open air to die. The old man Iolaus is thrown to the ground by Copreus in *Children of Heracles*. He is then dragged away from the altar where he has sought sanctuary, while endeavoring to protect the children, who are also seized. *Hippolytus* ends with Hippolytus' shattered body brought on stage for his death scene. In *Madness of Heracles* the hero is wheeled on mad and lashed to a pillar until he recovers his sanity. Orestes and Pylades are brought on in chains in *Iphigeneia in Tauris* and *Helen* ends with the king Theoclymenes being forcibly restrained by a servant as he tries to run indoors. Andromache is seized by soldiers at Menelaus' command in *Andromache*, the child torn from her grasp, and her wrists tied behind her back: "my hands running with blood from the bonds."[7] *Rhesus* has Odysseus captured by the Chorus. *Suppliants* stages Evadne flinging herself from the palace roof onto her husband's funeral pyre. *Orestes* opens with Orestes forcibly held down by his sister and works to a climax on the palace roof with Orestes' sword at the throat first of a Phrygian slave and then of Hermione, Pylades setting the palace on fire, while Menelaus tries desperately to break down the door.

All in all this is a fairly weighty catalog of violent action. The plays are not as static as is often implied. Characters are regularly embracing, restraining one another, beseeching by grabbing at knees and beard, suffering rejection, moving fast or slow according to prescription (or in the case of Iolaus, slowly when he thinks he is moving fast), collapsing to the ground, helping one another up, baring their breasts, and even taking off their shoes!

It cannot be denied either that much potential action does occur offstage and that some of the excuses used for getting characters offstage to be murdered are unimpressive. Almost every play contains at least one long descriptive speech by an eyewitness of action that has taken place elsewhere. Some plays have two Messenger speeches that may be of considerable length. In terms of dramatic writing, however, these features can be accounted for by reasons other than mere "taboos" on violence. Offstage action and the Messenger speech depend far more on theatrical reasoning than they do on religious decorum.

The amount of stage space generally available would surely be sufficient for fights and murders to be presented should the playwrights have wanted to present them. The problems encountered in trying to get a "dead" character off can be considerable, particularly if the body is dressed in fairly elaborate costume and wears a mask. "Dead" or "dying" characters are invariably carried or wheeled on so they need not be laid, physically, on the stage or on the ground.

Biers, shields, litters, and couches were all used for such a purpose as the texts indicate.

More significantly, offstage deaths in Greek tragedy tend to be spectacular. The defeat of the Persian fleet involves sea battle and shipwreck. Oedipus is mysteriously "translated." Pentheus takes refuge in a tree, until, spotted by his mother and his aunts, he is shaken out and torn limb from limb. It is in the nature of myth and tragedy to devise particularly bloody fates for their victims, and scarcely a scene described or commented on by a messenger is capable of physical staging.

As far as the structure of the plays is concerned, three points can be made. The first is conjectural and returns to the emergence and development of the first actor. Certain formal elements of tragedy (notably the *kommos*, or "lament") seem to be survivals from the infant drama of Athens. It is possible that the Messenger speech, which occurs with such regularity and in set form, is yet another throwback. If one accepts the connection between the bard and the actor, perhaps the relationships of messenger to chorus is the same in the fifth century as that between first actor and chorus was in the sixth century. The Messenger speech would then involve the development of a former physical response on the part of the chorus into an emotional response: not an extension of the story but rather a reaction to it. If this was so, the Messenger speech might well have been much more of a visual highlight in production than is usually assumed. This in turn would seem to explain why the device is used more frequently and more evocatively in the later plays.

The second justification for the restriction of violence is simply that the results of actions are usually of greater concern to the playwright than are those actions themselves. The realism of Euripides is a realism based not so much on what men do but on the effect of their actions upon themselves and others. One of the features that unites the Athenian tragedians is a common sense of dramatic tension, different to that of any later period, exemplified by the regularity with which a play is prolonged, when the physical action is complete.[8]

A third factor pleading for restraint of violence, is possibly the most important of all. In simple terms the theatre can make more out of what is implied than what is made explicit. What is physically repulsive does tend to alienate an audience, as Horace suggested, if given literal expression. The threat of force is more formidable than a manifestation of force. It is in the nature of fear that it lays hold of the imagination; it is in the nature of the imagination to conjure more dreadful mental images than the stage could ever present. The stage has usually acknowledged this by making its appeal more to reason or the emotions than to the senses, through the medium of image and suggestion.

One is justified in asking how this sense of "theatrical shorthand" can possibly be said to apply to classical Greek tragedies (those of Euripides in particular), when so much of nearly all the surviving texts is, to put it bluntly, lamentation of one form or another, and when no death is allowed to pass without an extreme elaboration of mourning. The answer lies in two factors. The first is the nature of performances that depended heavily on visual representation of primary emotions: in tragedy, this usually means the exhibition of grief. The second is the nature of "pity," that other Aristotelian emotion that, with "fear," requires "purification" (*katharsis*).[9] For the Greek, pity was reserved more for the person who had died than the person left to pick up the pieces. The sense of guilt felt by Creon in *Antigone* or Theseus in *Hippolytus* comes from a change of heart wrought by circumstance or by the intervention of a god, but the survivor lives on and sympathy was for the dead. That sympathy was enhanced, the more unpleasant the death. It was this aspect that was left to the imagination in a theatre whose staging practice was pragmatically antirealistic.

THE THREE-ACTOR RULE

One of the familiar arguments advanced to account for the rarity of deaths on stage in classical Greek drama is based on the supposed need to avoid immobilizing any actor who may be needed to reappear as a new character. The "rule" that no more than three actors were used in tragedy and comedy is generally accepted as absolute,[10] even though it is subject to occasional relaxation when the plays prove it to be inconvenient. It is backed by the authority of Aristotle. Aristotle refers in the *Poetics* to Sophocles' introduction of a third actor, after Aeschylus had first made use of a second, but does not mention a fourth actor.[11] The Soteric inscriptions from Delphi in the third century B.C. list Guild troupes of comic actors by threes, and Horace advises his protégé, "Let not a fourth actor speak."[12]

None of this is direct evidence for fifth-century practice, and the plays themselves offer a sounder guide. In the majority of tragedies and comedies parts can be cast among three speaking actors, although not invariably. If a fourth character is on stage he is either non-speaking or is given only a few lines, and there are scenes in which a character would logically be expected to speak, but in fact does not. At the end of *Orestes*, Pylades is asked by Menelaus whether he is in agreement with Orestes, but it is Orestes who replies, "He says so though silent. My speaking for him will suffice."[13] Certain exits seem contrived, and characters often fail to reappear later when they might reasonably be expected to do so. In other words, the plays seem to be written with only three actors in mind.

However, certain difficulties must be surmounted before asking why the three-actor rule should apply. First, some rather peculiar doubling is involved in the plays that might seem undesirable even allowing for a vocal delivery not consonant with characterization. *Oedipus Tyrannus* requires one actor to play Jocasta, the servant of Laius, and Teiresias. Even with three actors (some critics favor only two), *Alcestis* requires Alcestis to return after death as Heracles. In *Hippolytus*, Phaedra doubles as Theseus; in *Women of Trachis*, Deianira doubles as Heracles; and in *Bacchae*, Pentheus must return as his own mother, Agave, brandishing his own head. Apparently there was no fixed pattern of assigning roles to actors, although with casts of up to eleven speaking characters, the burden of the quick change would devolve mainly upon the least important actor. In several of the examples quoted above, complex and dissimilar parts fall to the second or third actor rather than to the first.

Even so, occasional scenes require odd lines to be spoken by a subsidiary performer of some kind, and a painstaking analysis of *Oedipus at Colonus* reveals that it would be extremely awkward to perform the play with only three actors. Although the play is episodic, with Oedipus an almost constant factor and Antigone present for most of the time, the rest of the characters could all be played by one actor, except for Theseus, who makes as many as five entrances. The only way out of the problem is to presume that Theseus was played by all three actors at one time or another, and that in one scene a substitute stood in for Ismene who is present, but does not speak. It is a solution unsatisfactory in many ways.

The usual apology for the three-actor rule against such infringements comes from the interpretation of the term *parachoregema* as "an extra actor" to play occasional lines not assigned to the "protagonist," "deuteragonist," and "tritagonist," the official first, second, and third actors. But the term *protagonist* is never used in the sense of "first actor" before Plutarch (writing in the first century A.D.). *Deuteragonist* and *tritagonist* appear occasionally in the works of Demosthenes (fourth century B.C.), but only with the slightly derogatory overtone of someone "playing second fiddle" or who is "third-rate."[14] The word *parachoregema* is a late usage meaning not "an extra actor" so much as "an extra expense," which on tour a fourth actor might well be. It is possible that it was through the emergence of this latter term that some of the confusion about the number of speaking actors originally arose.

ACTORS IN THE *ELECTRA* PLAYS

Libation-Bearers splits conveniently among three actors with the loads being spread as follows:

First actor:	Orestes	331 lines
Second Actor:	Electra	170 lines
	Clytemnestra	48 lines (although as the only running character in the trilogy, Clytemnestra might always have gone to the first actor)
Third Actor:	Servant	12 lines
	Nurse	39 lines
	Aegisthus	14 lines
	Pylades	3 lines (but on stage as much as Orestes, he might have been played by a fourth actor)

Sophocles' *Electra* offers no difficulty:

First actor:	Electra	600 lines
Second Actor:	Orestes	156 lines
	Chrysothemis	157 lines
	Clytemnestra	110 lines
Third Actor:	Tutor	148 lines
	Aegisthus	43 lines

It would greatly lessen the load on the second actor if a fourth actor were available so Orestes would not need to double, but the play could have been performed comfortably with three.

In the Euripides *Electra*, a fourth actor is required for Pylades, although he does not speak unless he is also the Messenger:

First Actor:	Electra	469 lines
Second Actor:	Orestes	217 lines
Third Actor:	Farmer	90 lines
	Old Man	90 lines
	Clytemnestra	74 lines
	Castor	86 lines
	?Messenger	91 lines
Fourth Actor:	Pylades	(nonspeaking)
	?Messenger	91 lines

Here the load for the third actor is abnormally high, even with four actors.

COMEDY

Applied to Old Comedy, the three-actor rule becomes ludicrous. Several of the plays of Aristophanes have twenty characters and in the opening lines of the first survivor, *Acharnians*, the third actor of three, would seem to be faced with the following directions:

Line 44: Enter as Amphitheus, first and second actor being occupied with Dicaiopolis and the Herald who remain on throughout the scene.

Line 55: Run off when the police are called.

Line 65: Enter as a Persian Ambassador, sumptuously dressed. (An "extra" character, Pseudartabas, who enters with him has two lines but they are gibberish.)

Line 110: The earliest the Ambassador can go off, more probably remain until 125.

Line 129: Return as Amphitheus at least to shout "Here I am" before retiring at line 132 to change to Theoros.

Line 134: Enter as Theoros and stay until at least line 166.

Line 175: Return as Amphitheus.

As this play involves eighteen speaking characters, distribution among three actors involves one as Diaeopolis and fifteen parts distributed between the remaining two, with two speaking "mutes"!

Every play of Aristophanes offers problems that can be solved only by the dual playing of one role or the widespread use of small-part players. Even with such contorted casting, *Lysistrata* and *Frogs* are not viable.

CONCLUSION

No good reason seems to exist for believing that the three-actor rule ever affected Old Comedy, although the majority of scenes show only a small number of speaking characters at any one time. Certainly, a number of extras and attendants are to be found in Old Comedy, but the same can be said of several tragedies. Exactly how actors were chosen for comedy is not known and no hints are given to the methods used for assigning parts. I can see no objection to the assumption that Old Comedy was played by a smallish acting group of no fixed number but extending to probably five or six persons on most occasions. To presume that Old Comedy employed only three actors would be to follow a precedent seemingly set by tragedy, but which is itself of questionable authenticity.

The case is stronger for an upper limit of three actors in tragedy: that Aeschylus introduced a second actor, as Aristotle tells us, and Sophocles a third, there is little reason to doubt. But why should the process have stopped there?

One sound reason might have been financial. It seems likely that from the middle of the fifth century, when prizes for actors were introduced, the state would undertake to pay for three actors.[15] Festival performances were still occasional. Presumably professional actors, although not excluded from citizen duties, commanded a high fee or even a state income. Beyond this, production costs were paid by a private individual, the *choregos*. The members of the chorus and the extras were amateurs. To employ a fourth actor would mean considerable extra expense that, if not grudged by the *choregos*, would certainly be unwelcome to him unless essential. To entrust any untrained actor with a sizeable part would be to risk exposing a lack of expertise.

By the fourth century the rise in status of the acting profession had led to troupes of actors touring Greece, Sicily, Asia Minor, and even North Africa, performing at various festivals. These troupes seem to have consisted of only three actors. If Lycurgus, at the end of the fourth century, found it necessary to pass a law that forbade tampering with texts, many of the extant plays may well include fourth-century revisions made to accommodate the practice of using only the three actors of the traveling troupe. This might explain the occasional contrived exits and the possible substitutions of nonspeaking actors for characters who remain silent in certain scenes—sequences composed not by the original playwrights at all, but by later producers with only three actors available.

Even if this argument is accepted, it fails to cover the remark of Horace, "Let not a fourth actor speak," but this surely refers to the three-hander scene. To write a triangular scene and examine its possibilities taxed the ingenuity of all three playwrights and such scenes are frequently duologues with occasional interpolations by the third actor. The four-hander scene, apart from being more difficult to handle, tends also to diminish the effect of conflict, and conflict reduced to its basic terms is the mainspring of tragedy.

Beyond all this the effect of performance in a large theatre must be considered. It was the size that dictated almost all dramatic development in the fifth century. With two onstage actors viewed at a range of up to a hundred yards, one can with comparative ease tell which of the two is speaking. When three actors are seen together at such a distance, the speaker becomes less clear. All the playwrights tend to meet this difficulty by balancing speeches in *stichomuthia*, almost always involving only two characters, or by long rhetorical speeches. For any audience to appreciate a four-hander scene (however carefully composed) when delivered at such a range in the open air and through masks is to require an exaggeration of reaction on the actor's part far more appropriate to comedy.

It may well have been the physical conditions of staging that limited the number of characters who appeared simultaneously. With more than three actors present, it would inevitably be difficult to tell who was speaking. That doubling of parts was regular and wholly acceptable to audience and actors alike cannot be doubted, and that some plays suffered from a limitation of the number of professional actors available to them seems likely. But the suggestion that the composition of entire plays was related solely to the number of available performers is a myth. I doubt if there was any absolute rule, and although few tragedies are likely to have been played by more than three professionals, I can find no adequate reason for assuming that the company working for a *choregos* in the latter part of the fifth century was invariably restricted to three actors. That this usually happened, with scenes seldom involving the presence of more than three principals together, is a feature of the play in performance, not the result of some vague aesthetic law.

ATTENDANTS

Many of the plays feature attendants, soldiers, and other supernumeraries (including children), in addition to the principal actors and chorus. In *Libation-Bearers*, Clytemnestra, offering hospitality, refers to Orestes' attendants, although up to this point in the text no allusion has been made to them. In Sophocles' *Electra*, Chrysothemis may have an attendant with her at her first entrance, and Clytemnestra instructs another to carry her fruit offering. These scenes can be matched in almost all of the plays, although Aeschylus seems to have been especially prodigal in the number of extras he employed.

Occasionally, attendants become briefly involved in the action, but for the most part they have little to do. But to what sort of convention did they belong? Did they wear masks, and did they react to the stage business?

If Orestes and Pylades in *Libation-Bearers* have attendants at the point when they approach the palace, it is not unreasonable to assume that they were thus accompanied at the beginning of the play. If so, what happened when Orestes and Pylades concealed themselves? Even if the action of "hiding" itself were purely symbolic, it would look equally odd for two attendants either to follow suit or to remain unaffected, unless some overall principle governed the action.

My own suggestion is that in performance, nonspeaking actors effectively did not exist until they were addressed. They simply did what they were required to do and were then conveniently ignored. Furthermore, I suggest that such nonspeaking actors were to all intents and purposes invisible, *since they did not wear masks*. Thus they were able to function as stagehands, supplying properties, moving furniture, or perhaps pushing the *ekkuklema* on and off as necessary. In such circumstances, they would not have needed to hide with Orestes and Pylades or to assume disguises with Orestes and Pylades. Quite simply they would be accepted as outside the action unless called upon to fit themselves into it.

A sequence in Euripides' *Electra* lends weight to this theory as applied to the latter part of the century. After the death of Aegisthus, a Messenger arrives, out of breath. At the end of his speech Orestes appears with the body of Aegisthus, presumably on a stretcher. Electra's first words to the Messenger, "Who are you? How do you show me these things are true?" meet with the reply, "Do you not know me, seeing your brother's attendant?" Electra answers, "My friend, through fear I had no recognition of your face."[16] The word for face used here is *prosopon*, also Greek for the "actor's mask." I would suggest that the Messenger, if not Pylades, was assumed to be one of the attendants now wearing a mask for the first time in the play. It would not need to be the same man who had in fact played the attendant, but it does provide a typically Euripidean moment combining Electra's confusion of mind with acknowledgment of a stage convention.

In such circumstances the fact that Electra herself has an attendant to take the water ("Take this jar from my hand")[17] involves no difficulty, even though she has been complaining about having to fetch the water herself and, although Orestes has seen only the one person, Electra herself, whom he has mistaken for a slave girl. He sees only one actor, because the other is in truth no more than a stagehand whose presence is purely functional. The likelihood of an attendant being present at this juncture is strengthened by Orestes expecting to overhear something:

Let us settle down and find out from this slave woman if we shall receive some word on the matter for which we have come to this land, Pylades.[18]

Is it reasonable for someone to expect a slave to mutter important information to herself as she walks along? In real life, the answer must be no, but in drama of this sort, Orestes' remark would not be inappropriate even if Electra were not overheard.

In the comedies of Plautus a character may overhear all, part, or nothing of a speech delivered to the audience in his presence. He may hear a snatch, wishing he could hear more, or even inform the audience that he wishes to sneak up closer to hear better. A soliloquy is just as audible to other characters as the playwright wishes and no more. Although such devices are more appropriate to comedy, Electra will cause no surprise by speaking out loud, even when alone.

Indeed, Euripides, by having an "invisible" attendant present as an apparent audience for Electra's complaints, seems to be working a convention both ways.

As the attendant is meant to be female, and probably not wearing a mask, it would have appeared distinctly odd for her to have been played by a man. There is no doubt actors and choruses were all male, but in comedy there are numbers of flute girls, dancing girls, and other female characters (such as Basileia in *Birds* and the Muse of Euripides in *Frogs*) who could have been played by women. These female characters in Aristophanes are treated in a different manner from that of the "drag" characters such as Lysistrata or the Women of *Women at the Thesmophoria*, far more as sexual objects. Citizen women would not have been involved, of course, but there is no reason why noncitizen women should have been prohibited from acting in festival plays as they did in mimes. If women could be so used for name parts in comedy, nothing is likely to have prevented their appearing as attendants in tragedy.

Euripides regularly introduced child characters of both sexes into his plays. *Alcestis*, *Medea*, *Children of Heracles*, *Hecuba*, *Andromache*, *Trojan Women*, and *Suppliants* all involve one or more children, several of whom speak, singly or in chorus, although always in a lyrical rhythm, which suggests recitative. In *Suppliants* this amounts to twenty-five lines. A. M. Dale believed that the lament of the child Eumelus mourning the death of his mother, Alcestis, was sung by the dead Alcestis herself;[19] others believed that children's lines were regularly sung from offstage. But surely such strange contortions were unnecessary. Children appear also in Sophocles and Aristophanes, but the prominence of children in Euripides' most bitter plays gives a clear indication that, as with law-court defenses of the following century, the introduction of children was regarded as a valid and effective way of twisting the knife in the emotional wound. As every single child in tragedy is either about to die, or to lose one of his or her parents, the stage device needs no further justification. The fact that the voice of a child might not carry is of minor importance. The quality of the voice would have. The only point at issue is whether children would have worn masks. Although no evidence can be found for the use of "mini masks," the children feature prominently in every scene in which they appear. In these circumstances I feel they would have looked even more strange without them than with them.

COSTUME

A number of vase paintings from the fifth and fourth centuries depict actors, but they require careful scrutiny before any generalizations can be made about stage costume. Several of the conventions of vase painting make literal interpretation of dramatic scenes risky. The mask, for instance, when it is not being carried in the hand, is often allowed to mold itself into the features of the face. The hang of garments is frequently emphasized by an outline of the naked body underneath, and several figures, particularly those of gods, appear nude when every other consideration makes it unlikely that they would have appeared so on stage.

Everyday wear in fifth-century Athens was simple and did not change much in several centuries. A rectangular piece of cloth, the *chiton*, wrapped round the body and pinned on each shoulder, is the chief basic article. Men wore the *chiton* to the knee, women to the ankle. Variations were possible. The material might be doubled at the top or belted at the waist, and various methods of pinning at the shoulders allowed freedom to the arms. In its simplest form the *chiton* amounted to no more than what James Laver described as "a kind of sack with openings for the head and arms."[20] The Doric and Ionic *chiton* varied, the latter being generally fuller, sometimes with sleeves and greater decoration.

The *himation* was a cloak that was wrapped round the body for warmth. Usually it was slung over one shoulder, fitted round the body from the back, and returned over the same shoulder. Pleated, tasseled, and variously decorated, the *himation*, too, was worn in a variety of styles by men and women.

The *chlamus* was a short cloak, pinned at one shoulder and worn exclusively by men and boys. It left the limbs free.

The *peplos* was an outer garment worn by women, again pinned at the shoulder. The final procession at the Panathenaic festival involved the escorting to the temple of Athene on the Acropolis of a massive *peplos*, woven and embroidered throughout the previous twelve months by the young girls of Athens.

The range of colors was probably wide. We know that statuary was vividly painted, as were some buildings, and in the theatre individual colors were perhaps used for identification of character and status. Greek writers seem to have been curiously restricted in the terms available for identifying colors. Obviously the range of color from modern dye processes was not available and most of the subtler tonal variations unknown. It has even been argued that the human eye might not at the time have been developed enough for major differences of shading even to be appreciated. Clothes for special occasions were to some extent defined by color but in private life decoration was dictated by cost and personal taste.

Sandals and slippers, or a soft boot, were worn on the feet. The head could be covered with a cap, but both sexes dressed their hair carefully and customarily left the head uncovered.

Lack of modesty in the wearing of clothes was frowned upon, but nudity itself meant little, and exercise was usually taken naked.

But what of costume in the theatre? Are we to assume that it bore some relation to everyday dress or did it have its own rules? In other areas, the theatre was nonrealistic. A late account tells of the priests at Eleusis copying Aeschylus' designs for their ceremonial robes. Might not all costumes have had a special kind of significance, being in themselves emblematic and traditional?

It has already been suggested that the theatre of the fifth century relied on strong visual presentation even though it did not attempt elaborate scenic effects. The relationship between chorus and actor and the distance from the audience suggest that kind of physical acting where the outline of the human figure needs to be established with clear definition. Bright colors and deliberate contrast between actors and setting seem probable. At this point many critics come to a full stop, leaving the actor with costumes so heavy and splendid that he could hardly move. If this notion of costuming is allied to the idea that the mask is incapable of being expressive, the actor must indeed have been immobilized, able to communicate only with his voice. But the amount of movement and the range of emotion implied in the texts suggest, at least in later plays, a far greater freedom for the actor, both in gesture and in movement, than would have been possible in constricting garments.

In *Illustrations of Greek Drama*, A. D. Trendall and T. B. L. Webster refer to no fewer than 498 visual representations, mainly on vases, associated with plays of the classical period. Of these illustrations, 175 are of fifth-century origin. The book presents examples relating to 40 plays of Aeschylus, 37 of Sophocles, and 48 of Euripides. Much of this evidence is, however, of dubious value in a study of the theatre: at worst the "scenes" are no more than an illustration of some story from mythology that the playwrights also used, at best a composite view of some particular aspect of a play, a "montage" rather than a "photographic" reproduction of performance. The number of illustrations from which any reliable information on costume can be gleaned is small. Nevertheless it is helpful.

The *Pronomos* vase (see figure 8), named after the musician, comes from late in the fifth century. Its illustration relates to a satyr play. The vase was perhaps painted to celebrate a victory. There are several points of note:

1. The view is generalized rather than related to a specific scene.
2. Ten chorus members, dressed only in loincloths with the *phallos*, are carrying or wearing identical masks. An eleventh has a similar mask but a more elaborate costume.
3. The chorus of twelve is completed by the leader Silenus, or Papposilenus, wearing an overall furry costume and an old man's mask.
4. Several individual characters are identified by name. Dionysus and Ariadne sit on a couch. The figure beside Silenus with a club and a leonine mask is Heracles. The god and demigod are recognizable from their emblems, *thursos*, club, and lionskin.
5. Two more masked figures, a man standing beside Dionysus and a second seated woman, are identified by name as Laomedon and Hesione.
6. The remaining figures appear to be playwright and musicians, Demetrios with the scroll, Pronomos the flute player, and Chorinos with the lyre.

As they all, including some members of the chorus, wear wreaths in their hair, and as a tripod is also featured, the scene is presumably in honor of the victory in a dramatic competition of one Demetrios, for which he had perhaps written only the satyr play for a tragedian's group of plays.

The *Andromeda* vase (see figure 9), of roughly the same date as the *Pronomos* vase, also takes its name from the central figure.[21] As with the *Pronomos*, the scene seems to be a composite view.

1. The central figure, Andromeda, wears a highly decorative sleeved garment reaching to her feet. A cloak hangs from her shoulders.[22]
2. Although no mask can be detected, Andromeda's headdress closely resembles that of the actor playing Hesione in the *Pronomos* vase, who holds his mask in his hand.

3. Perseus (who rescued Andromeda from the rock to which she had been tied and killed the sea monster to whom she was to be sacrificed) appears naked except for cap, high laceup boots, and cloak. He is identified by the sickle with which he decapitated the Gorgon Medusa. Hermes is similarly naked but barefoot. He carries his *caduceus*, a wand of office. The standing female figure is Aphrodite, who carries a staff.

4. The seated figure at Andromeda's feet depicts her father, Cepheus, and above Andromeda stands an oriental, probably a member of the chorus.

Figure 8.   a. b., and c. The Pronomos Vase (Naples, Museo Nazionale)

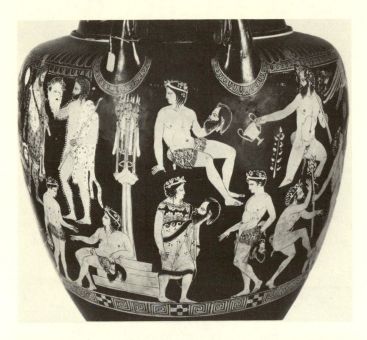

Figure 9.   The Andromeda Vase (Berlin, Staatliche Museen)

The indications are that a fairly loose form of costume, which could be highly decorative, was used on the stage of the latter part of the fifth century, allowing great physical freedom for the male characters in particular. No doubt the conventions affecting costume changed between the time of Aeschylus and that of Euripides. Such a change would be in keeping with the continuing development of both plays and conditions of performance. In 438 B.C., Euripides' group of four plays, of which *Alcestis* survives, included *Telephus*. The story of the wounded king of Mysia who could be cured only by Achilles, the man who had wounded him, had already been used by Aeschylus and probably by Sophocles. It seems that before revealing himself to the Greeks, Euripides' Telephus disguised himself as a beggar. Aristophanes repeatedly makes fun of Euripides for this practice of dressing his kings in rags. In Aristophanes' *Acharnians*, for instance, Dicaiopolis, with a cause to plead, goes to Euripides to borrow his tragic paraphernalia to make himself seem more pathetic:

I want some rags from your old play. I've got to make a long speech to the Chorus, and its death if I speak badly.[23]

Euripides questions Dicaeopolis further about which particular set of rags he requires before telling a servant to go and fetch the rags of Telephus, which he will find between those of Thyestes and Ino.

In *Frogs* one of Aeschylus' most pressing criticisms involves the same point. As far as Aeschylus is concerned:

If characters are demi-gods then that is the way they should talk, and dress if it comes to that. I showed how it should be done but you've degraded it.[24]

T. B. L. Webster regarded these references as ". . . a brilliant comic device for attacking the realism of Euripidean tragedy to show the poet among the rags in which he imagined *but did not in fact* [italics mine] dress his characters."[25]

This curiously backhanded piece of thinking is the least probable explanation of the point. A more reasonable explanation would be that until 438 B.C. costume had been associated with the status of the character wearing it. If a character in Aeschylus was a king disguised as a beggar, he was presented to the audience as a king carrying emblems of beggary, perhaps a staff and a begging bowl. But this did not meet the requirement of Euripides' realism: for Euripides Telephus had to look like a beggar. The point is obviously of real significance in comparing the *Electra* plays.

As far as Aeschylus is concerned, costume was, it would seem, more obviously "of the stage," appropriate to rank and more in keeping with what priests would wear at a ceremony than what ordinary people would wear in everyday life. If the satyr play is to be seen primarily as parody of what had already taken place in the tragedies, the same conventions probably applied here also.

It has already been noted that on vase paintings individual figures often appear naked in scenes inspired by tragedy. The tendency is even more pronounced in Old Comedy, but it is difficult to believe that any actor would risk appearing in the nude in the chills of January or even in March. What is more likely is that actors in the satyr play and comedy wore close-fitting, flesh-colored leotards. This may well have been the basic costume for the nude Perseus and Hermes too. Modesty has nothing to do with the matter, comedy and the elements have. To the leotard it would be possible to attach whatever male or female attributes the part happened to require. One must never forget that the essence of Aristophanic comedy is that it was written to be performed by men. The sexual organs of both sexes were clearly visible and from the treatment they receive one must hope that they were not real. It is still difficult to accept that *all* male characters in Aristophanes sported a *phallos*. Vases illustrating the *phlyax* plays of Sicily or later Greek comedy do show comic characters with grossly distorted features. Backsides protrude, bellies sag, *phalloi* stick up in the air, dangle on the ground, and even turn corners. The combination of realistic portrait masks and often sophisticated dialogue suggests to me that Aristophanes at least relied only minimally on the physical grotesqueries that obviously had wide appeal among his contemporaries.

THE KOTHORNOS AND THE MASK

In none of the illustrations of Greek tragedy surviving from the fifth century is there any indication that actors wore either boots with platform soles, or masks with the exaggerated forehead, or *onkos*. (See figure 10.) Yet almost all general histories of the theatre assert that the high-soled boot and the *onkos*, both part of the equipment of the Roman tragedian, were part of a legacy handed down from fifth-century Athens. The confusion arises partly from a mistaken use of terms and partly from the assumptions of classical authors writing much later. Horace associates the word *cothurnus* (Greek *kothornos*) with Aeschylus and one of the *Lives* gives him credit for increasing the size of its sole. Lucian writing in the second century A.D. dismisses tragedy in the following words:

We have to form our opinion of tragedy from its externals. How frightful and frightening a spectacle is a man of disproportionate size, lifted up on high boots (*embatais*), a mask extended above his head with a mouth gaping as though to swallow the audience: never mind padding for chest and stomach so that his own figure will not betray the height. And inside is a man moving to and fro, singing iambics.[26]

But Lucian was referring to the Roman tragedy of his own period.

The Greek word *kothornos* is used by Herodotus twice in the fifth century, several times by Aristophanes. In Herodotus' *Histories*, Croesus advises Cyrus to compel the Lydians to wear *kothornoi* so they will become unwarlike.[27] Also in Herodotus,[28] Alcmaeon, having been offered the reward of as much gold as he can carry, puts on *kothornoi* and fills them up with gold dust. Clearly *kothornoi* are boots that come up to the knee, but are soft and loose. Even more important, *kothornoi* are normally worn by women. In his advice to Cyrus, Croesus is not trying to turn the Lydians into actors.

The same conclusion is reached by examination of the passages in Aristophanes. The Chorus of women in *Lysistrata* are wearing *kothornoi*. Blepyrus in *Women in Assembly* complains that he will have to put on his wife's *kothornoi* because he cannot find his own shoes. The clearest evidence comes from *Frogs* where jokes are twice made at the expense of Dionysus for wearing *kothornoi* while attired as Heracles:

Heracles: I really can't stop laughing.
Dionysus: Please come back. I've something to ask you.
Heracles: I just can't help it. Fancy wearing a lionskin over that robe. And that club and those *kothornoi*.[29]

A little later a woman who accepts him as Heracles says:

I suppose you thought I wouldn't recognise you with those *kothornoi* on.[30]

Dionysus, god of the theatre, is in fact being mocked for his effeminacy. The *cothurnus* may perhaps have come to symbolize tragedy when the boot was eventually built up, its purpose being to help the audience in the *orchestra* to see the actors on the high Hellenistic stage.

A high sole would make many scenes of action difficult. In *Oedipus at Colonus*, Antigone is dragged away by soldiers. Is she taller than they because of her *cothurni*, or would extras have worn them too?

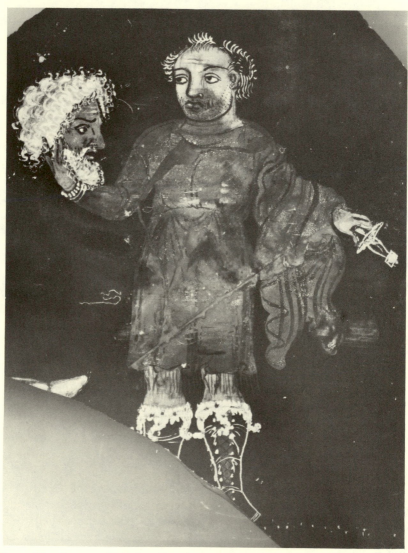

Figure 10. Actor and Mask, a Fourth-Century Vase (Würzburg, Martin V Wagner Museen)

What of the removal of Agamemnon's shoes before he treads the purple carpet in *Agamemnon*? Has he "symbolically diminished his stature"[31] as Peter Arnott suggested, or merely made his juxtaposition to Clytemnestra appear ludicrous? What of Evadne's leap to death in Euripides' *Suppliants*? To say the least, the stage action of the plays and the length of entrances and exits makes the wearing of the high-soled boot highly improbable.

That actors customarily wore a soft shoe reaching to the knee is clearly shown in vase illustrations (figure 8). The *cothurnus* came to be associated with the acting profession at a time when it was still everyday wear for women. Dionysus, as the god of the theatre, naturally wears *cothurni* in *Frogs* but in disguise as Heracles makes himself a figure of fun by not appearing barefoot.

In Lucian's time the actor was performing plays almost devoid of action, and he needed to increase his stature to compete with the scenic background. For similar reasons the Roman mask became exaggerated in feature. The famous statuette from Rieti (see figure 11) gives an excellent impression of a Roman actor, but one that is probably far removed from the fifth- or fourth-century Athenian actor. The "frightful spectacle" that Lucian complains of bears little resemblance to the relatively simple masks that can assume the contours of the face as a convention of vase painting (see figure 8). The masks first used by Thespis were thought to have been made of linen, but by the fifth century the whole head was covered and hair was attached. Carried on a cord, masks certainly appear to have been fairly substantial, made perhaps from cork or wood, but quite realistic.

Pollux includes in his extensive information on Greek tragedy a comprehensive list of types of mask in regular use. We have learned to be wary of Pollux as evidence for the fifth century, but one must assume masks of this sort were worn at some time.

For tragedy Pollux lists the following:

6 old men:	smooth-faced, white, grizzled, black-haired, flaxen and more flaxen
7 young men:	common, curled, more curled, graceful, horrid, pale and less pale
3 slaves:	leathern, peaked-beard, flat nose

10 women: hoary dishevelled, freed old woman, old domestic,
                               middle-aged, leathern, pale-dishevelled, pale
                               middle-aged, shaven virgin, second shaven virgin,
                               girl[32]

The list is irresistible and if in regular use would provide for an audience an immediate index of character (for example, Electra in Euripides' *Electra*: a married princess who would qualify, however, for "shaven virgin").

To this list Pollux adds specialist masks:

A horrid Actaeon, a blind Phineus, or Thamyris, one having a blue eye the other a black; a many-eyed Argus, or Tyro with mottled cheeks, as in Sophocles, which she suffered from the blows of a cruel stepmother; or Euippe, Chiron's daughter, changed into a horse in Euripides; or Achilles dishevelled when mourning for Patroclus; and Amymone, a river, mountain, Gorgon, Justice, Death, a fury, Madness, Guilt, Injury, Centaur, titan, giant, Indian, Triton; perhaps also a city, Priam, Persuasion, the Muses Hours, nymphs of Mithaeus, Pleiades, Deceit, Drunkenness, Idleness, Envy; which latter might likewise be comic masks. Satyric masks are an hoary satyr, bearded satyr, beardless satyr, Grandfather Silenus. The other masks are all alike unless where the names themselves show a peculiar distinction, as the Father Silenus has a more savage appearance. The comic masks, those especially of the Old Comedy, were as like as possible to true persons they represented, or made to appear more ridiculous.[33]

However unreliable Pollux may be, a number of conclusions can be drawn from his list. Masks seem to have been confined to standardized patterns, although for principal characters new masks were probably manufactured for each production. A character, moreover, could change mask in midperformance, so Oedipus and Polymestor, for instance, could both return "blind."

Tragic masks were used by the principals in the satyr play, which helps to reinforce the belief that the satyr play was primarily self-parody. In Old Comedy proper, living figures were represented by portrait masks, instantly recognizable as a Cleon, a Socrates, or a Euripides.

But the mask was not merely a substitute for the human face because the features of the latter could not be discerned at a distance. In any kind of theatre the mask is in reality one of the most powerful weapons at the actor's disposal, provided that he has been correctly

Figure 11. Roman Actor Perhaps in the Role of Clytemnestra (Paris, Musée du Petit Palais. Photograph J.E. Bulloz)

trained in its projection. The nature of performance by masked actors and masked chorus lies at the heart of any reconstruction of the original presentation of the plays. This performance can now be considered by direct reference to the range of emotion and activity that the playwrights expected their actors to convey.

NOTES

1. Aristophanes *Frogs*: lines 837–39.

2. Ibid., lines 841–42.

3. P. D. Arnott, *The Ancient Greek and Roman Theatre* (New York: Random House, 1971), p. 39.

4. Horace *On the Art of Poetry*: lines 180–85.

5. Ibid., line 188.

6. R. C. Flickinger, *The Greek Theater and Its Drama*, 4th ed. (Chicago: University of Chicago, 1936), p. 132.

7. Euripides *Andromache*: lines 501–2.

8. A notable exception is the Sophocles *Electra* in which the death of Aegisthus occurs almost after the end of the play.

9. Aristotle *Poetics*: 1449b.

10. K. Kelley Rees, *The So-called Rule of Three Actors in the Classical Drama* (Chicago, 1908).

11. Aristotle *Poetics*: 1449a.

12. Horace *On the Art of Poetry*: 192.

13. Euripides *Orestes*: line 1592.

14. Of Aeschines, Demosthenes' political rival and a former actor. *Demosthenes* : 344.8 and *De Corona*: 209.5, and so on.

15. See chapter 3.

16. Euripides *Electra*: lines 765–68.

17. Ibid., lines 140–41.

18. Ibid., lines 108–11.

19. Euripides *Alcestis*: lines 393–403, 406–15.

20. James Laver, *Costume in Antiquity* (London: Thames and Hudson, 1964), p. 8.

21. The play represented is almost certainly Euripides' *Andromeda*, although this has not survived.

22. This costume is much more in the Athenian tradition than that depicted on a vase of about 450 B.C. (identified by Trendall and Webster as Sophocles' *Andromeda*), where the look is decidedly oriental.

23. Aristophanes *Acharnians*: lines 415–16.

24. Aristophanes *Frogs*: lines 1060–62.

25. T. B. L. Webster, *Greek Theatre Production*, 2nd ed. (London: Methuen, 1970), p. 39.

26. Lucian *The Dance*: 27.

27. Herodotus *Histories*: I 155.

28. Ibid., VI 125.

29. Aristophanes *Frogs*: lines 43–47.

30. Ibid., line 557.

31. Arnott, *The Ancient Greek*, p. 52.

32. Pollux *Onomasticon*: IV 133–40. A full translation is included in A. M. Nagler, *A Sourcebook in Theatrical History* (New York: Dover, 1959), pp. 10–15.

33. Ibid., IV 141–42 (also in Nagler).

Chapter 7 Masked Acting and the Electras

In Sophocles' *Electra*, Orestes, after revealing himself to his sister, warns her:

So that our mother may not find you out, let us not enter the house with a joyful face. But, grieve at this invented disaster. As soon as we have succeeded then we may laugh.[1]

Electra replies:

Do not be afraid that she will ever see my face lit up with laughter.[2]

Dramatically and psychologically, Orestes' warning is timely to a sister whose extravagant manifestation of emotion might well threaten his well-laid plans. Critics over the years have chosen to see the exchange in a different light, however—an apology for Electra's grief-stricken mask, a mask that could register no emotion other than grief. Sufficient refutation can be found in the context. The lines occur at the conclusion of a scene in which Electra has been demonstrating her happiness for seventy lines.

More important is the basic misunderstanding such an attitude reveals of the way in which the mask is used by an actor. Regrettably Greek drama has often suffered at the hands of commentators whose experience has never extended to theatrical performance.

Fixed facial features are no more a limitation on the actor than they are on the puppet. The animation of the rod puppet covers all the basic emotions, and subtle refinements within them. Even the two-dimensional shadow puppet can demonstrate contrasts, all created by the juxtaposition of limb and stance. The glove puppet, more familiar in Western tradition, is still far from restricted by the expression on his face, and the marionette, worked in the Chinese marionette theatre by as many as forty strings, comes uncannily alive. Peter Arnott's own marionette versions of much of the classical repertoire, tragic and comic, have helped to convince audiences of the basic principles of masked acting as applied to Greek drama.

The Athenian playwrights at no time needed to apologize for the mask. Not that Greek actors were animated puppets, but more like the über-marionettes demanded by Gordon Craig: formal and precise but vibrantly alive.

The techniques of playing tragedy and comedy in a mask are subtly different, being related to the actor's relationship with his audience. Aristophanic comedy makes use of in-jokes, exhortations to stage-hands, and asides to individual members of the audience. The effect of direct address to those who are outside the play is to enhance comic values by frontal playing, encouraging a kind of mobile spontaneity alien to tragedy. Both kinds of acting, and that of the satyr play which used the techniques of comedy to burlesque tragedy, prescribe physical acting. All three tragic playwrights write with a physical performance in mind and none is fettered by it. Illusion was an alien concept in Greek theatre, and in Euripides, no less than in Aeschylus, the mask was the actor's first means of communication.

The amount of stage action involving more than one actor suggests a development from the drama of Aeschylus (where physical response fell mainly on the chorus) to the comparative busyness of the later plays of Euripides. The Orestes or Clytemnestra of Sophocles and Euripides is required to portray a greater range of feeling and more sudden shifts of thought than that of his Aeschylean counterpart. As the century progressed, all this may have resulted in some variations in the type of mask and in a corresponding adjustment of the way in which the mask was displayed. But this fact does not alter the basic nature of physical acting. If properly demonstrated the mask need never be impassive. Physical acting of the kind appropriate to a huge open-air theatre makes as much use of stance, the hang of the costume, relative positions of head, shoulder, and neck, as it does of the expression on the face of the mask itself.

The statuette from Rieti (see figure 11), although showing a Roman actor in Roman stage costume, is an excellent example of the way in which the essence of an emotion is conveyed through every part of the body. The cupped hand is as important as the way in which the neck withdraws the mask, and the balance of the stance and raising of the right shoulder complete the picture of dread. Fourth-century comic statuettes (see figure 12) confirm the impression that a masked actor is not restricted by his mask, and that in classical times he was always able to portray a range of emotions by creating a complete body picture. This even suggests that all movement of actors might have been stylized into a form of mimetic dance, relying for effect on the audience's familiarity with a whole range of expressive gesture, classifiable under the later Greek term of *cheironomia*.[3] If the meaning of a song could be danced by a group of dancers, it is not difficult to think in terms of the "plastic" acting-out of dialogue. A mask can appear to change its expression according to circumstances and even the play of light upon its contours can radically alter the emotion expressed. This fact may have led to the unsupported notion that some masks were made depicting joy on one side of the face and grief on the other, so the actor could offer to the audience whichever emotion was appropriate.

Many plays demand a considerable range of expression, and the display of quite intimate feelings. In *Alcestis*, Eumelus cries:

Hear me, hear me mother, I beseech you. It is I who call upon you, I your son pressing myself against your lips.[4]

Megara addresses her children in *Madness of Heracles*:

Which of you first, which latest shall I hold to my breast? Which of you shall I kiss? (*literally*, attach my mouth to)[5]

Andromache says to her son in *Trojan Women*:

Now, and never again after, embrace your mother, hold her; wind your arms round my waist and kiss me.[6]

Figure 12.   a., b. Greek Comic Actors, Fourth-Century Statuettes (New York, Metropolitan Museum of Art, Rogers Fund, 1913)

167

Figure 12. c., and d. Greek Comic Actors, Fourth-Century Statuettes

169

Physical acting, however, makes a kiss a simple gesture without actual contact, although the emotions so demonstrated can be quite as moving as literal display. The occasions on which masked actors are required to weep in Greek tragedy seem to have presented no difficulty. Set poses may well have been adopted: for instance in *Hecuba* the description of Hecuba with her head veiled suggests that the concealing of the face in the robe may have been a recognizable stock signal for the display of grief. The *Electras* offer numerous examples of action associated with the mask. The members of the Chorus in *Libation-Bearers* declare they are "tearing their cheeks with their nails."[7] In Sophocles' *Electra* the Chorus weeps for joy, while all three Electras weep from grief. Euripides' heroine also tears her cheeks with her nails and the Old Man wipes away his tears with his sleeve. Orestes in *Libation-Bearers* cuts off a lock of his hair, as an offering at his father's grave, and Sophocles' Electra offers a lock of hers to Chrysothemis for the same purpose.

In plays from the later part of the fifth century, which concentrate more specifically on human responses, more detailed actions affect the use of the mask. The way in which both Sophocles and Euripides deliberately direct attention to the mask suggests that what are so often regarded as the disadvantages of the mask for the actor are, in practice, quite the opposite. The mask remains in Euripidean tragedy and Menandrian comedy not as a kind of archaic survival, a sop to a religious tradition, but because it is a positive asset to both actors and audience in the only kind of acting style with which they are familiar. Why did the "unrealistic" mask remain, when tragedy itself had already become more realistic? Because, one presumes, the performance of tragedy or comedy by an unmasked actor would have seemed quite absurd and the unadorned face out of keeping with a physical acting style.

The mask was retained for other reasons too, but such reasons stem from the very sources of the mask tradition—some religious, some psychological, some practical, The tradition of the masked performer goes back far earlier than anything recognizable as "tragedy" or even as drama. The dancer in many African and American Indian tribes assumed a mask to induce the onlookers to accept him as the representative of higher powers or as a god. Over and above the compliance of the onlooker, the dancer may feel that he acquires some of the power of the mask itself, including protection from adverse gods or spirits. Hence the age-old use of the death mask to cover the features of a corpse. The mask was not originally used as a means of personification, but for the exaltation of the individual and to reveal the power of the god captured in its very essence. An analogous sense of mystery is the prime emotion of the animal mask, where individual or group wearing the mask assumes certain qualities of the beast itself, qualities also inherent in man, but suppressed under normal social conditions. In dance and in ritual these submerged qualities are allowed to surface, as everyday life is forgotten and the marvelous takes over.

In various Greek religions from earliest times, the mask was widely used, particularly in association with the worship of Dionysus. The more comic aspects of local festivals could combine the impersonation of particular individuals with the ridicule of officialdom. At first sight, the attribution of the dramatic mask by Horace to Aeschylus seems not unreasonable. But if Thespis' contribution to the history of the theatre was that he "invented" the first actor, by using direct speech to present one character at a time, the process of the actor's development was one of reduction from the narrative function of bard or chorus leader. At this point the mask would most likely have been introduced not only to subordinate the personality of the narrator to that of the character, but also so two or more characters might be imitated in quick succession. Dialogue between characters was, of course, impossible until Aeschylus' use of a second actor, and the chorus initially provided the character's immediate audience.

Thus the chorus, acquiring a personality to respond to the actor, would also have needed to assume masks. The personality of the chorus was essentially corporate, not individual: if individual, they would have become twelve or more actors. Chorus masks were made identical to demonstrate a group personality, despite the leadership of a single individual.

Paradoxically the importance of the actor was diminished by his emergence, or at least the emphasis on the playwright as author rather than performer grew stronger as the requirements of dramatic construction began to dominate. It is significant that not until eighty years after Thespis was the prize for tragic actors instituted at the

Great Dionysia: comic actors had to wait even longer. Not until the era of the great tragic playwrights had passed did the actor take over the public imagination.

Even during the last years of the fifth century, young actors were criticized for overelaborate use of gesture and lack of dignity. Oratorical style seems at this time to have become more fluid, but a comparison of *Libation-Bearers* and the *Electra*s shows how the manner of the composition of the later plays made a modification of acting style inevitable.

After Thespis the practical advantages of the mask are fairly obvious. Its features offered sufficient individuality to distinguish one character from another and to permit it to project at least one dominant emotion, without being restricted to it. The introduction of the female character is attributed to Phrynichus (writing about the turn of the sixth century) and with props and emblematic costume, a character would have required no introduction to be recognized.

It is not difficult to imagine Aeschylus testing the potentialities of the masked actor. His choruses too are allowed sensations of apprehension, exultation, fear, joy, anger, submission, or indeed a sort of nullity, according to the situation. A principal advantage of the mask is that although its function permits only one or a small number of dominant emotions, these emotions, or a reminder of them, are carried over into any situation. Far from being a hindrance to the presentation of emotion, the mask is essential to adequate performance of Aeschylus. Even in an indoor theatre, lack of the mask may damage the dramatic purpose of Sophocles and Euripides. It serves to focus the attention of the audience without distracting them with side issues.

VISUAL CONTRASTS

Conventions affecting the use of the mask are underlined by the way in which characters are portrayed. Here again the differences in method between the three playwrights are particularly noticeable. Aeschylus introduces an Old Nurse in *Libation-Bearers* at a moment when tension is mounting. The scene is almost bathetic. Both stage and real audience are aware that Orestes is not really dead; yet the Old Nurse is allowed to continue for over thirty lines with her reminiscences about Orestes' childhood. The Nurse suddenly brings the tragedy not down from but up to a level of common humanity, and this she does perhaps because she bears a closer resemblance to a comic rather than a tragic character. She follows a scene with Clytemnestra and emphasizes the love that the real mother has never displayed. Despite the mundane speech of the Nurse, there is no reason to believe that the delivery of her lines, and her physical attitudes, would have been out of keeping with those of the other characters. Her sentiments are, however, more immediately sympathetic. The stage picture is visually pointed by the contrast between the Nurse's long, slow, sad exit up the *parodos* and the arrival after a choral ode of the same actor as Aegisthus, bloodthirsty, eager, and excited. The reversal is completed with the awareness of both chorus and audience that Aegisthus' reasons for exultation are as ill-founded as were the Nurse's for despair.

Sophocles also concentrates on physical differences. The Tutor is described by Orestes as white-haired, perhaps in a mask resembling that of the fourth-century actor shown in figure 10; but his age and vigor are contrasted with Orestes' youth and near-casual attitude when reunited with his sister. Similarly, Electra and Chrysothemis are contrasted in character (and perhaps feature) but both are required to show reversals of emotion. Chrysothemis enters joyfully from the visit to her father's tomb, only to be thrown into despair by Electra who is lying on the ground prostrated by the news of Orestes' death. Sophocles employs the triangular scene to contrast reactions—Clytemnestra's reaction of relief, Electra's reaction of grief at the long, drawn-out description of the chariot race in which Orestes is meant to have died. Such reactions are far easier to portray in the poses of masked acting than in the shifting expressions of the human face, which is ill-suited to hold and focus a single all-pervading emotion.

In Euripides the "realism" of the language had been extended to the actors' dress but only within the existing conventions of costume. The style of the clothes and of the masks of the Farmer and of the Old Man were probably indicators of social class, although the decrepitude of the Old Man is strongly emphasized to contrast with the sturdiness of the Farmer whom he doubles. Orestes and Pylades wear traveling clothes and Orestes has his cloak fastened by a buckle, but "they look noble enough"[8] as the Old Man grudgingly admits.

Electra herself, however, is a real princess and in real rags. At first Orestes takes her for a slave girl, and her mask must have been appropriate, as she constantly reminds him:

See my dirty hair, and these rags of clothes.[9]
You see how withered my face [or frame] is.[10]
And my head and hair shaved with a razor.[11]
Tell Orestes first . . . what sort of clothes I am stabled in, and with how much filth I am weighed down.[12]

Her mother, herself resplendent, asks her:

Why are you so unwashed with your body so ill-clothed?[13]

Electra mentions at one point that she has to make her own clothes and is clearly not much good at the job! The picture painted of her is certainly that of a woman in mourning, but it hardly inclines one to anything but sympathy for Pylades condemned by the Dioscuri to marry her. Either Electra really did look as she describes herself, and this self-assessment is confirmed by what others say of her, or she is again exaggerating. Whichever was true of the first production of Euripides' *Electra*, the visual contrast between the heroine's status and her appearance is something that she as a character is at pains to stress.

At all times the three playwrights were writing for masked actors whose basic training made the mask as flexible and demonstrative for their theatre as does the unadorned face in today's theatre. The audience expected this mode of presentation just as they expected to see the action of the plays pass before a pillared facade. If the process of physical acting is properly understood, examination of the playwright's use of the theatre becomes simpler, and it becomes possible to make a significant comparison between the theatre of Aeschylus and that of the later fifth century.

CONCEALMENT AND DISGUISE

The amount of essential movement in *Libation-Bearers* is not great, but on many occasions the text reveals or at least indicates movement. When *Libation-Bearers* opens, Orestes and Pylades must be offstage, but their first lines indicate they have entered to a position where Orestes can address his father's grave in prayer. When they first see Electra and the Chorus, they hide and eavesdrop, hearing what she and the Chorus have to say. They then reveal themselves to her. Orestes and Pylades remain "hidden" for all of two hundred lines. What then is involved? The entrance from the *parodos* is long, but at the beginning of *Libation-Bearers* it presents no difficulty. To conceal themselves, the pair could hardly sprint thirty yards back the way they came, nor would they be likely to enter the palace by one of the doors. In either case they would be hard put to indicate they were capable of hearing what was being said by Electra and the Chorus. The set is unlikely to have provided any place where the newcomers would really be "hidden" from a chorus of twelve and Electra.

In terms of any formal stage presentation, of course, a token withdrawal would be sufficient, although this needs to be indicated by more than words alone. The proverbial ostrich makes use of a perfectly good theatrical convention when it hides by putting its head in the sand. A withdrawal by Orestes and Pylades to the *skene* could indicate concealment. So could the simple covering of the mask with a cloak or the turning away of the body. However, such specific gestures may carry other associations, for the display of grief and disbelief, whereas a full turn upstage accompanied by withdrawal of only a few paces could formally render Orestes and Pylades "invisible." Their revelation would then be a simple matter of reentry by a turn and a pace forward.

Such a solution may be acceptable for *Libation-Bearers*, but could the process of concealment be quite so formal in the similar scene in Euripides' *Electra*? Lines are taken literally by characters in Euripides and scenes like the recognition scene[14] show Euripides apparently mocking Aeschylus for suggesting that a brother and sister might have similar colored hair and the same size foot. That a formal acting convention might be modified in the direction of realism after forty-five years is entirely believable and seems to indicate that acting styles, although still appropriate to the wearing of the mask, had changed considerably by the century's end.

Because of Electra's appearance, Orestes believes he is in the presence of a slave girl. Since he cannot hide completely from the audience's view, must he not therefore visibly react to hearing the ragged figure's declaration that "I am Agamemnon's daughter"?[15] When Electra first sees the two men she indicates that they have been lurking close to the house and "are rising up from ambush."[16] This surely suggests a practical attempt at concealment (at least from Electra) perhaps beside one of the statues between the pillars flanking the doors. This would account for their being able to intercept her before she can get indoors.

A similar development in dramatic technique is suggested in a curious way when the two later dramatists avoid the issue of disguise. In *Libation-Bearers*, Orestes announces he will disguise himself:

Like a stranger, having all the equipment, I will come with Pylades here to the gates of the threshold, as stranger and spear-carrying stranger. And we will both use Parnassian accent imitating the speech of Phocis.[17]

Whether by "equipment" Orestes means actual disguise, with properties or costume, is not made clear, although any other form of disguise except traveling clothes would be pointless. If Orestes actually assumed an accent when talking to Clytemnestra, it is certainly not written into the text. Nor do the lines of Pylades suggest the Phocian accent that he, as a Phocian, would have anyway. What seems likely to have happened is that literal interpretation of detail would be avoided and, that, once referred to, the disguise would be taken to exist by virtue of having attendants appear with baggage. In the time of Aeschylus the setting was most probably created by description allied to some emblematic representation, so the need to consider the question of disguising Orestes and Pylades was indeed appropriate, although actually doing something about it was not. The disguise is nowhere referred to again, and although the moment of the character's return to normal speech would be dramatically strong and might perhaps be introduced into a modern production, the fact that Aeschylus thought it necessary must be regarded as very doubtful.

Sophocles and Euripides, aware perhaps that their theatre could no longer accommodate such an anomaly, write out the need for "disguise." In Sophocles' *Electra*, Orestes says that no one will recognize the Tutor after so much time now that his hair has turned white, and Euripides bases the whole of the recognition of a reluctant Orestes on the unforeseeable suspicions of the Old Man. Neither playwright permits his Orestes to meet Clytemnestra, whereas the confrontation in *Libation-Bearers* is the climax of the play.

All of the foregoing staging is conjectural, of course, but Aeschylus does seem to call for a style of performance more akin to an oriental than an occidental tradition. The later dramatists move toward subtlety of reference and an extension of emotional range reflected in a change of emphasis on the function of the chorus. Sophocles' closeness to the Homeric version of the Orestes story, restated to make sense in classical Athens, makes it understandable that the Aeschylus of Aristophanes' *Frogs* should accept Sophocles but reject Euripides. In terms of performance Sophocles and Euripides appear to make similar demands on their actors and audiences. But Euripides made his characters speak a new stage language, still verse, but sometimes colloquial and domestic, sometimes as controversial in sentiment as the dialectic of the contemporary sophist.

THE KOMMOS

The importance, throughout the fifth century, of the actor's vocal delivery is clearly evident. If this fact has been understressed so far, it is only so performance may first be visualized from the page. In a theatre like that at Epidaurus, acoustics are still superb, and clarity of diction was highly enough valued for an actor to be mocked in Aristophanes' *Frogs* for a minor mispronunciation that altered the sense of a phrase in a play of Euripides.

It is likely that considerable portions of the dialogue were performed to music. A chorus was accompanied by a musician,[18] who entered at the beginning of the play (or perhaps with them), and who took his place either in the center of the *orchestra* or at the side. He may have been sufficiently involved with the action to have played almost nonstop, not perhaps to accompany the lines with a tuneful backing, but as in Chinese Opera to supply an emotional pitch for the actor to play off and phrase against. The actual music is almost all lost and what little survives cannot be interpreted with any degree of certainty, but modern Greeks at least have some feeling for their musical heritage. Zouzou Nicoloudi, writing of his work with the Greek director Karolos Koun, mentioned in a 1965 program note:

We rediscovered the unlimited treasury of our folk traditions, the roots of which go far back and have their beginnings in primeval religious worship. We still find these unbelievably alive today in popular song and dance, in religious rituals, and especially in the very characteristic Greek rhythms, which are basically lop-sided—a lack of symmetry which perhaps gives Greek music its lively and primitive character. . . .

If indeed it was a characteristic of the music of classical tragedy, this lack of symmetry suggests that in the classical theatre, music was used primarily to highlight speech, particularly at moments of emotional stress when the rhythm of the lines tends to change from dialogue iambics to the more choral anapaests and dochmiacs. As a general rule, therefore, again as in Chinese Opera, dialogue and set speeches might be expected to have been delivered as speech, whereas formal laments and prayers were probably sung in a form of recitative. The suggestion is speculative in the extreme since clear evidence is nonexistent. A comparison of the *Electras* again suggests that practice may have changed as the century progressed.

Aeschylus' *Libation-Bearers* has only one passage, the *kommos*,[19] where main characters do not speak in iambics. This is a ritual lament surviving as a formal element in most tragedies and probably closely associated with primitive forms. Long and drawn out, it is of limited appeal to a modern audience as it stands, with its prayers and lamentation balanced between Orestes, Electra, and the Chorus. The strictness of the metrical pattern implies musical accompaniment and the lines of the Chorus are themselves graphic:

I beat an Arian lament in the manner of a Cissian mourner, and the hand could have been seen stretched out raining blows from above and below as my wretched head reverberates at the beating.[20]

The extravagance of the grief is real enough and the words of the Chorus seem to describe an externalizing of the lament of the principals. Perhaps Orestes and Electra knelt at the tomb—they refer to themselves as suppliants—while the Chorus danced the emotions they expressed.

But much more of *Libation-Bearers* seems to be suited to such a mode of performance than does either the *Electra* of Sophocles or that of Euripides. It has already been suggested that this externalizing of the sentiments in dance might have been the Chorus' main function before the time of Aeschylus and may even have affected *Persians* and *Seven Against Thebes*. The *kommos* of *Libation-Bearers* clearly had some accepted form of presentation that distinguished it from the rest of the play. Nor does this rule out the possibility of extensive choral involvement elsewhere during the dialogue scenes.

Sophocles has Electra entering with a lyrical lament that itself changes in rhythm when the Chorus joins in. The increasing parade of misery through seven sections, interspersed with choral response, suggests that this sort of treatment required no apology when first performed. Electra underscores the formality of the lamentation when she returns at its conclusion to iambics with the words:

I am ashamed, women, if I seem to you to bear it too hard in my lamentation.[21]

Almost the equivalent of "Now let's get back to the plot."

A similar change of rhythm occurs twice more. On the first occasion Electra and the Chorus share a passage that is split into the matching *strophe* and *antistrophe* of a full choral ode. The passage is the more remarkable for indicating twenty-eight changes of speaker in under fifty lines. Electra seems to break into lyrics simply because the extremity of her grief can be displayed in no other way, in precisely the same way that she reacts with joy after her reunion with her brother.

In Euripides' *Electra* (where so many of the sentiments have an almost naturalistic ring to them), Electra's first entrance is in the form of a *kommos* with the line "Stretch out the speed of your foot"[22] repeated in parallel sections, suggesting that her entrance from the *parodos* may have been a dance rather than a walk. But Euripides cannot resist the sharp contrast, and the joyful entrance of the Chorus was itself probably marked by a change in the quality of the music, leading up to the Chorus' eventual reproach to her:

Not by wailing, but reverencing the gods with prayers, will you obtain fair
weather.[23]

Throughout the somewhat abrupt prayers for success in their meeting with Aegisthus, the characters use iambics exclusively, but after the murder of Clytemnestra, Orestes and Electra both break into lyric iambic dimeters to express their horror at the murders that Electra herself has compelled upon them.

It seems, then, to be an acceptable usage that when action is suspended for the demonstration of profound emotion, the characters cease to use the iambic trimeter and move into more choric rhythms.

THE CHORUS

All manner of individual dances were known in classical Athens, several specifically connected with comedy and tragedy. But how and where they were used, it is virtually impossible to discover. No examination of the metres of the plays can suggest the original choreography, but it is reasonably safe to assume from the emphasis placed on the chorus trainer that new dances were elaborated for every production.

The fluidity of gesture and stance that an actor in a mask finds essential has already been described as a kind of dance. The language of gesture has also been mentioned and the theory put forward that choral movement was used at least during part of the action to give a visual extension to the spoken word. This theory directly contradicts the accepted view of the chorus as a strictly rigid unit. Oliver Taplin stated:

The choral dancing was normally in formation, either rectangular or circular in basis, and, while it might occasionally become quite wild and rapid . . . it was usually rather solemn and decorous. . . .[24]

Some evidence supports the arrival of the chorus in columns of three (*kata zuga*) or in lines of five (*kata stoichous*); but the varying entries in the extant plays make even this improbable. Some choruses arrive agitated, others apprehensive or stricken with grief, some in a hurry, some hesitantly. All of the literary evidence is of too late a date to relate to the original performances and applies rather to the time when the chorus was no longer rehearsed as an integral part of the whole production. A steady procession would be acceptable for the slave women of *Libation-Bearers*, and the local

women of Sophocles' *Electra*, but hardly for the joyful young girls
who enter running in the Euripides. Sophocles in *Oedipus at Colonus*
has the Chorus enter in some agitation:

Look about! Who is he? Where is he?
Where has he got to, this most shameless of men?
Look about, search him out, examine everywhere. . . .
I have looked round the whole of the grove without finding where he is.[25]

Surely such an entrance could not be in accordance with any formal
pattern, such as that parodied by Euripides in his *Orestes*:

Electra: Here come my friends again, companions in my dirges, but they will
    wake him up from his sleep, and fill my eye with tears to see my
    brother raving. Walk quietly, dear friends, and do not utter a sound.
Chorus: Hush, now, hush, gently place your slipper to the ground and
    do not utter a sound.
Electra: Get back, back from the bed.
Chorus: Right, I obey.
Electra: And your flute, my dear, do not play it so loud.
Chorus: There I make its note soft.
Electra: Yes, but bring it down softer, and tiptoe to me. . . .[26]

Even in Aeschylus the shock effect of the entrance of the Furies,
however staged, would have been impossible with orderly rows of
upright citizens "nosing out" their victim. They may not have
been so frightening as to cause a reduction of the chorus from fifty
to twelve (as Pollux suggests), but at least some of the Furies must
have entered from inside the main entrance and in a manner that a
later scholiast describes as "sporadically."

The choruses of Old Comedy had a multitude of identities and
were more concerned with acrobatics than were those of tragedy.
Other comic writers created choruses of Flies, Fish, and even Islands,
and in Aristophanes' surviving plays there are choruses of Clouds,
Wasps, Birds, and Frogs. A connection clearly exists between the
choruses of Old Comedy and the assumption of animal characteristics in older comic forms such as the satyr play. As their
prime purpose is more that of complicating the plot than of helping

individuals, the reactions of the comic chorus during normal dialogue scenes and in the choral odes seem to have centered upon specialized rude dances such as the *kordax* and a multitude of kickings, proddings, and slappings. The final "crab dance" of *Wasps* has members of the Chorus urging one another to spin like tops, fling their legs in the air, kick themselves in the stomach, and then ends with the disarming boast:

For nobody has ever done this before, danced out at the end of the comedy, leading the chorus behind him.[27]

Only once does the Chorus of *Libation-Bearers* affect the action directly, and this when the leader suggests to the Nurse that she should alter the message to Aegisthus, but it is so involved with individual scenes that it is difficult to conceive of as ever passive. Electra has to ask for advice and individuals share in the pouring of libations, thus giving the play its name. As a composite unit, it has half the lines of the *kommos*, yet can suddenly react realistically, as when Aegisthus' death cries are heard. Individual voices suddenly question the source of the sounds and suggest that they should all withdraw lest they seem to be accomplices. As successive odes sweep the Chorus into a fuller vision of past and future, and then drop it firmly back into the present, there is a constant mobility into and out of the plot of the play.

What at first sight appears to be an almost perversely irrational refusal by Aeschylus to single out the purpose and identity of any chorus is really his greatest achievement as a dramatist, permitting as it does great freedom to a chorus to stand both inside and outside the action. For this reason, if for no other, the Chorus' range of reaction must have been wide. When the leader talks of Clytemnestra's dream, might not the members have danced the dream? When the leader calls for an Ares "to wield the bent-backed Scythian bow and brandish the handled sword,"[28] might not one or more individuals have created these images as only a single voice describes them? Elsewhere she talks of the "arms of the sea teeming with monsters,"[29] "the sharp sword nearing the breast,"[30] and "the anvil of Justice planted firm,"[31] all of which cry out for physical presentation, not necessarily literal, but certainly identifiable.

From the arrival of Orestes and Pylades "in disguise," the Chorus becomes part of the conspiracy. Between the end of the ode previous to its arrival, and the beginning of the next, the Chorus has no lines. It obeys Orestes' injunctions to keep silent. But keeping silent, in stage terms, may well be an active rather than a passive state, involving a set pose with appropriate stance and gesture. Of this, no proof can be found other than Orestes' initial remarks to the Chorus, but if the Chorus has no reason to take part in the action, why require it to keep quiet? Why not ignore it on the simple assumption that it will do nothing? If the Chorus is occupied with demonstrating by voice or gesture a hostile attitude to Clytemnestra, Orestes' warning may well be appropriate and indeed necessary to avoid its complicity arousing Clytemnestra's suspicions. From this it follows that the Chorus might have displayed dislike towards Clytemnestra as soon as she appears, or it might have maintained a pose of deception when it effectively becomes a conspirator. By the play's end, might not the members of the Chorus have even become the Furies, which Orestes sees for the duration of his speeches, changing to sympathetic friends and comforters during their own remarks? I find it more and more easy to believe that the main purpose of the chorus, at least in *Libation-Bearers*, was to reflect the total action of the play by creating mood and extending the language into visual images. In terms of a complete theatrical performance, its contribution becomes a distraction from the main action only if it is not seen as itself a central part of that action.

In Sophocles and Euripides the contribution is a lot less, but it by no means disappears. The chorus of Sophocles can again react like a group of casual bystanders at one moment and immediately thereafter sing of the justice of God and expound on family morality. Yet it is its very freedom from a fixed persona that may have been its greatest asset. The triangular scene involving the description of the chariot race in Sophocles' *Electra* is something of a set-piece and uses the contrasting reactions of Electra and Clytemnestra as its dramatic springboard. But why should it continue for so long? Might not the Chorus have danced the whole description, not literally interpreting the race but extending the picture of excitement, challenge, and ultimate disaster? The whole speech is pure fiction, but in performance could have involved visual display above and beyond the rhetoric. Or might not the Chorus have reflected the contrast between the sisters, and between mother and sister, by dividing into semichoruses? Or perhaps it could have contrasted the nature of these family relationships by exploiting a neutral position as conciliator between Electra and Chrysothemis, while indicating quite clearly whom it favored in Electra's confrontation with Clytemnestra?

If in the Euripides version the Chorus again offers at first the line of sympathy that the audience might be expected to follow, only to turn against Electra in the final scenes of the play, this process could have been demonstrated without any ambivalence at all. By the time that Clytemnestra is sighted, Orestes is having second thoughts, and the reproof implicit in some of the earlier comments of the Chorus has no doubt become firm condemnation by the time that Castor and Pollux put in an appearance.

Sophocles is generally thought to have increased the number of the chorus from twelve to fifteen, and this number was probably maintained for tragedy, at least at the Great Dionysia. In a theatre the size of the Theatre of Dionysus, a chorus of twelve to fifteen is the right number to represent both composite and individual identity. Euripides may indeed have found it occasionally uncomfortable to have so many eavesdroppers on the private lives of his principals, but much of his reputation rested on the beauty of his lyrics, which so often have only the most tenuous links with his plot.

Certainly, the Chorus of Euripides' *Electra* is unlikely to have provided the intuitive and atmospheric inspiration of an Aeschylean chorus. In their own time Euripides' lyrics may have been as well known as the hit songs of a modern musical, being repeated in private solo performances. But the Chorus was masked and contributed directly to the mood and rhythm of the action of the play, so its reactions in movement or gesture were unlikely to have been confined to mere outbursts.

One section gives an indication of a full choral dance, when as the Messenger concludes his story of the death of Aegisthus, the Chorus breaks into song:

Place your footstep to the chorus, my dear, lightening your step, lifted into the air with joy like a fawn. Better than by the springs of Alpheius your brother has striven and achieved a victory of a crown. Sing a victory ode to accompany my dance.[32]

Electra speaks of her triumph, but in iambics, and the Chorus continues in *antistrophe*:

Fetch garlands for his head. Our happy dance will be set out for the Muses. Now our own true kings of earlier times will rule the land justly, having killed those who ruled unjustly. But let a shout for joy go forth accompanied by the flute.[33]

The vigor that such odes demand cannot be denied even if individual movements can never be known. Both sections are described by J. D. Denniston as examples of the *huporchema*,[34] a paean, Cretan in origin and explained in the Liddell & Scott lexicon as "accompanied with dancing and pantomimic action." Athenaeus compares the *huporchema* to the *kordax*, the ribald dance of Old Comedy.[35]

These views are self-evident. What needs changing is the belief that this *huporchema* stands in contrast to choral dances elsewhere. At this moment Electra is invited to join in a particularly lively dance. Whether or not it was a special dance normally associated with the worship of Zeus, Apollo, or Dionysus is only partly relevant. What is truly significant is that the Chorus gives a graphic impression of what its dance physically involves. In this it seems to conform to, rather than to contrast with, the two longer descriptive odes, both of which tell stories in words that seem almost to prescribe the dancers' movements.

A final comparison of the playwrights' approach can now be made by examining the manner in which each handles two key scenes.

NOTES

1. Sophocles *Electra*: lines 1296–1300.
2. Ibid., lines 1309–10.
3. See chapter 2.
4. Euripides *Alcestis*: lines 400–403.
5. Euripides *Madness of Heracles*: lines 485–86.
6. Euripides *Trojan Women*: lines 761–63.

7. Aeschylus *Libation-Bearers*: lines 24–25.

8. Euripides *Electra*: line 550.

9. Ibid., lines 184–85.

10. Ibid., line 239.

11. Ibid., line 241.

12. Ibid., lines 304–5.

13. Ibid., line 1107.

14. See chapter 8.

15. Euripides *Electra*: line 115.

16. Ibid., line 217.

17. Aeschylus *Libation-Bearers*: lines 560–64.

18. The *aulos* was a single or double pipe, played with a mouthpiece, and usually translated as "flute."

19. Aeschylus *Libation-Bearers*: lines 306–478.

20. Ibid., lines 423–28.

21. Sophocles *Electra*: lines 254–55.

22. Euripides *Electra*: lines 112 and 127.

23. Ibid., lines 195–97.

24. Oliver Taplin, *Greek Tragedy in Action* (London: Methuen, 1978), p. 12.

25. Sophocles *Oedipus at Colonus*: lines 118–22 and 135–37.

26. Euripides *Orestes*: lines 133–49.

27. Aristophanes *Wasps*: lines 1536–37.

28. Aeschylus *Libation-Bearers*: lines 161–63.

29. Ibid., line 587.

30. Ibid., line 639.

31. Ibid., line 646.

32. Euripides *Electra*: lines 859–65.

33. Ibid., lines 873–79.

34. Euripides *Electra* in the edition by J. D. Denniston (Oxford: Oxford University Press, 1939), p. 154.

35. Athenaeus *Deipnosophists*: XIV 630e.

Chapter 8 Recognition and Conclusion in the Electras

AESCHYLUS

The groundwork for *Libation-Bearers* is already laid in *Agamemnon*, and Aeschylus need therefore waste no time in uniting Electra with her brother. When Orestes offers prayers at the tomb of his father, he places a lock of hair as an offering and then has to retreat at the approach of Electra and the Chorus.[1] Electra does not see the lock until she has poured the libations, although it would presumably be in full view. Perhaps it is while she bends down to get rid of the vessels that Electra sees the hair. But upon the audience, the visual presence of this lock of hair would have as trifling an impact as the footprints Electra will next see. What is of prime importance is Electra's initial reaction, picking up the lock and comparing it with her own hair:

Electra: And it is the same texture to look upon.
Chorus: As what sort of hair? I wish to hear this.
Electra: As our own, very like it to look upon.
Chorus: Can this be a gift from Orestes, secretly given?
Electra: It is his hair that this is most like.[2]

The lock of hair could be left by the tomb but Electra probably picks it up during this sequence and holds it against the hair of her own mask. The lock is referred to several times in the next thirty lines, and even if scarcely visible in Electra's open hand, it still serves as a focus for the attention of the audience.

The second sign needs an equally strong reaction:

And here are footprints, a second proof, resembling my own.[3]

No actual footprint would be visible or needs to be. All that is necessary is that Electra "see" the prints where Orestes has stepped. As she places her own foot where Orestes has already stood, Orestes confronts his sister. Perhaps Electra even approaches his place of "concealment."

Forty years later this recognition scene was to be derided by Euripides for patent absurdity if taken literally. In terms of performance, where action, reaction, and implication are presented formally, its incongruities simply pass unremarked. What Aeschylus presents is a series of indications of recognition, no more. The pattern of performance makes it entirely reasonable that the hair of a brother's mask should be identical to that of a sister's, even though, as Euripides' Electra points out sarcastically:

How can you match hair with hair, one lock a well-born man's brought up in the wrestling-ring, the other a woman's and combed?[4]

Similarly, placing a foot where another's foot has trodden is an acceptable recognition symbol because Electra is retracing Orestes' steps, not because they share the same size in shoes. Certainly there is no need to defend Aeschylus as did at least one editor on the grounds that Orestes was employing the methods of the "black trackers" of Australia![5]

With the revelation of Orestes the recognition is still far from complete. Electra is immediately plunged into doubt and needs Orestes to reiterate the proof:

Electra: Do I really address Orestes?

Orestes: You are slow to learn even when you see me. Seeing this shorn lock of mourning hair, and looking at the tracks of my footprints, your heart took wing and you seemed to see me. Place this hair against where it was cut and see how it matches your brother's. And see this piece of cloth woven by your hand, the work of your shuttle, and the beast designed upon it. Contain yourself and do not be distraught from joy. For I know that those most close to us are bitter enemies.[6]

If it were possible to see only this short passage as it was originally performed, much of the essential style of the Greek performance would become clear. Electra is initially suspicious; Orestes offers the proofs. The footprints are insufficient for her so she compares the hair to his, as he suggests. A pause seems necessary after "your brother's" for the comparison to be performed, particularly if Electra has put the lock back upon the tomb before catching sight of the footprint. Still she is unconvinced. Finally Orestes offers the third proof: a piece of woven cloth he has brought with him.

In his later parody, Euripides seems to imply that in Aeschylus Orestes was wearing the garment, although it was woven for him when he was a child. The word *uphasma* is used elsewhere in the play to denote the garments torn by members of the Chorus in their mourning, as well as the garment in which Agamemnon was murdered. A kind of cloak is indicated, although Orestes may be carrying rather than wearing it to reveal it at the apposite moment. That Orestes does this is implied by a scholiast's note, which is probably correct. The only inconvenience to Orestes is caused by his needing to carry this prop, although it may have been with Pylades or an "invisible" attendant from the beginning of the play.

More important than the signs themselves is Electra's acceptance of them. Being shown the cloak, she reacts strongly enough to induce Orestes to tell her not to break down, and here any number of expressions of joy on the part of Electra are possible, from weeping to embracing her brother. Perhaps it might merely be the cloak to which she reacts by performing an action no more emphatic than laying her head against it. The significance of this act and of her acceptance of her brother needs clarifying by action performed between the lines, not together with them.

The emotional impact of the scene is reinforced by Electra's speech expressing love for her brother and urging him to action. When Electra speaks of love, she must be capable of kindling sympathy for that love in the minds of the audience. But here again the nature of the performance to inspire such an audience reaction demands not a realistic imitation of love or joy but a formal and no less affecting presentation of these emotions.

The Chorus appears to have little to do. It speaks only five lines and these are bracketed by two speeches of Orestes. The Chorus suggests to Orestes and Electra that they should both keep quiet in case they are overheard. This remark is interesting for the way in which it situates the scene in its physical context, and the possibility of eavesdroppers is to be picked up and expanded by Sophocles. Up to this point the Chorus has allied the pattern of its emotional reactions to that of Electra. The Chorus has given Electra instructions and she has offered them information, but the attitudes of both coincide. The recognition scene is clearly centered upon the two principals, but might not the Chorus have had a part to play in it? The Chorus might stand stock still during the recognition scene. It is equally possible that it transmitted the emotional flow of the characters with whom it most sympathized, or responded in the role of spectators to an action whose outcome it could not predict. Such disparate responses are not mutually exclusive.

What of Pylades? Scarcely noticed until later, he may have adopted a passive attitude wherever possible, reacting little if at all. But if Pylades is a genuine Aeschylean "still figure," how can he be differentiated from the attendants other than by wearing the mask? How much more effective it would be were he also to reflect, in movement, the actions of Orestes. His dramatic purpose is to support Orestes, and when he does speak, it is with the force of Apollo. Perhaps when Orestes kneels, Pylades kneels also; when Orestes reacts, he too reacts; when Orestes draws his sword, so does Pylades: but always a pace behind, almost as a shadow.

That Pylades should be merely passive might seem more appropriate to Aeschylean drama, but some movement is required from the character that makes him function very differently from Cassandra during the Queen's greeting to her in *Agamemnon*. Even with so few lines to speak, in performance, Pylades' presence is constantly felt, and I prefer to think of him, as I do of the Chorus, as consistently active in the development of the play. Thus without losing the shock effect of his three lines, surely the audience is better prepared for his important function when Orestes, faced with his mother, seems to weaken. The fact of his having spoken places a new emphasis on Pylades during the final scene of the play. His single speech occurs just after the Servant has summoned Clytem-

nestra with the news of the murder of Aegisthus, and has run off to
fetch her an axe. Orestes enters from the central entrance, Pylades
close behind:

Orestes: Do you love the man? Then you shall lie in the same tomb. You
    shall not abandon him even when he is dead.
Clytemnestra: Hold, my child. Have respect for this breast at which you
    slumbered and sucked nourishing milk with your gums.
Orestes: Pylades, what am I to do? Am I to refrain from killing my mother
    from reverence?
Pylades: Where then are the oracles of Apollo, spoken by the Pythian
    priestess and our trusted oaths? Make all men your enemies rather
    than the gods.
Orestes: I judge that you prevail and give me good advice.[7]

The action here is relatively complex as the play builds to its
dramatic climax. A scholiast's note suggests that Pylades delayed
his entrance until actually addressed by Orestes, because he had to
make a rapid change from playing the attendant.[8] It seems more
reasonable to assume that the scholiast's note refers to the practice
of fourth-century troupes, where Pylades and the Servant would
have to double, rather than to Aeschylus' original intention.

Clytemnestra's appeal to her son suggests that she is confronted
by immediate threat of personal violence: perhaps Orestes raised
his sword, while Clytemnestra dropped to her knees. Exposure of
her breast reaffirms the importance of describing an action while
merely indicating it physically. One can hardly imagine that a male
actor would have opened his dress to display an artificial bosom! A
mere gesture towards the costume would suffice to augment the
words. Her reaction has the effect of stopping Orestes in his tracks.
Perhaps the sword is slowly lowered while he appeals to Pylades
for advice. Then in that moment of supreme dramatic potency, the
hitherto silent figure reaffirms Orestes' resolution. Only then, when
the audience already knows that it will be unavailing, does Aeschylus
allow Clytemnestra to put her argument. At last she comprehends
her dream while Pylades stands implacably before her, representative
of Apollo, symbol of justice.

A passage of *stichomuthia* follows before Clytemnestra is driven or, perhaps more suitably, makes a dignified exit into the palace to meet death at Aegisthus' side. This time no cries come from indoors: Clytemnestra's death is certain and in a sense already complete.

Orestes' first line on his return indicates the stage action:

Behold the double tyranny of this land, and the slayers of my father, destroyers of the house. . . . And see again, you who hear of these misfortunes, the device, a fetter for my wretched father, bonds for his hands and a yoke for his feet. Spread it out and standing round in a circle display the man's covering.[9]

Orestes refers to this "covering" again:

Is it a trap for a wild animal, or the bath curtain (*or* funeral pall) drawn over the feet of a corpse? It is a net rather, what you would call both hunting-net and robes to tangle the feet.[10]

Although the use of the image is complicated and a single property capable of serving all of its functions is difficult to imagine, the visual impression cannot fail to be powerful.

A scholiast suggests the use of the *ekkuklema* to reveal the dead bodies of Aegisthus and Clytemnestra, and there is no good reason why the device should not have been used. A tableau is clearly intended, and the only alternative would be for the bodies to be carried forward. What is important is that the bodies should be displayed, and wheeling them forward on the platform provides an entirely satisfactory stage picture. It is usually assumed that the actor or actors playing Aegisthus and Clytemnestra would not themselves have appeared in the tableau, that a demonstration of death through substitutes would suffice. A display of the masks alone would indeed provide an effective enough tableau, although perhaps dummies were used to represent the whole of the body. The audience will have little doubt who the corpses are if sufficient indication is given that they are indeed corpses.

The use of the "device" that snared Agamemnon is interesting: it may have been a real net. A red-figure vase from about the period of the first performance depicts the scene that occurs offstage and links the murder of Clytemnestra with that of Agamemnon. The "device" shown there is a thin, all-encompassing garment. Similar wall paintings show Clytemnestra, with her axe, and the murder of Aegisthus. (See figures 13a and b.)

Precisely how Orestes exhibits the robe and net during his speech is not clear. He orders it to be spread out on the ground, perhaps where Clytemnestra spread the red carpet for Agamemnon to tread underfoot. Such links to the murder of Agamemnon are found in the text and may well have had their visual counterparts. Most probably the Chorus surrounds the "device" at Orestes' request, although later it is implied that Orestes holds the robe, displays it, and uses it as Antony uses the robe of Caesar:

> Look in this place ran Cassius' dagger through;
> See what a rent the envious Casca made;
> Through this the well-beloved Brutus stabbed;
> And as he pluck'd his cursed steel away,
> Mark how the blood of Caesar followed it
> As rushing out of doors, to be resolv'd
> If Brutus so unkindly knock'd or no.[11]

Did she do it or not? This garment is my witness, where the sword of Aegisthus was bathed. The stain of blood combines with time, destroying the many colours of the embroidery.[12]

Orestes refers only twenty lines later to an olive branch and garland of supplication with which he has furnished himself as he makes for the sanctuary of Apollo's temple. Either he brings these on when he enters, and holds them throughout or is given them only when he has again laid down the robe. The concluding lines of the play imply comparatively swift action and the necessity for a more flexible form of acting than that required earlier. Handling of properties and rapid movements indicate that each scene was played according to its dramatic requirements. The Chorus surely would have played differently in a choral ode from the manner in which it played the scene with the Nurse. Orestes may have adopted a greater formality in the *kommos* than in the passages preceding and following the murder of Clytemnestra. At every turn one is brought back to the requirements of masked acting and the hard fact of the sheer

Figure 13. a. and b. Clytemnestra Restrained as Orestes Kills Aegisthus (Vienna, Kunsthistorisches Museen)

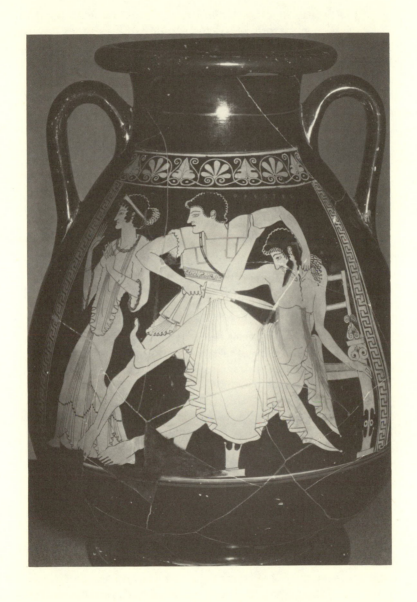

size of the theatre. If Orestes handled the robe, his reactions to it must have been in the form of a demonstration of his attitude towards it. If the robe remained on the ground by the tomb, or formed part of the tableau with the bodies, Orestes' references to it could still be as affecting as if he were actually holding it.

The garland and branch need have no existence until they are brought into play, just as the robe, once Orestes has stopped speaking about it, is no more than a visual reminder of Agamemnon. A modern production might leave the robe in full view to the end of the play, along with the tableau.

Orestes' incipient derangement demands a series of strong reactions on the part of the actor. The suggestion made earlier that the Chorus might have contributed by "becoming" the Furies during its own lines is pure conjecture,[13] but it is unthinkable that the Furies should have appeared in real form at this point. Orestes' exit is difficult, implying a haste that hardly seems appropriate. A hotfoot departure up the *parodos* does not appear to lend dignity to the occasion. But here again it is perhaps possible to demonstrate urgency with means other than running. The *wayang wong* dancers of the Ramayana Ballet can present a wonderful impression of speed with a walking step rising on the balls of their feet and accelerating over twenty to thirty yards. A movement of no great elaboration involving chorus and actor could enable Orestes to exit without forfeiting the emotional overtones that the moment requires.

In *Libation-Bearers*, on only the rarest occasions does the need for or even the possibility of realistic acting occur. Although much of any reconstruction must be personal preference, a consistency of performance can be noted, which suggests at once points of similarity with performance requirements for Sophocles and Euripides, and particular differences from them.

SOPHOCLES

In Aeschylus' *Libation-Bearers*, Orestes and Electra are seen together on stage from line 20, speak to one another at line 212, and perform a recognition scene during the next fifteen lines. By arranging for them to miss one another at this same point, Sophocles delays their meeting until line 1097, with his recognition scene coming 120 lines later.

Sophocles thus emphasizes Electra's predicament, allowing her to remain in ignorance of her brother's return for over two-thirds of the play. It is a daring piece of dramatic writing in that the audience, knowing that Electra's claims to desolation are now ill-founded, might be less inclined to sympathize with her. Orestes and Pylades make their second entrance at line 1087. Unsure whether the Chorus will be kindly disposed towards him, Orestes initially confirms the news of his own "death" in the chariot race. The scene that follows is a particularly fine example of stagecraft, focused upon the urn reputed to contain Orestes' ashes. Brought in, perhaps by Pylades, the urn is handed to Electra at her request. Although the Chorus has described her as "closest to Orestes,"[14] the latter does not appear to realize that Electra is his sister until he puts the urn into her hands. (See figure 14.) This might be caution on the part of Orestes, but Electra proceeds to deliver a long and moving speech over the urn, which affects her brother considerably. Electra's reaction to the urn is matched by Orestes' reaction to Electra. At the conclusion of her speech his resolve to keep quiet has weakened. "Why do you lament so, staring at me in this way?"[15] asks Electra. Orestes replies by detailing his troubles and hers. Electra retorts:

And yet you see a trifling part of my afflictions.[16]

The *stichomuthia* scene lasts in all for over fifty lines, ending in half-line question and answer. The whole scene including the recognition is warmer and more intimate than are similar passages in Aeschylus. The urn is the focal point of attention throughout, and Sophocles makes the urn the pivot of Orestes' abandoning his resolve to keep his identity hidden. The scene is worth quoting in full:

Orestes: Give back the urn, so that I may tell you all.
Electra: Do not force me to do this, stranger, by the gods.
Orestes: Obey my words and you will not regret it.
Electra: Do not deprive me, I beseech you by your chin, of what is most dear.[17]

Orestes: I tell you I will not allow it.

Electra: Wretched as I am, Orestes [*addressing the urn*]
    I am to be deprived of the right to bury you.

Orestes: Speak auspiciously: you have no right to mourn.

Electra: How do I have no right to mourn my dead brother?

Orestes: It is not fitting for you to utter these words.

Electra: Am I so dishonoured by the dead?

Orestes: You are dishonoured by none. But this is not your duty.

Electra: Even if I hold here the body of Orestes?

Orestes: But it is not Orestes, except in so far as it is dressed up in such
    words.

Electra: Where then is that poor man's grave?

Orestes: There is none: for a man who is alive there is no grave.

Electra: What did you say, young man?

Orestes: There is no deceit in what I say.

Electra: And the man is alive?

Orestes: Yes he is, if I am alive.

Electra: Are you that man?

Orestes: Look at this ring of my father's and learn if I speak plainly.

Electra: Oh, blessed day![18]

Orestes could take the urn in at least four places during the above
passage. On the other hand, the urn could remain with Electra until
it has changed from an object evoking grief to one indicative of joy.
It could be used to emphasize the moment of decision on Orestes'
part or of the recognition of Orestes on the part of Electra. What is
certain is that once the urn has been given the significance that
Sophocles intends it to have, action involving it must also acquire
special significance. The robe of Nessus in *Women of Trachis* and
the bow in *Philoctetes* function similarly. Recognition is established
by the manner in which the urn is handled.

Presumably the urn has been disposed of by the time Electra says
to Orestes: "I hold you in my hands."[19] It still has its part to play in
the plot, but its immediate significance is diminished. Orestes is
more concerned about keeping Electra quiet during their joyful
reunion—and not without reason. Electra is as extravagant in joy
as she has been in grief, and Orestes spends the next seventy lines
attempting to calm her.

Figure 14. Orestes, Electra, and the Urn (Vienna, Kunsthistorisches Museen)

Figure 15. Aeschylus' *Libation-Bearers*, the Recognition (Brynmor Jones Library Photographic Department, University of Hull)

We do not know the attitude of the Chorus to this scene. It might remain still, although elsewhere stillness seems to be used actively rather than to provide a neutral gear when the Chorus has nothing specific to do. A choral "freeze" to enhance the central action can be effective only for a short time, after which it becomes an empty gesture. Stillness designed to concentrate attention on the urn, for instance, or counterpointing the actual moment of recognition, would only make itself felt in contrast with movement elsewhere. No doubt for much of the central action of this play, the Chorus was ignored. In terms of modern production (although this is a dangerous criterion) the Chorus could enhance all the scenes in the play by concentrating the emotional tenor.

This is especially true of the final scene of the play, which Sophocles handles so differently from the death of Aegisthus in *Libation-Bearers*. In Aeschylus the Chorus is unsure of the outcome of this first murder and reacts by retiring from the action. In Sophocles, Clytemnestra is killed first, with the minimum of fuss, and Electra remains onstage. The Chorus has no fears for the outcome and when Orestes and Pylades reenter, the leader announces that they cannot condemn their actions. Five lines later, one member catches sight of Aegisthus and urges Orestes and Pylades back indoors to complete the deed. Another tells Electra she must speak submissively to Aegisthus to persuade him to enter the palace.

Once the final scene has begun the Chorus has no more lines until the last four, which conclude the play on a note of triumph. This last scene is one of remarkable power and one point only requires emphasis. The quality of tension generated with the sheeted body of Clytemnestra onstage embraces all those present. Unless the Chorus were to be effectively removed from the main action, its contribution to the scene is a factor that cannot be ignored, although nowhere is it indicated in the text. The relationship of the chorus in the Athenian theatre to the acting area and to the auditorium was such that a chorus could not easily be "switched off" when no longer required. It is only reasonable to assume that the dramatists, sensibly enough, made use of a fact they could not simply ignore.

When Aegisthus' approach is announced, at least one member of the Chorus must be in a suitable position to look along the stage-left *parodos*. Electra's catching sight of Aegisthus implies that she

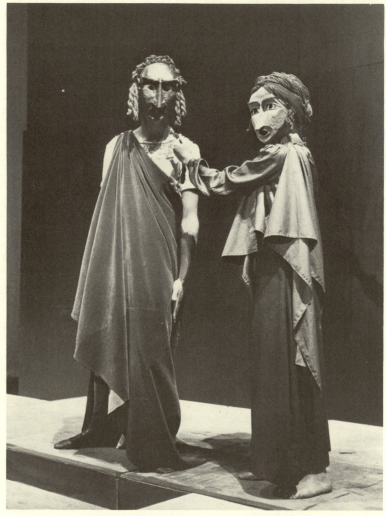

Figure 16. Aeschylus' *Libation-Bearers,* the Confrontation (Brynmor Jones Library Photographic Department, University of Hull)

Figure 17. Aeschylus' *Libation-Bearers*, the Deception (Brynmor Jones Library Photographic Department, University of Hull)

moves towards the stage-left *parodos*, while Orestes and Pylades stay at the door. Clearly Aegisthus cannot be seen by the audience before he is first seen by the Chorus or indeed until Orestes and Pylades have disappeared from view and the doors have closed, ten lines later. The remaining two lines give barely enough time for Aegisthus to enter and cover the forty-odd feet from *parodos* to the center of the *skene*.

Electra feigns grief and docility, and even when Aegisthus addresses them, the Chorus refrains from involving itself directly. Aegisthus calls for the doors to be opened, and by means of the *ekkuklema* the body of Clytemnestra is revealed under the sheet, Orestes and Pylades standing beside it. In terms of how to murder your stepfather, the remainder of the scene is gratuitous; in terms of pure theatre, it builds to the most thrilling moment in Sophocles:

Aegisthus: Remove the cover from the eyes, so that a kinsman's lament may come from me.
Orestes: Lift it yourself. It is not my job but yours to see what is here and greet it fondly.
Aegisthus: You speak well and I will be persuaded. But, you there, if Clytemnestra is in the house, call her.
Orestes: She is close beside you. No longer look elsewhere.
Aegisthus: What do I see?
Orestes: Who are you afraid of? Who do you not know?[20]

The staging of the scene needs to be carefully handled, but it is difficult to go far wrong with such a splendid ploy. The corpse is that of Aegisthus' own wife and the man whose vengeance he thinks he has escaped stands at his side.

Orestes threatens to drive him inside, but Aegisthus asks why this "noble deed" cannot be carried out then and there. Orestes' reply is that Aegisthus is to be killed where he slew Agamemnon. In a moment of grim humor, Aegisthus invites Orestes to lead the way and then makes his final exit.

The departure of Aegisthus, Orestes, and Pylades leaves only three lines to the end of the play, during which the Chorus quits the *orchestra*. That it leaves Electra alone with the body of Clytemnestra to be drawn inside on the *ekkuklema* is only conjectural but would place the emphasis of the play where Sophocles puts it, on the character and person of Electra.

The differences in approach of Aeschylus and Sophocles are clear enough, but it would be a simplification to say that what has occurred is merely a shift toward realism. In Sophocles there is still a complex blend of patterns of behavior, as well as a reaction away from some of the more formal elements of early tragedy. A comparison of the work of the two older writers with Euripides shows how an actual move toward realism created a completely new dimension in Greek tragedy.

EURIPIDES

In Euripides' *Electra*, Orestes and Electra appear on stage together at line 82 and meet at line 215, but the recognition does not take place for a further 350 lines. Even then this recognition is effected by a third person and in rather odd circumstances.

When Orestes and Pylades emerge from hiding and first confront Electra, they block her retreat into her house. Falling on her knees Electra prays to Apollo, and Orestes takes her by the hand as she shrinks away. All this is written into the lines, but when Electra is again standing submissively, ". . . for you are the stronger,"[21] a moment of crisis occurs. This is surely the point at which recognition should take place, but it does not. Orestes fails to admit who he is:

I have come bringing news of your brother.[22]

In fact, he never attempts to reveal himself. He is recognized and "unmasked" by the Old Man. This is a major departure from the approach of the other two dramatists and needs explanation.

In his first speech to Pylades, Orestes admits he has come to search for his sister, who lives nearby. He already knows that Electra is married. The only possible reason for his failure to identify himself is that after taking a close look at Electra, he no longer wishes to reveal himself as her brother. Who is to blame him?

Orestes: What are you to your brother, do you think?
Electra: Though absent and not here he is dear to me.
Orestes: And why do you live here far from the city?[23]

A little later:

Orestes: You talked of him [*that is* your husband] as a good man, one to
    be well treated.
Electra: Yes, if he who is absent shall ever return home.
Orestes: And your mother, does she put up with these things?[24]

On both occasions Orestes deliberately changes the subject, and later
he avoids yet another opportunity to reveal himself. The presence
of the Chorus can hardly deter Orestes, as he accepts a guarantee of
their loyalty:

Orestes: Are these women who hear our words friendly to you?
Electra: So as to keep your words and mine carefully.
Orestes: What would Orestes do were he to come to Argos?
Electra: Do you ask this? You speak basely. Is the time not ripe?
Orestes: And if he came here, how would he kill his father's murderers?
Electra: By daring such things as were dared against his father.
Orestes: And would you take the risk of killing your mother with him?
Electra: With the same axe as my father was killed with.
Orestes: I will tell him these things, and your firm words.
Electra: I would be happy to die after shedding my mother's blood.
Orestes: I wish Orestes were near to hear these things.
Electra: I would not know him if I saw him, friend.
Orestes: No wonder. . . .[25]

The passage continues in the same vein. Not only does Orestes
manage to avoid revealing himself, but it can hardly fail to be clear
to the audience that he does so. Hesitation and obvious change of
subject are shown in stage terms by means of vocal inflection and
appropriate physical responses. Those who are being deceived on
stage habitually become inordinately unintelligent and miss the
signals the deceiver supplies for the necessary enlightenment of the
audience. So here, one presumes. But what of Pylades? Was he
merely a "dumb personage"? Euripides implies that it is Pylades
and his family who have been responsible for pushing Orestes this
far. Might there even be a suggestion that Electra suspects Pylades
of being Orestes? Certainly the eventual revelation is one against
which she fights, since it fails to accord with her vision of her brother.

Euripides' play appears to require the most subtle acting if it is to be presented on any level other than the most superficial. If the nuances of character suggested above are to be dismissed as purely modern interpretations, the alternative is to see *Electra* as a fourth-rate piece written by a man with no sense of dramatic construction or stage logic. The play demands only a careful investigation of motives to reveal it as a remarkable piece of theatre, of direct relevance to its own time and dramatically strong for any other. That a new and more subtle acting line was now required does not mean that the mask had become a hindrance. The mask is still an invaluable device when used for contrasting word and implication. Euripides' chief gift as a playmaker was that he could construct plays based on realistic human emotions and responses, by contrasting the conventional stories drawn from myth with contemporary reactions to those stories.

Euripides' recognition scene occurs after the arrival of the Old Man who has passed Agamemnon's grave on his way to the farm. The Old Man thinks that Orestes may have come back, because a newly sacrificed ewe lay by the grave and upon it a lock of hair. Perhaps the hair would match Electra's? Electra scornfully rejects the idea. Orestes would never return secretly, and anyway, why should their hair match? Orestes has had an athlete's training, while her hair is "feminine" with combing.[26] The Old Man then suggests they should check footprints. Again, Electra will not hear of such nonsense. Footprints on rocky ground? Anyway, women have smaller feet than men.[27] The Old Man persists: perhaps Orestes might be wearing a cloak Electra had woven for him? Her sarcastic rejoinder is that he would hardly be wearing it still![28]

The scene refers the audience directly, of course, to *Libation-Bearers* where these three tokens—a lock of hair, footprints, and woven cloth— serve to reunite Electra and Orestes. Euripides' purpose in rejecting them is three-fold. The fact of parody makes the scene in part comic, and that Euripides' audience would have recognized and responded to the mockery can be in no doubt. More important, Euripides' treatment of his theme serves to emphasize for the audience the difference in dramatic method between Aeschylus and himself. Euripides is not concerned solely with the consequences of an action. If the action is illogical in terms of human response, let it be seen to be so, and let some more plausible device be used. Finally, within this play, Electra, by rejecting the possibility of Orestes having already arrived, underscores the difference between this real Orestes and her romantic expectation.

When Orestes emerges from the house he is taken aback to find out who the Old Man is:

Orestes: Electra, whose friend is this antique relic of mankind?
Electra: This is the man, stranger, who brought up my father.[29]

Things go from bad to worse for Orestes:

Why is he staring at me. . . . Why is he circling round me?[30]

The Old Man recognizes him by a scar, thus forcing Electra re-luctantly to acknowledge her equally reluctant brother. After such a scene the mutual protestations of affection sound not a little hollow and the lengthy embrace is unconvincing.

Beyond a short ode to celebrate the reunion of the brother and sister, the Chorus is little involved. But its words have an ironic ring:

You have come, you have come. You have shone out, a timely dawn, like a flashing beacon from the city. . . .[31]

By the end of the play, the attitude of the Chorus is one of horror at what has come about.

You suffered badly, perhaps, but what you have done is unholy, wretched woman.[32]

Throughout the *kommos* it is Electra the Chorus upbraids.

After Clytemnestra's death cries have been heard, and Orestes and Electra have returned from the killing, the Chorus refers to them as "stained with newly-shed blood."[33] This might refer to visible staining of hands or costume or it might simply be a formal statement. From the description that emerges, the killing has been particularly unpleasant. Clytemnestra failed to die at the first blow and instead opened her dress to expose her breast to Orestes (as she does onstage in *Libation-Bearers*). Orestes seized her by the hair while she was still on her knees. Clytemnestra then put her arms round Electra's neck so that the latter dropped her sword. Finally Orestes covered his eyes with his cloak while Electra guided the sword into their mother's throat. That they should appear in blood-stained garments might well be appropriate for this play, although inappropriate for the comparatively clinical executions of Aeschylus and Sophocles.

The bodies are brought on together, presumably on the *ekkuklema*, although Orestes refers to them as "lying on the ground."[34] The grief of brother and sister continues through the *kommos*, as the Chorus condemns Electra for what she has forced Orestes to do. Orestes instructs Electra to cover her mother's body. Although both bodies are in view, that of Aegisthus is no longer important and is never directly alluded to. As Electra starts to obey her brother's instructions, the Dioscuri appear on the *mechane* "above the topmost house. . . . This is no place for mortals."[35] They may have been swung only to the edge of the roof or perhaps right out over the action. What is of importance are the reactions of Electra and Orestes, presumably facing front even with the gods above and behind them.

The purpose of the gods' arrival is to return the myth to its original state, and this they do despite the broken lives in clear evidence below. Electra's marriage to Pylades, Orestes' acquittal by the Areopagus, the absolution of Helen, and the enrichment of the Farmer all have a desolate ring when faced by the emotional realities of the de-nouement. Castor even interrupts Orestes' farewell to his sister:

She has a home and husband. She has suffered nothing that she might be pitied for, except that she leaves the city of Argos.[36]

The final embrace of Electra and Orestes seems as empty as their reunion earlier in the play, and Electra leaves with Pylades. Castor then tells Orestes to set out for Athens and announces that he and his brother Pollux are going to succour the fleet in Sicily.[37] A tidy little ending is then tagged on, plus a final scene that presents numerous problems involving allocation of lines and identification of references. One should never forget that Euripides frames his plot with a prologue and with a *deus ex machina* to sustain the myth. The meat lies in between.

The *Electra*s amply demonstrate the extent to which dramatic writing developed during the course of the fifth century and also show how Euripides, for many the finest playwright of the trio, wrote in such a way that, after him, further development on "classical" lines became impossible. The dialogue of Aeschylus never attempts any subtlety greater than the deception of one character by another, with both chorus and audience aware of the truth. So a style of acting has been suggested for Aeschylus that externalized the emotions and perhaps relied on an operatic type of delivery.

Sophocles involves deeper emotions in a series of responses between characters and in ironic reference. In Euripides whole scenes take place where the subtext contradicts the apparent value of the words. This can be emphasized physically and may have been reinforced by less extravagant costumes and masks. But the method of delivery implies a new concentration on vocal tones if only because the shifts of thought and mood are so much more rapid than those to be found in Aeschylus.

For the following century "realism" was to be the pattern, with Euripides in revival the most popular playwright. The actor came to dominate the tragic stage, a position of superiority in which he was to continue for the next thousand years.

NOTES

1. As so much of the stage action proposed in this chapter is at best conjectural, I have chosen to describe it for the most part in the present tense, rather than imply a spurious authority.

2. Aeschylus *Libation-Bearers*: lines 174–78.

3. Ibid., line 205.

4. Euripides *Electra*: lines 527–29.

5. Aeschylus *Choephori* (*Libation-Bearers*), in the edition by T. G. Tucker (Cambridge: At the University Press, 1901), Introduction, p. lxvi.

6. Aeschylus *Libation-Bearers*: lines 224–34.

7. Ibid., lines 894–903.

8. See chapter 5.

9. Aeschylus *Libation-Bearers*: lines 973–74 and 980–84.

10. Ibid., lines 997–1000.

11. Shakespeare *Julius Caesar*: III 2. 179–85.

12. Aeschylus *Libation-Bearers*: lines 1010–13.

13. See chapter 7.

14. Sophocles *Electra*: line 1105.

15. Ibid., line 1184.

16. Ibid., line 1188.

17. One of the formal gestures of supplication was for the suppliant to clasp the knees and beard of the patron.

18. Sophocles *Electra*: lines 1205–24.

19. Ibid., line 1226.

20. Ibid., lines 1468–75.

21. Euripides *Electra*: line 227.

22. Ibid., line 228.

23. Ibid., lines 244–46.

24. Ibid., lines 262–64.

25. Ibid., lines 272–84.

26. Ibid., lines 524–31.

27. Ibid., lines 534–37.

28. Ibid., lines 541–44.

29. Ibid., lines 553–55.

30. Ibid., lines 558 and 561.

31. Ibid., lines 585–87.

32. Ibid., lines 1170–71.

33. Ibid., lines 1172–73.

34. Ibid., lines 279–80.

35. Ibid., lines 1233–36.

36. Ibid., lines 1311–13.

37. This is thought to be a contemporary reference and has been used to date the play to 413 B.C. when the Athenian fleet was engaged in the expedition to Sicily.

Chapter 9 The Fourth Century and Beyond

In the preceding chapters, I made an attempt to examine the main factors affecting public performance of the work of the major Greek playwrights. By and large I returned to the plays themselves as being the most likely place to find evidence of the aims of the playwrights and of the Athenian audience's expectations and requirements. In so doing I rejected many of the assumptions of later Greek and Roman critics.

Such apparent rashness needs little apology because these critics patently refer to periods later than those when the plays received their first performance. When Vitruvius and Pollux discuss "the Greek theatre," it is unlikely to be the Athenian theatre of the time of Pericles, which they have in mind, so much as the theatre of the entire Greek world in the fourth and third centuries B.C.

Athens remained a cultural capital, but after defeat in the Peloponnesian War, it was politically never the same again. For Aeschylus, Sophocles, and Euripides, the fourth century nurtured Plato, Aristotle, and Demosthenes. No fewer plays were written, but fewer new works were successful. Performances in fact multiplied in number as actors traveled farther and farther afield.

LATER TRAGEDY

Whatever one believes about the development of tragedy in the fifth century, one feature dominates. The conspicuously choral performance of earlier times was overtaken by a new emphasis on character. From Aeschylus to Sophocles and Euripides, the proportion of text devoted to choral speech was reduced from one-half to one-quarter. The move towards realism still allowed for a chorus to underscore the rhythms of the play but probably diminished its original function of commenting on the action through movement.

Many people think this fifth-century progression is a decline in itself, but it represents surely no more than a substitution of a new set of dramatic terms and conventions from those that Aeschylus employed. With the advent of Sophoclean irony and tension came not an improvement on the methods of Aeschylus, but a concentration on a new set of dramatic values. When Aeschylus and Euripides squabble in Aristophanes' *Frogs* about who is the better playwright, their arguments are those that even a modern audience might make in support of one dramatist against another. About the moral and didactic purpose of the theatre, the two "dead" playwrights are in absolute agreement. It is their approach that sets them apart. As god of the theatre, Dionysus cannot separate the pair, and perhaps we can assume that Aristophanes, himself a man of the theatre, also had the healthiest respect for both his illustrious forebears. The eventual choice of Aeschylus as the one to return to Athens is made less on grounds of the weight of lines (strictly farcical) as on the political advice (deadly earnest).

To say that tragedy declined from Aeschylus to Euripides is to contradict not only the opinion of the fourth century, but of most subsequent centuries. Yet after Euripides a decline is perceivable, and this, ironically enough, may be most easily accounted for in terms of Euripides' contribution to the theatre. Euripides wrote new kinds of plays, plays that defied convenient categorization, and that, although produced as "tragedies," contravene any acceptable definitions of that term and wreak havoc with preconceived ideas of Greek tragic form. Euripides introduced contemporary thought garbed in contemporary language; he turned traditional myths on their heads by considering them in terms of fifth-century rationalism; he challenged beliefs and moral codes that the majority of Athenians had for centuries held sacred.

All this he achieved in the classical theatre within a conventional framework that served his purpose because it militated against innovation. The open-air performance, the size of the audience, the religious occasion with its contingent rituals, the chorus, the use of the mask and masked acting—all were taken by Euripides and employed to surprise audiences and impel them to think about what they saw. To say that established convention restrained Euripides is to underestimate his skill as a playmaker. It would be more correct to say that Euripides' novel exploitation of his medium made unlikely the emergence of successors of equal status.

New tragedians did emerge in the fourth century, but experimentation was rare. Attempts at historical drama or the fictional plot were short-lived and little was thought worth preserving at the time. Revivals of the fifth-century masters were common and, as so often happens, appear to have treated the originals with scant respect. Stage conditions and the requirements of a touring system caused such a rash of textual emendation that at the end of the fourth century, official copies were deposited in the archives in Athens, copies the actors were forbidden to vary. How much the plays had already been bowdlerized we cannot know: it is a popular scholarly pastime to try to deduce what passages are late interpolations. Certainly, to dismiss any passages as "late" that interfere with a theory is a convenient if facile way of solving problems concerning dating, acting, and production. It is also exceedingly seductive.[1] Such an attitude does serve to emphasize the important fact that all the texts we possess are "folio" versions of what may have been rudimentary rehearsal scripts.

From the fourth century not a single tragedy is extant and there remain only a small number of fragments from playwrights whose names need not detain us. Aristotle refers to them on occasions, sometimes in praise, sometimes (more informatively) to castigate.

The tragedies of our most recent playwrights are characterless. . . . The older poets made their characters talk like statesmen . . . those of today make them talk like rhetoricians.[2]

A more telling remark occurs not in the *Poetics* but in the *Rhetoric*, where Aristotle asserts that: "actors hold greater power today than playwrights."[3] Integration of chorus with the drama disappeared as the influence from oratory and philosophy played their part in removing emphasis away from the playwrights. Not so differently from the native British tradition, it was not until the period of real genius in the Greek theatre had passed that the age of the actor began.

Theatrical performances continued to flourish for centuries. Plutarch attended the Great Dionysia in 96 A.D., by which time plays were also being performed in Athens at the Panathenaia. Changes in organization had taken place, and the office of *choregos* was replaced by various state and tribal arrangements. About 310 B.C. the office of *agonothetes* was created for the management of theatrical performances, but in many of its essentials, the Great Dionysia retained its traditional format well into the second century A.D. The Lenaea probably went into decline much earlier, but records that establish its persistence exist up to the time of Terence in the second century B.C.

Athens and its Great Dionysia continued to formulate the criteria of quality, although challenged by Syracuse and Macedon. In the fourth century B.C. no less than in the fifth century, to be a successful actor meant to be successful in Athens. At the same time interest in theatre began to spread throughout the Greek world, until ultimately every township of size or importance boasted its own theatre and promoted its own local dramatic festivals in honor of Dionysus (in one or another of his various embodiments) or any of several other gods, Apollo in particular. Records from several localities, including Delos and Delphi, are more complete than those for Athens and supply valuable information.

Already by the end of the fourth century, tragedies were being performed on other than public occasions, significant among them the wedding feast of Philip of Macedon for his daughter, the festival at which Philip was assassinated. By invitation actors might travel to any part of the Greek-speaking world from Spain to Alexandria to perform their repertoire at both secular and religious festivities.

LATER COMEDY

No longer associated with the other plays of a set, the satyr play surrendered its traditional position as fourth play. If performed at all, the satyr play usually opened the program and it maintained a popularity until the time of the Roman Empire, although more often superseded, especially in Italy, by local farce.

Comedy proper, however, projected two new forms of which examples have survived.

Middle Comedy extends from the end of the Peloponnesian War until about 325 B.C. when Menander first began to write. It is very much a transitional form, and the two last plays of Aristophanes fall into this category rather than into the category of Old Comedy. *Women in Assembly* and *Wealth* (produced between 392 and 388 B.C.) are near enough to *Frogs* in time to possess the same bizarre combination of fantasy, farce, and social comment as Old Comedy, although in a noticeably emasculated form.

In the nine surviving Old Comedies first staged between 425 and 405 B.C. Aristophanes directed much of his humor against his contemporaries, Athenian personalities familiar to and often members of his audience, so close-knit was the community of Athens. This kind of familiarity is one of the elements of Aristophanic comedy most difficult, if not impossible, to recreate, because its practice was dependent upon the immediacy of the situation. In a cast of only five principals plus chorus, *Knights* features Nicias and Demosthenes, the Athenian generals, with Paphlagon (a transparent disguise for the statesman Cleon) as slaves of the Athenian people, personified as Demos. The only other character is the Sausage Seller destined to usurp Cleon's position in the state. *Peace* introduces an Athenian farmer, Trygaeus, who has dealings not only with the god Hermes and the personifications of War, Riot, and Peace herself, but also with two children who sing warlike songs and introduce themselves as sons of Cleonymus the demagogue and Lamachus the general. *Women at the Thesmophoria* includes Euripides and Agathon and at one point Echo. *Birds* offers Iris, the messenger of Zeus, Heracles, Poseidon, and Prometheus, with the latter carrying an umbrella to avoid detection from above; *Clouds* offers a Socrates representing the "new learning," unfairly identified as a leading Sophist. *Frogs* opens with a meeting between Dionysus and Heracles in the Athens of 405 B.C. after which Dionysus visits Hades, by way of Charon's ferry, to judge the competition between Aeschylus and Euripides. The sense of anachronism was traded upon by the mixture of contemporary characters with gods and heroes.

Women in Assembly and *Wealth* are different. Both plays are set in Athens, with human choruses, but no contemporary Athenians figure in either play. *Women in Assembly* employs the "drag" joke in extended form, with male actors dressed as women disguising themselves as men. Discounting the Chorus, twice as many of the characters are female as are male. Aristophanes pokes fun at the idea of women taking over the state and instituting Platonic communism carried to its logical and illogical conclusions. Some local figures are mentioned in passing and the play ends, as does all Old Comedy, with a feast. But the atmosphere is different. One might attribute *Women in Assembly* to Aristophanes writing on an off-day were it not for his last play *Wealth*, which simply falls short of Aristophanic comic inspiration. The god of Wealth is discovered blind and is restored to sight, but only at the very end of the play does the succession of incidents that result recall Aristophanes' former comic mastery.

As the flights of fancy diminish, so too do direct address, multiplicity of incident, and spectacular exuberance. Instead the plays tend to investigate social attitudes that, even if not considered deeply, remain at least viable moral issues. Perhaps Aristophanes was growing old, becoming less frivolous. Perhaps war provided the stimulus his genius required, or perhaps nothing in Athens seemed quite so secure any more and the government was disinclined to put up with immediate and serious criticism.

The transitional phase to New Comedy, however, is as well represented by the less obviously "tragic" plays of Euripides. From *Alcestis* in 438 B.C. through *Helen* and *Ion*, Euripides is trying out a different kind of play, a play with a happy ending, humorous passages, and mythical personages who attempt to validate their activities against the *mores* of a contemporary Athens. It is in these plays that Euripides first looks forward to New Comedy, particularly when the processes of marriage, education, and getting on with one's neighbors are under scrutiny. In *Helen*, Menelaus, confronted with his real wife in Egypt after the end of the ten-year war against Troy, discovers that the Helen over whom the Trojan War was fought was no more than a phantom created by Hera. The real Helen has stayed in Egypt, chaste and loyal, and the play revolves around her efforts to escape from her captor with her husband, Menelaus. A whole series of comic recognitions are played out against a growing awareness of the utter futility of the whole ten years of the war against Troy.

In *Ion* the foundling Ion is eventually reunited with the mother from whom he was parted as a baby, a stock situation in New Comedy. Euripides offers a comic and ambiguous ending with Ion attempting, with limited success, to discover whether his father was god or mortal. The subtlety of inference in such plays must have required a performance style far from that needed for Aeschylus, but quite suitable for the social comedies of Menander in the later part of the fourth century.

Menander is the sole author of New Comedy of whose work a complete play survives. His reputation in the ancient world was exceptionally high, but until recently only fragments of his plays were known. The discovery of *The Bad-Tempered Man* and, more recently, enough of the lost portions of *The Girl from Samos* for the text to be regarded as complete have better enabled modern scholars to reassess Menander's worth.

Despite the domestic formula of these two extant plays and substantial portions of others, it is clear that the basic structure of performance remained as in the previous century. The theatre for the Great Dionysia and Lenaea was still the Theatre of Dionysus. Masks were still worn, and setting requirements were no more elaborate than for Euripides. Exclusive concentration on character comedy probably accounts for Menander's winning only a comparatively small number of first prizes (for eight out of over one hundred reputed plays), although masked acting can comfortably handle intimate as well as emphatic styles of writing. The list of masks that Pollux conjectures for New Comedy[4] may well be reliable, including as it does nine old men, eleven young men, seven slaves, three old women, and fourteen young women, characters whose whole personality depends upon age, social status, profession, or obsession. Human failings rather than fantastic situations now became the mainspring for comic action.

The emphasis on character shows where the "new drama" of Euripides and the late Aristophanes was heading. For all of Aristotle's strictures about characterless tragedies, the stock comic characters of Menander are far more recognizably human than are their descendants in New Comedy adaptations of Plautus.

The absence of politics, outrageous characters, and even blue jokes is matched by the virtual disappearance of the chorus as a force to be reckoned with in the plays. Menander uses choruses but texts supply merely a stage direction, stating "choral interlude" between scenes. The chorus is introduced if at all by a remark like that of Chaerestratos in *Arbitrants*: "Let's go. Here comes a gang of young drunks I'd rather not tangle with."[5]

The most certain feature to be picked out distinguishing drama of the fifth from that of the fourth century is its gradual genteelization. In both comedy and tragedy, extremes of character and behavior were toned down. Aristophanes had used ordinary citizens for leading characters, but what befell them was far from ordinary.

The religious aspects of the Great Dionysia were still observed, but the concern of the playwrights with the relationship between man and the gods diminished. Onesimos in *Arbitrants* has a contemplative speech that typifies the new mood:

I'll make it clear for you. There are about a thousand cities in the world, three hundred thousand souls live in each. Do the gods punish or protect each and every individual? . . . And don't the gods care about us at all? you will say. Each man has his Character given by them, as Guardian of his soul, that's what brings him to ruin or looks after him. That is "god" to us, responsible for good luck or bad. He's the one to propitiate by behaving decently and doing nothing outlandish or thoughtless.[6]

THE THEATRE

Imagine that this place is Phyle in Attica, and this cave I've just entered from is a shrine of the Nymphs belonging to the farmers of Phyle, who manage to coax a living out of these rocks. Here on the right is the home of Cnemon. . . .[7]

Thus the god Pan opens Menander's *The Bad-Tempered Man*. Visualized within a setting suggested for the Periclean theatre,[8] this passage creates no great problem. The wooden pillars of the facade would present a doorless central entrance. Painted panels between the pillars would perhaps indicate the countryside and the shrine of the Nymphs, or this might be shown by means of an adjacent altar and statues. A statue of Pan is also required. Stage right and stage left, the two *paraskenia* could have been put in place to represent the farm of Cnemon and the house of Gorgias later referred to —a straightforward set, with perhaps some differentiation between farm and house.

However, the year 324 B.C., which probably saw the first performance of a play by Menander, also saw the death of Lycurgus. In the twelve years following 338 B.C. Lycurgus, in charge of Athenian finance, oversaw the construction of the first stone theatre building in the Precinct of Dionysus. This was a momentous period, which included the defeat of Athens by Philip of Macedon and the writing of the *Poetics*. New building in the theatre precinct may even have been initiated as a morale booster, as had been the rebuilding of the city after its destruction by the Persians in 480 B.C. The decision to make the theatre "permanent" was most probably dictated by the nature of the precinct rather than by any desire for a single, fixed setting. The Athenians had had nearly one hundred years to decide which elements of the impermanent theatre needed to become permanent, and what compromises would be most necessary as flexibility was diminished.

The Lycurgan theatre incorporated a new stone auditorium. With as many as seventy-eight rows of seats, the angle of inclination was just under one in three, a gradient accounted for by the shifting of the whole *orchestra* northwards farther into the hillside, to accommodate extensions to the stage building on its other side. Only the lower part of the auditorium remains today as it was built under Lycurgus. The upper half, confined at the top by a perpendicular cleft in the rock where the sanctuary of Thrasyllus was placed, has now been destroyed. The retaining walls at the eastern and western limits of the auditorium were also modified to accommodate the new placement of the seating. The transverse gangway proposed in figure 3 for the Periclean theatre was confirmed with perhaps a second gangway lower down. Twelve stairways running from top to bottom gave access to the thirteen blocks of seats, the same number as envisaged for the theatre of Pericles.

Each row of seats was a thirteen-inch platform backing on a thirteen-inch risesr. Behind this seating platform the level dropped two inches and extended backwards to accommodate the feet of the person sitting in the row behind. The actual depth of each row was about thirty-six inches, with the platform of the seat on an overhang to give extra room for feet or belongings.[9]

The seats of honor at the front of the auditorium included the luxury of backs and were occupied by priests, archons, special guests, perhaps playwrights, and judges. These seats constituted the front rows from the *orchestra*, which again had been shrunk from seventy-eight feet across to a mere sixty-six feet. A drainage channel surrounded the *orchestra* but the present paved surface dates from much later. In the Lycurgan theatre the *orchestra* was probably clay-covered or lightly paved. The end walls of the auditorium are situated to allow for an opening from the *parodos* of about eight feet six inches up to the edge of the *paraskenia*.

The stage building seems to have resembled the removable facade of the Periclean theatre. Two *paraskenia*, probably columned and backed by doors, protruded sixteen feet, six inches from a rear wall. The space they enclosed (*proskenion*) exactly matched the diameter of the *orchestra*—sixty-six feet. Each *paraskenion* had a frontage of twenty-three feet, four inches and a height of perhaps thirteen feet with a pedimented roof. These *paraskenia* were enlarged and permanent versions of the movable pieces postulated for earlier theatres.

The appearance of the rest of the *skene* presents the same problems as that of the Periclean theatre. Was there a *prothuron*? Was there a second story, with columns and doors or an upstairs area? In the Periclean theatre the answer appears to lie in the availability of several removable architectural elements, and such a solution also may be applied to the Lycurgan theatre. It is risky to assume that every feature of the scenic facade was necessarily fashioned in stone at the time of the general reconstruction. Fifth-century plays were regularly revived and the implication is that any permanent theatre would permit their production in a convenient manner. The arguments for a high stage of ten to twelve feet at this period hold little weight so long as the chorus has an integral part to play in the action. But did the form of the Lycurgan stage building make the evolution of a high stage a logical process? By the following century, theatre practice outside Athens may have caused the actor to be substantially elevated above the floor of the *orchestra*.

Despite the seniority of the Theatre of Dionysus, there is clearly no reason by this time for all theatres to resemble one another in any detail, more than is necessary to allow for the performances upon them of the same plays. As any actor who has played on tour knows, the most extensive alterations can be made in a short time to a production with even complex technical requirements.

ACTORS

The changes in dramatic technique from Aeschylus through to Euripides must have made considerable demands on actors. From the time when Aeschylus himself was an actor, and throughout the Classical period, references to individual actors are few. Later reports associate individual actors with particular dramatists, but this association must have ended with the introduction of the lottery. Names are known of numbers of actors who won prizes at the Great Dionysia and Lenaea from the time when they were first awarded, but few actors seem to have achieved fame in the fifth century as actors, even when they had effectively become professionals.

If Plato can be relied upon,[10] the same actors did not play tragedy and comedy. Versatility must still have been of a high order. Different portions of the plays required different forms of delivery, and although emphasis has been placed on the physical nature of masked acting, the voice had to be trained with the greatest care.

It was only with the passing of the Classical age that the actor came into his own, a fact that may in part account for the decline of the theatre. The art of the actor, even when preserved on film or tape, is essentially ephemeral. Actors can only survive by reputation. Style in acting changes so rapidly that with the exception of a few genuinely charismatic film actors and comics, the stars of one generation hold little appeal for the audiences of another.

From the fourth century onward, odd passing references show how highly actors of that time could be regarded. In this respect criticism can often be as revealing as praise, and stories of mispronunciations, of drying up, and missing entrances indicate as demanding an audience as is to be found in any period of the theatre's history.

Aristotle seems to complain about excessive realism:

People become wary of those who are out to trick them as they are of mixing drinks. That is what happened to the voice of Theodorus, compared with other actors. His voice actually seemed to be that of the speaker, that of the others the voice of someone else. It is a clever trick for a speaker to make use of ordinary language, as indeed Euripides was the first to demonstrate.[11]

Aristotle certainly considered *hupokrisis* ("delivery") to be a late art. *Hupokrites* meaning "answerer" or "actor" is found as a word in the fifth century only in Aristophanes. This reinforces the idea that Greek acting became primarily vocal long after its association with other forms of recitation. To Aristotle, writing in the second half of the fourth century, the art of the "actor" was still closely associated with that of the "rhapsode," or epic reciter. Euripides was seen as the father of the dramatic line, which, while sounding natural and ordinary, was still recognizably dramatic language in strict rhythm.

Stories abound of actors being held in esteem in the fourth century, but it is not until the end of the fourth century and during the third and second centuries that actors banded together for mutual benefit.

THE GUILDS

As ever more theatres were constructed and dramatic festivals proliferated, the actor began to feel himself in need of protection—protection from unscrupulous festival organizers, from unlicensed performers, and from the limitation on free travel between states and countries. Employers began to require a guarantee that actors would turn up, and that their performances would be adequate when they did. The establishment of a central agency that would arrange itineraries for actors, and to which application could be made for a company, became a necessity. The guilds were formed as the forefathers of Actors' Equity.

The practice of having companies of three became established with this centralization of control. A troupe would travel together, perhaps with a musician and a fixed repertoire. They could play a circuit with advance bookings guaranteed and on the mutual understanding that sanctions would be imposed for breach of contract. Reputations no doubt depended almost as much on reliability as on quality.

As individual actors made names for themselves throughout the Mediterranean basin, so their status increased and they extended the scope of their activities through their position of privilege to the political field. Some of them, exempt from military service, made use of their diplomatic immunity as servants of Dionysus to act as intermediaries and negotiators. Not that all of them enhanced the good name of their profession. Aristotle in *Problems* asks for the first time but not for the last why it is that *technitai* ("artists of Dionysus") are for the most part so dissipated and blames it on the kind of life they lead and its financial insecurity.

The process by which actors became organized was obviously gradual. Formation of the guilds is dated by A. W. Pickard-Cambridge[12] to between 288 B.C., when festival arrangements from Euboea give details of private contracts, and 279 B.C. , when decrees from Delphi cite one of the guilds. The theatre at Delphi is fourth century and may have been used for dramatic and musical performances for up to a hundred years before the institution of the Soteria in 279 B.C. to commemorate the defeat of the Gauls and the preservation of the oracle. The Soteria took place in late summer in honor of Apollo, whose temple stands just below the theatre, and an inscription setting out certain guarantees concerning the Athenian Guild of actors survives. The organization of the festival may have been in the hands of the Amphictyonic League, to which Delphi belonged, but the detailed records of a non-Athenian festival make an interesting point of comparison.[13]

Programs of musical, dithyrambic, and dramatic performances sometimes involved hundreds of artists from all over the Greek world. Alongside these other artists two or three acting companies would compete, each company comprised of three actors, a musician, and a *didaskalos* ("director" or perhaps "company manager").[14] Comedy had similar arrangements but with larger companies and occasionally a small professional chorus.[15] Menander's comedies could manage with even less. No tragic chorus is mentioned, although G. M. Sifakis suggested[16] that the dithyrambic choruses served for tragedy too.

About the same time that the Athenian Guild was formed, the Isthmian-Nemean Guild also came into being. It maintained a position of importance equal to the Athenian Guild at least until the next century, but how strong the rivalry between the two guilds may have been is not clear. As several smaller guilds were formed later, it seems likely that private arrangements were made concerning the allocation of territory, but that for a certain number of major festivals, artists might come from all over. Strangely enough, third-century records of dramatic performances in Athens make no mention of the guilds, which perhaps indicates that the local guild took for granted its involvement in Athenian festivals.

In the later years of the third century two more large guilds came to prominence, one in Egypt, based probably at Alexandria, and the second, the Ionian-Hellespontic, at Teos. Large guilds had several local branches, and centers of activity are known as far apart as Cyprus, Corcyra (Corfu), and eventually Naples. The second century witnessed a heady dispute between the Athenian and Isthmian-Nemean guilds. Successive Roman proconsuls failed to restore peace, and it took direct appeal to the Senate in Rome by Athens and a *senatus consultum ultimum*, that most solemn of decrees, to break the deadlock in 112 B.C.

Later, a single organization of artists was created, but probably not until the Christian era. Membership was still fairly exclusive but included actors, musicians, reciters, producers, directors, and possibly costume hirers. Excluded from becoming *technitai*, there remained the horde of mimes, pantomimes, and performers of those more or less bizarre offerings that enraptured Roman audiences. The guild provided stability and could demand high fees for its members. Organization was strict enough to permit artists to be allocated to festivals even without their approval. By 133 B.C. a permanent administration with secretarial assistance was available, and powers were exercised to impose fines on a guild member for nonappearance or unsatisfactory performance. The guild served primarily as a protection for both parties in what, for want of a better term, may be described as the legitimate side of the theatre business.

This state of affairs lasted until the third century A.D. when the Artists Guild combined with the Guild of Athletes, a union that Pickard-Cambridge described as resembling "a fusion of the Old Vic and the Football League." As he pointed out, it does demonstrate the range of interests held in common by performers once the entertainment complex goes commercial.

ROME

Greek tragedy reached Rome in the third century B.C. and so long
as the guilds were in existence was often included in Roman festivals.
Tragedy in Greek managed to outlive its Roman counterpart whose
competition was negligible. What by then it had itself become
can only be conjectured. The plays of the Athenian masters, deprived
of religious background and chorus, the actors concealed by padding
and hugely exaggerated masks, set against the massive forty-foot
facade of the Roman theatre, must have become virtually un-
recognizable.

The Roman author Seneca composed his dramas for private
consumption only, but if Seneca's maunderings can claim a foundation in the work of Euripides, the notorious Roman philistinism had
certainly submerged the genius of Athens.

Pantomime and elaborate balletic performance were to replace
tragedy and relegate it to the study. Descriptions of such performances
provide an interesting account of the application of Roman practicality to theatre devices, but the bulk of the end product was sensation
and an endless search for new varieties of sexual oddity and blood-
letting.

With the deterioration of the classical theatre, the works of Aeschylus, Sophocles, and Euripides finally disappeared into the school-
room. Only a small fraction was ever to reemerge, together with
some work of the boisterous Aristophanes, still too ribald for many
sensibilities. Swamped in debate on matters of metrical intricacy and
grammatical peculiarity, the drama itself lay dormant. When the
dramatic potential of the plays reasserted itself, it was in the teeth
of a nineteenth-century tradition, basically romantic, but heading
towards naturalism. The heroic endeavor of Gilbert Murray to
rehabilitate this drama is still hampered by a series of stilted translations that, however admirable in their time, created of Greek tragedy
for many people a daunting mass of recalcitrant verse, bordering
on self-parody. More recent translations are wearing better, but
too many have revealed themselves more interested in the preoccupations of the translator than in the original. A new emphasis
on the open stage suggests that the time is right to rediscover the
Greek theatre in the terms in which it was created. Developments
in modern dance point a way forward for the theatre, and much

interesting work is being done on the techniques of masked acting, its association with physical expression, and with nonarticulate communication.

The value of Aeschylus, Sophocles, and Euripides lies as much in their creation of valid modes of dramatic expression as in their intellectual concerns. "I say that the stage is a concrete physical place which asks to be filled, and to be given its own concrete language to speak," declared Antonin Artaud.[17] The concrete language of Greek tragedy needs to be rediscovered. Only then may the rash productions "based on Euripides" or "adapted from Sophocles" give way to a climate of informed opinion in which theatre companies will dare to take on Greek classical theatre and justify its position as the cornerstone of all Western theatre.

NOTES

1. See chapter 6.

2. Aristotle *Poetics*: 1450a–b.

3. Aristotle *Rhetoric*: 1403b.

4. See chapter 6.

5. Menander *Arbitrants*: lines 33–35 (line numbering according to the Loeb edition of F. G. Allinson [Cambridge: Harvard University Press, 1964]).

6. Ibid., lines 875–87.

7. Menander *Bad-Tempered Man*: lines 1–5.

8. See chapter 5.

9. See A. W. Pickard-Cambridge, *The Theatre of Dionysus in Athens* (Oxford: Oxford University Press, Clarendon Press, 1946), pp. 140–43.

10. The characters in the *Republic* generally agree that the same actor cannot play tragedy and comedy.

11. Aristotle *Rhetoric*: 1404b.

12. A. W. Pickard-Cambridge, *The Dramatic Festivals of Athens*, 2nd ed., rev. by John Gould and D. M. Lewis (Oxford: Oxford University Press, Clarendon Press, 1968), ch. 7.

13. See G. M. Sifakis, *Studies in the History of Hellenistic Drama* (London: Athlone Press of the University of London, 1967).

14. *Didaskalos*, literally meaning "teacher," does suggest fairly strict artistic control.

15. A chorus of only seven is mentioned with reference to Delphi.

16. Sifakis, *Studies*, app. 1.

17. Antonin Artaud, "Metaphysics and the Mise-en-scène", in *The Theater and its Double*, translated by Mary C. Richards (New York: Grove, 1958).

Selected Bibliography

FOR THE GENERAL READER

J. T. Allen, *Stage Antiquities of the Greeks and Romans* (London: Harrap, 1927).

P. D. Arnott, *An Introduction to the Greek Theatre* (London: Macmillan, 1959).

_____, *The Ancient Greek and Roman Theatre* (New York: Random House, 1971).

H. C. Baldry, *The Greek Tragic Theatre* (London: Chatto and Windus, 1971).

Margarete Bieber, *The History of the Greek and Roman Theater*, 2nd ed. (Princeton, N.J.: Princeton University Press, 1961).

Iris Brooke, *Costume in Greek Classic Drama* (London: Methuen, 1962).

K. J. Dover, *Aristophanic Drama* (London: Batsford, 1972).

R. C. Flickinger, *The Greek Theater and Its Drama*, 4th ed. (Chicago: University of Chicago Press, 1936).

R. J. Hathorn, *The Handbook of Classical Drama* (London: Arthur Barker Ltd., 1967).

James Laver, *Costume in Antiquity* (London: Thames and Hudson, 1964).

L. B. Lawler, *The Dance of the Ancient Greek Theatre* (Iowa City: University of Iowa Press, 1964).

A. W. Pickard-Cambridge, *The Dramatic Festivals of Athens*, 2nd ed. rev. by John Gould and D. M. Lewis (Oxford: Oxford University Press, Clarendon Press, 1968).

F. H. Sandbach, *The Comic Theatre of Greece and Rome* (London: Chatto and Windus, 1977).

Oliver Taplin, *Greek Tragedy in Action* (New York: Methuen, 1978).

A. D. Trendall and T. B. L. Webster, *Illustrations of Greek Drama* (London: Phaidon, 1971).

T. B. L. Webster, *Greek Theatre Production*, 2nd ed. (London: Methuen, 1970).

FOR THE SPECIALIST

J. T. Allen, *The Greek Theatre of the Fifth Century Before Christ* (New York: Haskell House, 1966).

P. D. Arnott, *Greek Scenic Conventions* (Oxford University Press, 1962; reprinted Westport, Conn.: Greenwood Press, 1979).

David Bain, *Actors and Audience* (Oxford: Oxford University Press, 1977).

A. M. Dale, *Collected Papers* (Cambridge: At the University Press, 1969).

C. W. Dearden, *The Stage of Aristophanes* (London: Athlone Press of the University of London, 1976).

G. F. Else, *The Origin and Early Form of Greek Tragedy* (Cambridge: Harvard University Press, 1967).

A. E. Haigh, *The Attic Theatre*, 3rd ed., rev. by A. W. Pickard-Cambridge (Oxford: Oxford University Press, Clarendon Press, 1907).

N. C. Hourmouziades, *Production and Imagination in Euripides* (Athens: Greek Society for Humanistic Studies, 1965).

J. L. Huddilston, *Greek Tragedy in the Light of Vase Painting* (London: Macmillan, 1898).

A. W. Pickard-Cambridge, *The Theatre of Dionysus in Athens* (Oxford: Oxford University Press, Clarendon Press, 1946).

———, *Dithyramb, Tragedy and Comedy*, 2nd ed., rev. by T. B. L. Webster (Oxford: Oxford University Press, 1962).

William Ridgeway, *The Dramas and Dramatic Dances of Non-European Races* (Cambridge: At the University Press, 1915).

G. M. Sifakis, *Studies in the History of Hellenistic Drama* (London: Athlone Press of the University of London, 1967).

Oliver Taplin, *The Stagecraft of Aeschylus* (Oxford: Oxford University Press, Clarendon Press, 1977).

George Thomson, *Aeschylus and Athens*, 3rd ed. (London: Lawrence and Wishart, 1966).

Peter Walcot, *Greek Drama in Its Theatrical and Social Context* (Cardiff: University of Wales Press, 1976).

T. B. L. Webster, *The Greek Chorus* (London: Methuen, 1970).

Index

About the Author

J. MICHAEL WALTON is a Lecturer in Drama at the University of Hull in England. He was Visiting Professor in Theatre at the University of Denver, and his articles have appeared in such publications as *New Theatre Magazine*, *Recherches Théatrales*, and *Theatre Research International*.